Truth and Lives
on Film

Truth and Lives on Film

The Legal Problems of Depicting Real Persons and Events in a Fictional Medium

JOHN T. AQUINO

McFarland & Company, Inc., Publishers
Jefferson, North Carolina, and London

LIBRARY OF CONGRESS CATALOGUING-IN-PUBLICATION DATA

Aquino, John T.
  Truth and lives on film: the legal problems of depicting real
persons and events in a fictional medium / John T. Aquino.
      p.   cm.
  Includes bibliographical references and index.

  ISBN-13: 978-0-7864-2044-5
  (softcover : 50# alkaline paper) ∞

  1. Biographical films—History and criticism. 2. Justice,
Administration of, in motion pictures.   3. Motion pictures—Law
and legislation.   I. Title.
PN1995.9.B55A78   2005
791.43'6554—dc22   2004030530

British Library cataloguing data are available

Cover photograph ©2005 Corbis Images

Manufactured in the United States of America

McFarland & Company, Inc., Publishers
  Box 611, Jefferson, North Carolina 28640
  www.mcfarlandpub.com

To my wife, my inspiration, my love,
Deborah Curren-Aquino, who makes my world go 'round;

to my mother Philomena Zappi Aquino
and my late father Sylvester J. Aquino,
who together taught me to love and respect the movies and the law,
for their endless love and support;

and to my second father, the late Robert R. Curren,
and my second mother, Adelaide Curren,
who gave me their treasure,
for their love, prayers, and constant encouragement

Acknowledgments

First and last, I want to thank my Deborah for her eagerness to help, her discerning ear, her perceptive and receptive mind, her patience, and her love.

I wish to thank two attorney professors at the Columbus School of Law, the Catholic University of America, Washington, D.C.: Harvey Zuckman and Shira Perlmutter. Chapters I and IV began as papers in their respective classes a number of years ago. Their support and guidance got me started with this book. As a teenager, I was fascinated with the incongruity when movies based on the lives of well-known people included disclaimers describing them as "fictitious." Professor Zuckman gave me the opportunity to explore this fascination in a class project.

My undergraduate concentrations at that university were literature, drama, and film. For the influence they had on this book in their lectures on modern drama and film, respectively, I fondly and gratefully remember the late Dr. Richard Foley and the late Leo Brady.

Mother Maria Immaculata Matarese, O.S.B., Subprioress of the Abbey of Regina Laudis, who was an attorney before entering monastic life, has always been a gracious listener, and I remain grateful for her prayerful support and wise and constructive advice. Richard Willing of *USA Today*, in interviewing me for an article, engaged in a lot of back and forth that I found very useful. My friend Harry Regan was very helpful in assisting me in accessing an e-book of N.P. Chipman's 1911 account of the Andersonville trial. I would also like to thank an anonymous reviewer of a university press who commented on a very early draft of this book for his or her insights and suggestions. Thanks to Steve Calvacca and Ned McLeod for bringing me into the *Tyne* case where I was able to get a closer look. Mary Claycomb has long provided me with excellent literary advice. Finally, I send my gratitude to Janet Benrey, my agent.

Some of the ideas for this book appeared in several of my articles, including "Socko! Boffo! And Wrong!" *Washington Post*, July 1, 2001, B1, and "Whose Characters Are These, Anyway?" *Washington Post*, May 19, 2002, B04. I thank Frances Sellers and the other editors for the "Outlook" section of the *Post* for their help with these articles.

John T. Aquino
Washington, D.C.
December 2004

Contents

Introduction

> Truth and falsehood, it has been well said, are not
> always opposed to each other like black and white, but
> oftentimes, and by design, are made to resemble each
> other so as to be hardly distinguishable, just as the
> counterfeit thing is counterfeit because it resembles
> the genuine thing.
>
>
>
> Sir Anthony Cleasby
> English Jurist
> *Johnson v. Emerson* (1871)
> *L.R. 6 Ex. Ca. 357*
>
>

In the 1976 film *From Noon to Three*,[1] an outlaw seduces a woman and later fakes his own death. She goes on to write a torrid best seller about her few passionate hours with this now supposedly deceased stranger. Toward the end of the film, the outlaw finds himself hiding in a theater where a stage adaptation of the woman's book is being performed. Seeing the liberties taken with an event that he experienced, he rushes onstage and shouts at the actors, "That's not the way it happened!"

In a cut scene from the 1969 film *Butch Cassidy and the Sundance Kid*,[2] the titled characters—again, both outlaws—watch a silent film based on their exploits, and Sundance cries out to an uninterested audience, "We didn't do that—never—."[3]

In the 1940 *The Return of Frank James*,[4] a sequel to the 1939 *Jesse James*,[5] Frank James attends a performance of a play about the death of his brother Jesse; in the play, his brothers' killers are portraying themselves, and they are shown as heroes who shoot an evil Jesse James while he is molesting a woman. In the earlier film, these men, played by the same actors, shoot Jesse James in the back while he is taking a picture off the wall, in contrast to what the play claims. And so it is understood that Frank James—stoic though he may seem as played by Henry Fonda—is watching a false and self-gratifying portrayal of events.

Those who have found themselves portrayed in fact-based films have often reacted like the characters in *From Noon to Three* and *Butch Cassidy and the Sundance Kid,* shouting that the portrayal in the movie was false. Spouses, relatives, and friends of deceased people depicted in fact-based films have felt as protective as Frank James did to the memory of his brother in *The Return of Frank James* and may even have wished that they could have acted as decisively as Frank James does in the movie — he chases the false portrayers of his brother's life off the stage and kills them.

But the comparison of reality versus film and theatrical performances becomes even more complicated: Two of these films that are based on actual people and events—*Butch Cassidy and the Sundance Kid* and *The Return of Frank James*— while exhibiting implicit outrage at the false depiction of real-life people, themselves romanticize and thus falsify the people and events they portray. Jesse James was, by all accounts, a cold-blooded killer and not the Robin Hood of the Old West of both *Jesse James* and its sequel,[6] and the movie Butch Cassidy and the Sundance Kid are more late 20th century rebels— who amiably shoot guns and ride horses and bicycles to a pop score by Burt Bacharach — than authentic early twentieth century outlaws.[7]

It is not an insult to filmmakers to say that their job is to both to tell the truth and to lie. They must make the action convincing and believable — especially if the movie is meant to be realistic and reflect everyday life or historical events, even if it is science fiction or fantasy and even if it surrealistic or impressionistic. Audience must *connect* with they are seeing.

Yet filmmakers, and indeed all makers of fiction, must, in many ways, lie. Filmmakers rely on certain conventions. As in the theater, audiences must suspend disbelief. In the movies, summations to a jury last minutes rather than hours. Movies tend to show prosecutors working with the investigators as they try to solve a crime (active is better than passive in films); while that may, rarely, happen, prosecutors usually leave the investigation to their investigators so that the prosecutors will not find themselves being called as witnesses by the defense. Call them conventions. Call them liberties. The falsehood here is that things don't really happen this way." In making a film about an actual event and actual people, filmmakers may have to "lie" even more, so that the falsehood progresses from "things *don't* happen this way" to "things *didn't* happen this way." If nothing else, filmmakers must take events that may have actually taken place over a thirty-year period and somehow compress them to a running time of two hours. Oliver Stone's 1991 film *JFK*[8] shows New Orleans district attorney Jim Garrison and his team uncovering evidence suggesting a conspiracy in the 1963 assassination of President Kennedy. The evidence was actually largely amassed by others prior to Garrison's investigation, but a "lone investigator" is more dramatically effective than a number of writers and analysts working over a five-year period.[9] Oliver Cromwell's "witchhunter" Matthew Hopkins died in bed of tuberculosis in 1644, but it was thought to be a better story — not only poetic license but poetic justice — if he himself was burned at the stake, which is what was shown in the 1968 horror film *The Conqueror Worm*.[10] In the film *Glory*,[11] which is about the 54th Massachusetts, one of the first black regiments in the Civil War, the 54th is made up mostly of runaway slaves, while in reality it was a regiment of freed men.[12] To tell a good story, it is sometimes necessary to lie — who wants to get mired down in "details"? Filmmakers largely appear to have relied on an axiom articulated by the newspaper editor in John Ford's 1962 western *The Man Who Shot Liberty Valance*[13] when he finds that the actual facts are less exciting and inspirational than the story that everyone believed was true: "When the legend becomes fact, print the legend."

Pablo Picasso is quoted as saying, "Art is a lie that tells the truth." Storytellers snatch elements of the truth — as they've heard it and as they've felt it — appropriate them, and then manipulate them. Artists may argue that after this appropriation and manipulation the result "tells the truth." John Fowles framed his novel *The Magus*, which is about illusion and reality, truth and lies, around a quote from the poet T.S. Eliot from "The Little Gidding" section of "The Four Quartets":

> And the end of all our exploring
> Will be to arrive where we started
> And know the place for the first time.

There is indeed a modern trend in film scholarship which, while critical of the "conventional Hollywood historical film," defends a postmodern history film that, according to historian Robert A. Rosenstone, "uses the medium [of film] to revision, even reinvent history."[14] As examples of this type of film Rosenstone cites among others *Glory*, *Mississippi Burning*[15], *Walker*[16], and *JFK*. In an essay on *Walker* and *Mississippi Burning* in

Rosenstone's collection, Sumiko Higashi notes the criticism *Mississippi Burning* received for "gross distortions in the film"— namely that the film glorified FBI agents who had actually thwarted civil rights workers in the early 1960s and that it ignored the black activism in the civil rights movement. Higashi observes in response, "Put simply, such views equate history with objectivity and truth."[17]

In an interview with historian Mark C. Carnes, filmmaker Oliver Stone, director of *JFK* and *Nixon*,[18] answers the accusation that his manipulation of actual film footage of President Kennedy in *JFK* was "sneaky," by saying,

> [W]e as dramatists are undertaking a deconstruction of history, questioning some of the given realities. What you call "sneaky" is, to me, an ambivalent and shifting style that makes people aware they are watching a movie and that reality is in question.... We play with your mind.[19]

Director and screenwriter John Sayles compares this movement:

> what happened in the 1960s with the New Journalism. Tom Wolfe was one of the first guys to do it at *Esquire*; Gay Talese was another. The idea they had was that if you were true to the spirit of the story, you didn't have to get all the facts exactly right. Their work led to a lot of what I consider creative writing.... In films, [history] is a story bin to be plundered and depending on who you are and what your agenda is, it's either useful or not.[20]

Higashi comments that those who criticize historical films for distorting facts assume audiences will believe that what they see is what actually happened. The makers of commercial Hollywood historical films have argued that the audience is smart enough to know that a movie is "only a movie" and not a history lesson. The disclaimers asserting that a movie — even if apparently based on fact — is wholly or in part "fictitious and any resemblance to characters living or dead is purely coincidental" support this argument since the audience is "on notice" about fictionalization. And yet it is a common tenet of advertising that repeating a message over and over again makes the audience believe that the product does what the ad says it does— until the audience finds out otherwise. In the case of an historical event, a widely shown movie based on that event may be the last word on the subject for a very long time.[21]

Terry Treachout, the drama critic for the *Wall Street Journal*, claims that the film *JFK* appears to have persuaded a number of people that there was a conspiracy to kill President Kennedy. "Film has a special capacity for [doing] this because of the nature of the medium. Because it consists of photographs. Because all film creates the illusion of a documentary reality."[22]

Legally, filmmakers argue that they are protected by the First Amendment of the U.S. Constitution, which promotes freedom of speech. That protection *does* exist — with limitations. The idea of this protection apparently has governed the actions of many filmmakers.[23] An attorney for a movie studio, talking to me about another studio's obviously unfactual treatment of the character of politician and attorney Thomas Dewey in the film *Hoodlum*,[24] said, "But we're entitled to our 'take' on Thomas Dewey!" Giving just that example of the portrayal of Dewey — which is so false — will make the filmmaker's argument look irrational. In fairness, Oliver Stone is basically saying, "We are entitled to our take on Richard Nixon."

To the writer and filmmaker, their work may — in some way — deliver "a truth." It is in these contexts where "being true to the spirit" of the actual events is a phrase that comes up. In the 1970 film *Patton*,[25] a film biography of General George Patton, there is a scene after Patton arrives in Morocco where a Nazi plane bombs Patton's headquarters. Patton runs out and shoots at the plane with his revolver while the bullets from the plane somehow miss him. An historian interviewed for a television discussion about history and the movies said Patton's headquarters were indeed bombed soon after he arrived in Morocco and that everyone ran out, but Patton did not shoot at the plane because it had flown away by then. Yet, he added, shooting at the plane was something Patton would have done.[26]

Perhaps the film portrayal of Butch Cassidy and the Sundance Kid, while not true to all the facts, is true to their essence. It is interesting that screenwriter William Goldman begins the published version of the screenplay for *Butch Cassidy and the Sundance Kid* with a kind of reverse disclaimer: "Not that it matters, but most of what follows is true."[27] One can argue, as noted earlier, over what is meant by "true," but noteworthy is Goldman's use of the word "most" and of the phrase "Not that it matters."

Sometimes the old-Hollywood "tell-a-good-story" and the postmodern revision-to-tell-the-truth approaches are offered as justification at the same time. The families of some of those portrayed in the 2000 movie *The Perfect Storm*[28] sued the filmmakers over misuse of their loved ones' names and images and false portrayal, and the deposition of the film's director Wolfgang Petersen included the following exchange:

Q: So we tell a greater truth if we exaggerate or distort the actual facts?

A: Absolutely, absolutely.

Q: History becomes just what you, as a filmmaker, choose it to
be...?

A: This is not a documentary. This is a motion picture, largely
fictionalized, to tell a story about fishermen in Gloucester, Massachusetts ... and how their life is, and not an accurate recreation
and retelling of every single element of the story. Because if you
do that — right? — you might have a story that is accurate but not
very dramatic.... If you just go with the facts, very often — very,
very often, you get a film that just doesn't really get into your
heart. Is it correct in every detail? Of course not, because we had
to — make up a lot of things.[29]

While filmmakers can argue for a need or even a right for commercial, aesthetic, or polemic reasons to amend and revise the details of a factual event, to an individual portrayed in the story or to his or her family
or friends, if what is on the screen is not what really happened, it is untrue.
Thomas Dewey's family worried that an entire generation of moviegoers
would think that this upright public figure was instead a crooked politician as shown in the movie *Hoodlum*. Individuals portrayed or their families may seek remedy from the legal system for libel, invasion of privacy,
violation of their right of publicity, and commercial misappropriation as
well as other torts. The law may prove them right, or they may find that
the law is either not clear cut or is still catching up.

By the end of the twentieth century, there appeared to be increased
activity by the living and the families of the dead in suing filmmakers for
fictionalized depictions in fact-based films. So great was this increase that
insurance companies raised premiums for "errors and omissions" actions
by filmmakers.[30]

Looking at the larger picture, we come back to the issue of truth.
Critics of these films claim, as Max Frankel is quoted as saying in Chapter I of this book, "[These films] damage the appeal of fiction and corrode
the meaning of truth."[31] Referring specifically to the film *JFK* and a cable
History Channel's 2003 documentary that presented as fact President Johnson's complicity in President Kennedy's assassination, Jack Valenti, president of the Motion Picture Association of America and a special assistant
to President Johnson, wrote,

> The power to dissolve reason in an ever-ascending reach of story-
> telling oftentimes empowered by digital legerdemain makes it
> harder and harder to distinguish what is right and plainly what is
> wrong.[32]

This book begins with a history of legal issues concerning fictionalization in fact-based films, continues with my own account of legal actions concerning the movie *The Perfect Storm* based on my limited participation, and then presents a comparison of fact and fiction in films for which there is, in court documents, a clear historical record: courtroom dramas based on actual trials. A coda chapter discusses an aspect of fictionalization that is part of the alternative universe created when actor and roles merge. Actors who are so strongly identified with characters they play in motion pictures and television that they blend with the fictional characters— Groucho Marx, Bela Lugosi as Dracula — have found their personas taken and have fought to claim some legal right in these fictional creations.

There is a sense that when filmmakers start to tell a fact-based story they feel that the story — indeed the whole process— is theirs to do with as they wish. Some call Hollywood the "fantasy factory," and in the manufacturing process rights can be abused. Or not.

Such tension is the focus of this book.

I

Fictionalization in
Movies and Television

*I love a ballad in print o' life, for then we are sure they
are true.*

—*The Winter's Tale*

In 1997, the science fiction movie *Contact*,[1] based on the novel by Carl
Sagan, utilized actual footage of President Clinton giving a press conference. The president was never referred to by name. Certain words of his
speech were dubbed so that it was made to seem that he was referring to
the alien beings in the movie. The White House responded in a release
that, "Although President Clinton is a public figure, we believe that use
of the President's image is inappropriate."[2] The producer of the movie
said in return, "[We] used the president in good fun and in a fictitious
setting."[3]

Similarly, in 1975, footage of Queen Elizabeth of Great Britain was
inserted into the movie *Hennessy*,[4] which was about an Irish terrorist,
played by Rod Steiger, who attempts to blow up the Queen. In the actual
footage, the Queen looks up in reaction to a noise. In editing the film of
the Queen into the action of the movie, the filmmakers arranged to have
the section in which the Queen reacts to the noise immediately follow the
scene where the police jump on the bomber, thereby making it seem as if
the Queen was actually in the scene when the police stop Rod Steiger from

setting off the bomb. It was thought to be so realistic that the British government insisted that the film carry a disclaimer that the Queen was not an actor in the movie.

In 1997, the family of former New York district attorney and presidential candidate Thomas Dewey complained that he was portrayed in the movie *Hoodlum*[5] as being corrupt and in league with gangsters. Dewey had in fact gained national attention from his relentless battle with organized crime in the 1930s as district attorney of New York County. When his family complained in writing, the attorneys for the motion picture replied that the family had no cause of action since Dewey was dead and the dead cannot sue for defamation.

In January 1993, foreign correspondent Georgie Anne Geyer threatened suit against Harry Thomason and Linda Bloodworth-Thomason, television producers and friends of President Clinton, claiming that the character of Georgie Anne Lahti in the Thomasons' CBS television series *Hearts Afire* was based on Geyer and that the depiction was causing injury to her reputation. As indicators of this "identification," Geyer noted that both she and Lahti had the same first names, were foreign correspondents, were from Chicago, were specialists in the Middle East, interviewed noted foreign leaders, wore their hair in bangs, and had written a book on Cuban dictator Fidel Castro. A major difference between her and the Georgie Anne Lahti character, according to Geyer, was that in the series Lahti confessed to having slept with Castro and the other leaders she had interviewed.[6] As proof that other people had identified her with Lahti, Geyer said that she had been getting letters from viewers.[7] Steven Huff, the Thomasons' attorney, responded that these were "not actionable similarities" and that Geyer's settlement offer had been "unreasonable."[8]

In 2000, the ex-wife and daughters of the captain of a fishing boat that went down off the coast of Nova Scotia in 1990 brought suit against Warner Brothers for the film *The Perfect Storm* for commercial misappropriation and invasion of privacy, claiming the portrayal of the captain was false in that it showed him as heroic but reckless and that it was done without permission.[9]

In 2003, CBS television set November 16 and 18 broadcast dates for its two-part miniseries called *The Reagans*, which was based on the lives of former President Ronald Reagan and his wife Nancy. Both were still alive, but President Reagan was suffering from Alzheimer's disease. Although no one had yet seen the film, the Republic National Committee (RNC) chairman, based on a *New York Times* article that cited some scenes from the script, denounced the film for its inaccuracies (the *Times* noted a line from the script that the screenwriters admitted was fictitious in which President Reagan appeared to equate the AIDS epidemic with divine retribution against homosexuals since they were "living in sin") and for one-sided characterizations of the two Reagans—President Reagan was reportedly seen to be well-meaning but ineffectual and Nancy Reagan as controlling. The RNC chairman insisted that either a panel of historians screen the work for "historical inaccuracies" or that a disclaimer be run every ten minutes at the bottom of the screen announcing that the film was fictitious. There was a subsequent firestorm of criticism from mostly conservative sources, and ultimately, CBS announced that it was pulling the film because it too found the portrayal unbalanced.[10] CBS ultimately had the film shown on its cable network Showtime — which reached a smaller audience — on November 30, 2003.[11]

Contact, Hennessy, Hoodlum, The Perfect Storm, Hearts Afire, and The Reagans, like virtually all U.S. films and television series, end with the disclaimer — or some variation: "The characters and events depicted in this program (or film) are fictitious. Any similarity with (or resemblance to) persons living or dead is purely coincidental (or unintentional)." The philosophy behind the disclaimer is the reason why the president is not really the president, the queen is not the queen, and the details of the life and actual character of Thomas Dewey can be seemingly changed at the whim of the filmmakers. The background is a long and tortured one that wends its way through ancient Greece, Elizabethan England, an American film that was the basis for a British defamation suit, and the subsequent pushing of the envelope in regard to rewriting history for dramatic effect.

"A Libertie Used by All Good Wrighters"

The tension between reality and fiction is not new. The earliest attempts in ancient Greece to present dramas based on contemporary events produced negative reactions. The Greek poet Phrynicus's play Capture of Miletus, written in 492 B.C., explored a real-life massacre of two years earlier, and, according to the historian Herodotus, there was such a public outcry that Phrynicus was eventually fined and the play was banned.[12] As a result, Aeschylus, Sophocles, and Euripides turned to mythology for their subject matter — Prometheus, Oedipus, Agamemnon — and shaped the Greek drama that is known today.

In the Renaissance, as revolutionary thoughts were starting to be explored and promulgated through the popularization of printed books and the rebirth of drama, the courts of England became concerned about how historical figures as well as those living were being portrayed. A Privy

Council order exists that states that in Middlesex "certaine players ... do represent upon the stage in their interludes the persons of some gentlemen of good desert and quality that are yet alive under some obscure manner, but yet in such sorte as all the hearers may take notice both of the matter and the persons that are meant thereby."[13] In a late eighteenth-century treatise that looked back on the history of the Star Council, a British court in the sixteenth and seventeenth century that ended up persecuting disobedience to the king and queen, the author wrote that, "Libels are of several kinds, either by scoffing at the person of another in rhymes or prose, or by the personating him, thereby to make him ridiculous."[14]

It was in this atmosphere in 1600 that the noted jurist Sir Edward Coke (1592–1634) reviewed a situation involving a writer of histories who was said to have rearranged and embellished the facts.

At the time, Coke was England's attorney general. In this role, he would prosecute Sir Walter Raleigh in 1603 and interrogate Guy Fawkes and the other papists on trial for the 1605 gunpowder plot to blow up the king and queen and the members of Parliament. He would become Chief Justice of Common Pleas in 1606 and of King's Bench in 1613. King James would dismiss him in 1616 after years in which Coke quarreled over the role of the court. Coke's *Notes* and *Institutes*, in which he recast, explained, and defended the common law, were later published and proved very influential in their legal concepts for many years thereafter.

However, on July 11, 1600, and January 22, 1601, Coke interrogated the writer Sir John Hayward (1564?–1627) concerning his history, *The First Part of the Life and Raigne of King Henrie III*, reportedly because the ministers of Queen Elizabeth I thought that Hayward had rearranged events and invented speeches to help foster a rebellion against the queen by the earl of Essex. The book had been dedicated to Lord Essex.[15] The queen herself was reported to have been offended. By way of context, it should be stated that two weeks after Coke's last interrogation of Hayward, on February 7, 1601, Essex and his followers began their rebellion and failed, and Hayward's book was cited in Essex's treason trial by Sir Francis Bacon.[16] The day before the rebellion, Essex's followers had paid for a presentation of William Shakespeare's play *Richard II*, which also, according to some, rearranged events of a previous time and put speeches in characters' mouths to glorify Lord Essex.[17]

Coke asked Hayward about invented speeches, speeches that had no source in histories closer to the reign of Henry III. One of Coke's specific concerns was that Hayward "selecteth a storie 200 yere olde, and publisheth it this last yere: intendinge the application of it to this tyme." Hayward answered that "it is a libertie used by all good wrighters of historie to adde & to invent reasons & speaches according to the matter, " adding that it is "lawfull for any historiographer to insert any historie of former tyme into that hystorie he wright albeit no other hystorian of that matter have meued the same."[18]

Some commentators have noted that Hayward's answer suggests that he felt that the historian could play the poet.[19] In fact, even though it was historical prose, Hayward's history has been compared to the plays of Shakespeare in that both were "imaginative and invented texts, not one factual work, one fictive work." Even the histories of the period were works of imagination.[20]

Hayward was imprisoned for his history. The queen died in 1603, and Hayward was released. He wrote other histories, including *The Beginning of the Reign of Elizabeth*— whom he had displeased. This suggests that Hayward was having quiet vengeance and showing that history is indeed written by the survivors.

The tension between fact and fiction has been with us since the birth of drama, and it exists in other arts. Walter Scott, for example, inserted historical characters in his otherwise fictionalized novels, as he did with Richard the Lionheart in *Ivanhoe* (1819). Before the invention of photography, paintings, sculpture, and drawings were how historical images were recorded. But the artist John Trumbull wrote James Madison in 1824 to tell him that even though Madison had not been present in Annapolis in 1783 when General George Washington formally resigned his army commission, Trumbull had drawn him into his painting about the event along with Martha Washington and her children, who also weren't there. Trumbull wanted, he told Madison, to symbolically have four Virginia presidents in the painting, and Madison made four.[21] In another example, while William F. Cody had indeed been an Indian scout, he collaborated with the writer Ned Buntline on a series of dime novels and later on an 1872 play called the *Indian Scout* about "Buffalo Bill" Cody that were largely fictitious. Cody went on to develop the popular open-air entertainment known as "Buffalo Bill's Wild West Show," complete with fictitious Indian raids. In 1914, Cody founded "The W.F. Cody Historical Pictures Corp." to produce motion pictures.[22]

The invention and popularization of motion pictures pulled the string between fact and fiction tauter than ever. Early motion pictures showed real persons kissing and sneezing. When movies began to tell stories, the audience saw people like themselves projected on a screen, usually behaving in a manner approaching reality.

It was not long before people began to sue for invasion of privacy and defamation because of the manner in which they claimed characters based on them were portrayed in films. The New York Right of Privacy Act was enacted in 1903 and was first utilized in a motion picture situation in 1913 in *Binns v. Vitagraph*[23] which held that motion pictures are not "true pictures of a current event, but mainly a product of the imagination."

But the most influential case involving the portrayal of real-life personages in motion pictures was tried in Great Britain in 1934. It was a very sensational and contained unusual facts. Yet, it raised questions, issues, and precedents that still have a substantial effect on film and television today, particularly on how characters, especially historical ones, are represented in the visual media.

Youssoupoff v. MGM

On December 15, 1916, Prince Felix Youssoupoff, arguably the richest man in Russia;[24] Grand Duke Dimitrii Alexandrovich, Czar Nicholas II's cousin; V.M. Pourichkevich; and Captain Soukhotin killed Grigorii Efmovich Rasputin, mesmerist and counselor to the Czarina, at the Moika Palace, Youssoupoff's home. In doing so, they said, they felt that they were saving Russia from the hands of a mad and evil man. Prince Felix was exiled from Petrograd by the czar, thus saving him from the consequences of the 1917 revolution. Grand Duke Dimitrii was also exiled in effect, since he was assigned to serve with the army in Persia. Youssoupoff's wife, Princess Irina, a niece of Czar Nicholas, followed her husband into exile; ultimately, they settled in Paris. In 1917, the czarist regime was overthrown in the Socialist revolution. In 1918, the czar, his wife, and their children were executed.[25]

Filmmakers were quick to see the dramatic potential of these events. One year after the murder, Poly-World issued a silent film account. In 1930, *Rasputin* was released in Germany[26] starring Conrad Veidt.[27] Two years later, Metro-Goldwyn-Mayer (MGM) began filming *Rasputin and the Empress*. Following up on the successful teaming of John and Lionel Barrymore in the studio's *Arsene Lupin* and *Grand Hotel*, MGM's creative head Irving Thalberg planned the film as a starring vehicle for the three Barrymores, John, Lionel, and Ethel, who were cast, respectively, as Prince Paul Chegodieff, Rasputin, and the czarina. The Barrymores were known as the "Royal Family of Broadway" and were satirized in a 1927 play of that name by George S. Kaufman and Edna Ferber, which had been filmed in 1930.[28] John and Lionel were noted stage performers (John in such plays as *Hamlet* and *Richard III*, Lionel in *The Copperhead*), but they had also acquired great success in Hollywood, especially with the coming of sound pictures in 1927. An almost legendary stage actress, Ethel had only made one silent film (in 1919), and so *Rasputin and the Empress* would feature the first film recording of her famous voice and would costar the three Barrymores for the first time in a motion picture.

Ethel had only agreed to make the film on the condition that it be finished in time for her to return to the stage in the fall. As a result, filming began without a completed script, and playwright Charles MacArthur (author with Ben Hecht of 1927 newspaper play *The Front Page*) turned in pages each day. (Another reason for MacArthur's continual rewriting was his task of making sure that the scenes were evenly distributed among the Barrymores, fearful that they would become temperamental and jealous of one another.[29]) The original director, Charles Brabin, was fired, reportedly for working too slowly; he was replaced by Richard Boleskavsky, a Polish actor who had appeared at the Moscow Arts Theatre during czarist times. Ethel Barrymore objected during the filming to the script's depiction of the czarina, claiming that she had known her personally, having met her several times in London through the duchess of Sutherland.[30]

There were attempts to make the film historically accurate — a New York jeweler recreated the crown jewels to their exact scale; sets and costumes were duplicated painstakingly under the supervision of Natalie Bucknail, an exiled Russian aristocrat,[31] and the studio reportedly had releases from exiled members of the czarist court.[32] But there were also clear fictionalizations, mostly notably that of John Barrymore playing a nonhistorical Prince Paul Chegodieff, a seeming composite of Prince Felix and the Grand Duke Dimitrii. In the film, one man kills Rasputin, not four, and that man is Prince Chegodieff. In addition, crucial scenes and inferences were added to the script to the effect that a lady-in-waiting named "Natasha," played by Diana Wynard, was either raped or seduced while under hypnosis by Rasputin. (Rasputin leeringly tells Natasha that he will punish Paul; she sends Paul a note that states that she is no longer fit to be his wife, and she tells him that she remembers, while in a trance, Rasputin's beard brushing against her cheek.) Natasha is the love interest of Prince Paul Chegodieff and, according to MGM's later argument, was also either a fictional or composite character.

One reason given for the inclusion of these scenes suggesting that Rasputin raped Natasha, ironic in light of the ultimate lawsuit in a British court, was Thalberg's recognition that the Russian royal family was related to the British royal family and that 50 percent of MGM's foreign receipts came from Great Britain. By depicting Rasputin villainously, Thalberg hoped he would make the film's portrayal of Czar Nicholas more sympathetic. Thalberg was also reportedly concerned that since he and studio head Louis B. Mayer were Jewish, and Czar Nicholas had treated Russian Jews badly, any less than sympathetic treatment of the czar would be interpreted as revenge.[33]

According to Maria de Acosta, who did research for Thalberg on the screenplay, she saw an identification between Princess Irina and "Natasha" and told Thalberg that the princess and Rasputin had, to her knowledge, never met. But Thalberg insisted that the rape scene remain.[34] By other accounts, the rape scene was inserted "for shock progression" by the producer (supervisor) Bernie Hyman.[35] Hyman also, for reasons that are unclear, unless it was to capitalize on the relative topicality of the real-life event, added a prologue to the film:[36] "This concerns the destruction of an empire, brought about by the mad ambitions of one man. A few of the characters are still alive. The rest met their death by violence."[37]

Prince Youssoupoff and his wife Princess Irina were living in genteel poverty in Paris. In 1925, he had unsuccessfully sued an American art collector for art treasures the man had agreed to sell but then refused to return.[38] In 1927, he had written a book about Rasputin[39] and then overcome a suit by Rasputin's daughter in French court for damages for the murder of her father.[40] Knowing that Youssoupoff was in Paris, de Acosta wrote Prince Agoutinsky, a czarist émigré living there, and asked him to discuss the matter with Youssoupoff. The word came back that the Prince would sue if the film were released. But Thalberg was not dissuaded and instead terminated de Acosta's contract.[41] This report, however, suggests that, unlike later filmmakers who took comfort in the fact that it is well established that the dead cannot sue for libel only to find out that people portrayed in their films were still living, MGM knew that the Youssoupoffs were alive and yet proceeded anyway.

Rasputin and the Empress premiered in the United States on December 23, 1932, at the Astor Theatre in New York City. Critical reaction was mixed, and, given its expense, the box office reception disappointed studio executives.[42] The movie was not nominated for Best Picture and in fact received only one Academy Award nomination — again, ironically, in light of the later litigation, for "best story" for Charles MacArthur. But *Rasputin and the Empress* still was selected by critics in the *Film Daily* poll as one of the ten best movies of 1933[43] and was also one of the top grossing films of 1933.[44] MGM executive David O. Selznick was impressed enough with the teaming of the three Barrymores to plan another film for the trio, a version of John Galsworthy's *The Forsyte Saga*, promising that this time there would be a finished script and not "the grief of *Rasputin*."[45]

Meanwhile the Youssoupoffs, through the New York firm of Neufeld & Schlechter, had notified MGM that the film had defamed Prince Felix by depicting the murder of Rasputin unfairly and unjustly. When MGM repudiated the action, the firm changed its approach, doubtless because, since Youssoupoff had admitted and even boasted of having killed Rasputin, the falsity of the portrayal of the murder's method could be seen as irrelevant.[46] MGM was next informed that the princess had been defamed. Brooklyn-born attorney Fanny Holtzman was later contacted by Princess Irina and then by Prince Felix who asked her to represent the princess in a libel suit against MGM.

Libel is one of two types of defamation. Libel is a written (or otherwise fixed with some permanence) false statement of and concerning the plaintiff that is defamatory — that is, tending to lower the plaintiff's reputation in the community, that has caused harm to the plaintiff by the defendant's publication to a third party, that the third party knew to refer to the plaintiff, and that was caused by the plaintiff's negligence. For slander, which is oral defamation, proof of damage is required before the case will be sent to trial on the assumption that if a plaintiff cannot prove damages prior to trial then he or she will not be able to prove them at trial. But for libel, because the alleged defamation is written and potentially still doing the damage the plaintiff is claiming, absence of damages will survive a motion to dismiss. Another way of saying this is that damages are assumed in libel for trial purposes.

Youssoupoff had not seen the film but had only heard about it from Prince Agoutinsky. Holtzman arranged a screening, and at the film's end, Youssoupoff told her, "Le prince, c'est moi. 'Natasha,' c'est Irène."[47]

Since the character names had been changed, Holtzman was skeptical about being able to show the identification necessary for libel — basically that the libel "be of and concerning" the plaintiff and that a third person would reasonably identify the plaintiff with the character[48] — except for one thing: the prologue that Bernie Hyman had added, which claimed, "A few of the characters are still alive — the rest met death by violence." This seemed to Holtzman to be a negation of any claim to fiction, almost a reverse disclaimer that stated that the film characterizations were based on real people. Also, by simple subtraction, if Rasputin, the czar, and the czarina were all dead, then, Holtzman reasoned, of the film's principal characters that only left Prince Chegodieff and Natasha and provided some basis for the identification with Prince Felix and Princess Irina.[49]

The major argument for identification was this: Youssoupoff had written his book in which he established a claim as "the man who killed Rasputin." Since "Prince Chegodieff" in the film is the man who kills Rasputin and is married to a character named "Natasha" who, in the film, is evidently raped by Rasputin, then, the Youssoupoffs argued, audiences would identify "Natasha" with Youssoupoff's wife Irina. The defamatory statement was a false depiction of rape.

Papers were filed in the New York Supreme Court. But, tactically, Holtzman suggested that the initial case be tried in England where the film was due to premiere in early 1933 under the title *Rasputin the Mad Monk*. Holtzman felt that by first presenting the case in England the Youssoupoffs could take advantage of the British sense of privacy and Holtzman's impression that, in contrast to the United States, in Great Britain "libel laws were taken seriously and rigidly enforced."[50] She was also relying on the fact that the Grand Duchess Xenia, Princess Irina's mother, and Queen Alexandra, mother of King George V, had been sisters, with the logical result that the plaintiff and the British king were cousins. In fact, according to Holtzman, bond money and the initial fee for British counsel for the Youssoupoffs were supplied by Buckingham Palace.[51]

MGM had refused to consider a settlement. J. Robert Rubin, the MGM vice president and general counsel in New York, told Holtzman, "The movie is fiction, and we're protected by clearances."[52] But, while MGM had some releases, they had none from the Youssoupoffs.

The trial began on February 27, 1934, before Justice William Avory and a special jury, with Princess Irina testifying.[53] In a preliminary affidavit, the princess had stated that she had never even met Rasputin and that depicting her as Rasputin's sexual pawn "was not only grossly untrue but grossly defamatory."[54] At trial, she testified that the character of Natasha was "portrayed in such a manner that it must inevitably be "taken to be her" and "showed me not to be fit to be the wife of the man I loved."[55] This testimony echoed dialogue from the end of the film where Natasha says to Prince Chegodieff, "I thought this man was a man from God, and now I know that he was only a man, and I am not fit to be your wife."[56]

Back and forth the question of identification was debated by plaintiff and defendant's counsels— Sir Patrick Hastings and Sir William Jowitt, respectively. Defense claimed that Natasha was a lady-in-waiting in the film, not a princess; plaintiff noted that Natasha is called "her highness," that she was of the same age Princess Irina was at the time of Rasputin's death, and even dressed in a gown evidently modeled on Princess Irina's attire from just before the Revolution. Prince Felix testified about Rasputin's murder, and it was covered on page one of *The New York Times* with the subhead, "Says he acted for Nation." Under cross-examination from Jowitt, Youssoupoff admitted that there were four men involved in the murder of Rasputin, not one; that there were similarities between Natasha and other ladies-in-waiting in the czarist court; and that Prince Chegodieff did indeed have much in common with Grand Duke Dimitrii.[57] Jowitt later argued that the claim that a woman had been raped could not come under the Slander of a Woman Act of 1891 since that statute was confined to imputations of "unchastity or adultery" and cited Shakespeare's "Rape of Lucrece" for support.[58] What he was evidently arguing to the jury was that accusation of rape, since the act was forced upon a woman and did not therefore involve unchastity or adultery under the Slander of a Woman Act, was not defamatory: "Whatever else anybody may feel in regard to this great poem, I cannot myself conceive the frame of mind of a man who could feel toward [the raped] Lucrece either hatred, ridicule or contempt."[59]

In his summation to the jury, the presiding judge, Sir William Avory, said that the only question they had to decide was whether, regardless of intent, a substantial number of people would conclude that "Natasha" represented Princess Irina. He also refuted Jowitt's reading of Shakespeare's poem, quoting instead the lines, "Pure chastity is rifled of her store."[60]

On March 5, the jury deliberated less than an hour and found for the plaintiffs in the sum of £25,000 ($125,000).[61] On July 17, the court of appeals upheld the award.[62]

The appeal addressed these three issues:

1. *Is motion picture defamation libel or slander?* Both Lord Justice Scrutton and Lord Justice Slesser found the action properly framed as libel. The decision that the action was for libel was significant because, excepting statements concerning unchastity and adultery, injury had to be proved in slander cases. As previously noted, proof of injury was and is not necessary for libel. Lord Justice Greer stated for the record that there was no evidence of injury, that the plaintiff was a lady who "lives in Paris, and who has not lost, so far as we know, a single friend, and who has not been able to show that her reputation has in any way suffered from the publication of this unfortunate picture play...." [63] In confirming the action as libel, Slesser commented, "There can be no doubt that, so far as the photographic part of the exhibition is concerned, that it is a permanent matter to be seen by the eye, and is the proper subject for an action for libel."[64]

This ruling of libel for film defamation action had first been made in an American case nearly twenty years before, *Merle v. Sociological Film Corporation*,[65] but even the judges in the case found it to be a "somewhat novel proceeding."[66] Contemporaneously with *Youssoupoff*, *Brown v. Paramount Public Corporation*,[67] supported *Merle* in finding an action for libel justified in a case regarding Joseph von Sternberg's 1931 film version of Theodore Dreiser's novel *An American Tragedy*.

2. *Is the accusation of rape sufficient for slander?* Assuming, in the alternative, that it was slander, Lord Justice Scrutton noted that "it takes some

courage"[68] to argue, as the defense did, that accusations of rape were not defamatory under the Slander of a Woman Act in that such accusations did not involve claims of "unchastity or adultery" under the Act. "That argument was solemnly presented to the jury," Scrutton added with unveiled disdain, "and I only wish the jury could have expressed, and that we could know, what they thought of it because it seems to me to be one of the most legal arguments that were ever addressed to, I will not say a business body, but a sensible body.... I really have no language to express my opinion of that argument."[69] In a final note on the issue of slander versus libel, Sir Patrick Hastings for the plaintiff commented during the arguments that it was possible in motion pictures to create libel and slander at one and the same time.[70]

3. *Was there identification?* All three judges stated, as Lord Justice Scrutton observed, that "there was ground for the jury thinking that many people would naturally, in light of the book published by Prince Youssoupoff, take the view that the Prince Chegodieff in the film was intended to be and would be reasonably understood to be the Prince Youssoupoff who was one of the murderers."[71] He also cited the film's prologue and, just as Fanny Holtzman reportedly had done earlier, subtracted those murdered to come up with a reasonable assumption that Prince Felix and Princess Irina would be understood to be depicted in the film. Lord Justice Scrutton strongly suggested, however, that if the film had had a disclaimer such as often appeared in fiction stating that all events depicted were fictitious, then the identification might have failed.[72] In this way, Scrutton appeared to contradict the instructions of Sir William Avory at trial, who stated that intent was of no importance.

Faced with the $125,000 award against the film in Great Britain — which, at the value of the dollar at the end of the twentieth century, was the equivalent of $1,000,000 — and with both the impending New York suit and the possibility of actions in every country where *Rasputin and the Empress* had played, MGM settled with the Youssoupoffs for a "large sum" in return for their dropping all present and future actions.[73] While the actual settlement figure was never officially disclosed, Fanny Holtzman did not deny the report that it was around $900,000[74] — roughly $10 million when converted to late-twentieth-century dollars.

Reaction in American legal circles to *Youssoupoff* appears to have been cautious. In looking at the possible effect of the case, the *Michigan Law Review* suggested, "In reality, it would seem that a production which caused theater audiences to connect a character and his behavior with some actual person instead of considering the matter offered as purely fiction would be exceptional. Because of the practical aspect, it may well be doubted if our courts would allow many cases to reach the jury. Furthermore, most of the productions which make any attempt to concern themselves with actual persons deal with historical subjects, so that suitors would be confronted with rulings which disallow civil cases for libels of the dead."[75]

In retrospect, it is difficult to know how much effect the British sense of privacy that Fanny Holtzman had banked on had on the jury's decision or if there was any influence from the royal family on any of the proceedings. It should be noted that this was a time when the public, filmmakers, and the courts were all struggling with the great popularity of talking pictures and of their presumed impact. In 1934, the same year as the *Rasputin* decision, the Catholic Legion of Decency was formed in the United States to review the morality of individual films before they were released. With the Hays Office, as developed by the Hollywood studios, the Legion formed a two-pronged morality review to protect audiences from being influenced by what was shown on the screen.[76] Rather than what would later be the custom of having music on the film's soundtrack to highlight dramatic moments, filmmakers were still arranging to have a visible source for music in movies (performers, radio, phonograph) so that the audience would not get confused and ask, "Where is the music coming from?"[77] The assumption was that movie audience would take films very literally and believe what they saw to be absolutely true. Emphasizing his awareness of the tremendous impact libel in motion pictures could have, trial judge Avory said in his instructions to the jury, "It is certainly equally difficult ... to estimate the consequences of libel in a film which is being exhibited not only all over the country but in foreign countries in well."[78] (The judge's instructions were an element in the appeal, with the defendant's counsel arguing that the jury may have felt that they were to compute damages for all of the countries in which the film was shown and not just Great Britain. But the appeal court found any apparent contradiction harmless since, according to the trial transcript, Sir Patrick Hastings had evidently noticed the implications of the instructions and stated to the court that his action was limited to Great Britain; in response, Sir William Avory corrected himself before the jury.)[79]

In the immediate aftermath of the decision, Diana Wynard, who played Natasha, found that her contract with MGM was not renewed. Ethel Barrymore's contract had been allowed to expire immediately before the U.S. premiere; she had been critical of the film throughout the trial and she had claimed to be a great friend of the Youssoupoffs.[80] The second teaming of the Barrymores in *The Forsyte Saga* was never developed.[81]

While *Youssoupoff v. M.G.M.* surely was his most successful litigation experience, it was not Prince Felix Youssoupoff's last brush with the courts concerning a dramatization of the murder of Rasputin. In January 1962, the Columbia Broadcasting System (CBS) telecast the play "If I Should Die," in which Prince Felix Youssoupoff was portrayed by an actor using his name. Although the coauthors of the script later claimed to have made every effort to be historically accurate, their research, as they testified at the trial, did not include the fact that Prince Felix Youssoupoff and his wife were still alive.[82] Youssoupoff did not sue for libel, presumably because the thirty-minute drama portrayed him as a hero. Instead, he sued for invasion of privacy, asking for $1.5 million in damages.[83] One of his attorneys was once again Fanny Holtzman.

Both parties moved for summary judgment. Since use of a person's name or likeness was allowable in news situations but not in fictional formats under the New York invasion of privacy statute as interpreted by the courts,[84] the motions turned on whether the broadcast was a "fictionalization." Ironically, whereas in *Youssoupoff v. MGM*, MGM had argued in defense of libel that the film was fiction; here, claiming invasion of privacy, it was Youssoupoff who argued that the broadcast was a fictionalization, with "dialogue and action fictional in form"[85] and not a reporting of an actual event. A particular alleged falsehood in the teleplay that Youssoupoff raised was that the program suggested that he used his wife as bait to lure Rasputin to Youssoupoff's home the night of the murder.[86]

The court denied Youssoupoff's motion for summary judgment, holding that proof that an actor impersonated Youssoupoff was insufficient for summary judgment, adding, that to its reading, "while the dialogue is necessarily fictional, it is entirely innocuous as far as plaintiff's reputation, personality, or character is concerned."[87] Picking up on Youssoupoff's complaint that he had been depicted as the murderer of Rasputin for all to see, the court responded, much more coldly than the British court had, to the fact of Youssoupoff's self-generating identification, "Plaintiff may not complain, for the killing by plaintiff is an historical fact, in the public domain, where plaintiff, by his own writings, helped to put it."[88] But since CBS had "no personal knowledge of the facts, and can only express their belief, based on research," that the presentation was historically accurate, the court dismissed CBS's motion for summary judgment as well.[89] The joint denial of motions was affirmed by the appellate division.[90]

The trial was once again front-page news in *The New York Times* with the headline "Rasputin Assassin Is Here to Sue CBS."[91] The trial was lengthy — 18 days — and arduous; at one point, the 78-year-old Prince Felix collapsed under the weight of the defense attorney's cross examination, and his testimony was postponed. The state Supreme Court jury deliberated for no longer than the British jury had in 1934, only it found in favor of CBS.[92]

Prince Felix Youssoupoff died at the age of eighty on September 27, 1967,[93] a strange figure, whose act of murder did not save the country that he loved and who spent a good portion of his remaining life replaying and arguing against fictional presentations of that one December night in 1916.

The Idea of "Fictionalizations"

From its perspective, MGM, in developing *Rasputin and the Empress*, did what at the time was standard practice: it took a historical event and fictionalized portions of it, not, at least then, for legal protection, but simply to make it a better story. The creation of the character of Prince Chegodieff, had, by Youssoupoff's admission, combined elements of Youssoupoff and Grand Duke Dimitrii. The end result was a standard, dashing romantic hero played by John Barrymore that was in contrast to the actual Prince Felix Youssoupoff, who was, by all accounts, effeminate and bisexual.[94]

MGM treated this historical drama in the same way they had treated portrayals of *Billy the Kid* (1930) and *Mata Hari* (1931), combining some facts with stock melodrama.[95] In the latter film, MGM had greatly fictionalized the story of Mata Hari, and yet it had not faced any litigation. The problem with this practice, of course, in regard to *Rasputin* was that Youssoupoff and his wife were still alive, litigious, royalty, and friends of royalty, while Mata Hari had been executed as a spy in 1917 and could not sue. (It is a tenet of law that the "dead cannot sue for libel," since their ability to be personally compensated for damage to their reputations ends with death. In other words, only the person defamed, rather than his or her family members, would have standing to sue, and "the dead cannot sue for libel.") The creators of *Rasputin and the Empress* and of any dramatization of historical events have as their forefather Sir John Hayward, who felt it essential to fictionalize historical events for his audience and his medium of expression.

Interpretations of history will also reflect the time in which they are created. In 1942, with the world at war, Warner Bros. produced *They Died with Their Boots On* about the life and death of General Armstrong Custer.[96] Custer was portrayed by Errol Flynn in the same boyish manner with which he had played Robin Hood and Captain Blood for the same studio—as a visionary and a selfless hero. Thirty years later, in a revisionist look at the story, *Little Big Man* presented Custer as a selfish, vainglorious lunatic.[97]

Writing about his 1991 film *JFK*, the director and screenwriter Oliver Stone echoed Sir John Hayward, when he claimed, "Artists certainly have the right — and possibly the obligation — to step in and reinterpret the history of our times."[98]

Yet, while history must be compressed in a movie, made dramatic, and even reinterpreted by artists, the medium of film is lifelike and apt to be mistaken for reality. Subject matter that has a nearly contemporary historical basis, with actual people represented, is especially prone to the accusation that audiences will mistake the fruits of the adaptive process of moviemaking for the reality; as a result, living people could claim defamation.

Writing specifically about films and television movies of the 1970s, 1980s, and 1990s called "docudramas"— which, like documentaries, are based on actual events but "dramatized"— Max Frankel wrote,

> [They] misappropriate public figures and events…. They abuse the mass power of movie imagery; unlike books, they will not soon be rebutted, amended or corrected by rival visions of history. Docudramas put indelible words, thoughts, and motives into their characters' mouths, heads, and hearts. They damage the appeal of fiction and corrode the meaning of truth.[99]

After the *Rasputin* case, filmmakers responded in a variety of ways. They paid more attention to whether or not those portrayed in films were still alive — although they sometimes still made mistakes— and if the film's subjects were alive, then the studios often worked to obtain their cooperation. For example, Billie Burke, Florenz Ziegfeld's widow, was hired as a consultant for the 1936 film biography *The Great Ziegfeld*[100] in which she was portrayed by Myrna Loy and was also given an MGM contract that resulted in her playing the Good Witch Gilda in *The Wizard of Oz* in 1939. The studio also hired the comedian and singer Fanny Brice to play herself. Songwriter and entertainer George M. Cohan sold the rights to his life story — which was finally called *Yankee Doodle Dandy*,[101] — permission to use his songs, and his cooperation to Warner Bros. in return for a contract in which Warner agreed that Cohan would have "the final decision in connection with characterization, dialogue and all references to" himself and his family. For his part, Cohan agreed to provide approval for a script "which may be wholly or partly fiction, as finally edited and approved by Mr. Cohan."[102] But more often than not, filmmakers waited until the major personages in a story were dead before they filmed it.

Filmmakers also identified their intentions with disclaimers. By classifying their respective actions as libel, the *Merle, Youssoupoff,* and *Brown* courts brought to suits against films the precedents of actions and holdings concerning reported libel in fiction.[103] Fifteen years before *Rasputin v. MGM*, the prevalent view in these matters had been summed up in this way: "In a play or novel there is, practically speaking, a *prima facie* presumption that the characters are fictitious."[104] Since MGM, according to its New York vice president and general counsel, had always felt that the Rasputin film was a work of fiction, it made perfect sense for filmmakers to announce this understanding and to align it with the *prima facie* presumption concerning characters in plays or novels.[105] Taking the hint from Lord Justice Scrutton in the *Youssoupoff v. MGM* appeal that with a disclaimer that disavowed any intent to represent actual personages or events the case might have been decided differently, the American movie industry acted accordingly. Soon after the *Rasputin* decision, films began to carry disclaimers that largely read: "The characters and events presented in this film [or photoplay] are fictitious. Any resemblance to persons and events living or dead is purely coincidental [or unintended]." For films that did indeed portray historical events, the disclaimer seems to echo the philosophy of Sir John Hayward that divergences from actual facts are "liberties" that filmmakers openly take.

The incongruity of this soon became readily apparent. Films in the 1930s and 1940s that were based on historical events—*Juarez, The Story of Louis Pasteur, The Adventures of Mark Twain, Wilson*—just as *Rasputin* had been, as well as those that were strongly suggested by them, carried the disclaimer that said they were fictions, fantasia, riffs, or romanticized retellings of the event. For example, the 1937 film *The Life of Emile Zola*,[106] whose very title states that it will tell the story of the noted nineteenth-century journalist, begins with the disclaimer, "No such resemblance is real or inferred to actual persons or events."

The incongruity of such disclaimers was evident in another very early one, which comes at the beginning of the 1936 Warner Brothers' film, *The Charge of the Light Brigade*,[107] which also starred Errol Flynn as a visionary and selfless hero.[108] The film was inspired by the poem by Alfred Lord Tennyson, which was itself inspired by an actual incident during the Crimean War in 1854. The film quotes the poem but generally creates an entirely fictitious story in which, rather than a "blunder," as Tennyson called the charge, it is a bold, self-sacrificial plan by Flynn's character to save the day. The disclaimer that starts the film, obviously written in the aftermath of the *Rasputin* decision, reads,

> This production has its basis in history. The historical basis,
> however, has been fictionized [*sic*] for the purposes of this picture,
> and the names of many characters, many characters themselves, the

story, incidents, and institutions, are fictitious. With the exception
of known historical characters, whose actual names are herein
used, no identification with actual persons, living or dead, is
intended or should be inferred.

Virtually every U.S. film, whether based on a factual event or not,
began to carry disclaimers. The disconnect — the film *Gentleman Jim* is
based on the life of James J. Corbett, heavyweight champion from 1892 to
1897, but the disclaimer says the movie's characters and events are "fictitious"— was not unnoticed. In the 1940 Broadway musical *Louisiana Purchase,* the two opening scenes lampoon the disclaimer. The musical,
produced by B.G. de Sylva with music and lyrics by Irving Berlin and book
by Morris Ryskind, is about corruption in Louisiana politics and begins
in an attorney's office with a secretary typing a letter from the attorney,
expressing concern to the musical's creators that since the show is based
on Louisiana politics and on facts they will all be sued. But he concludes
that there is a way out — if they say "It's based on fiction." In response to
the attorney's advice, a chorus of men and women enter and sing a version of a film disclaimer, adding that they have invented a place called
"New Orleans" and that "if there is such a place, it's certainly news to us."
The chorus concludes, "Don't go out and sue. We don't mean you."[109]

Even twenty years later, films that were blatantly based on actual people and events carried the blanket disclaimer that the characters were fictitious and any resemblance to people living or dead was coincidental. A
prime example is the 1957 film *Wings of Eagles,*[110] which was a biography
of Commander Frank "Spig" Wead. Wead was a record-setting Navy flyer
who broke his back in mid-life and, thus crippled, became a screenwriter
and playwright, writing about the types of adventures that he had once
experienced but no longer could. Wead often wrote screenplays for John
Ford, the director of *Wings of Eagles,* who worked with Wead on the movie
They Were Expendable, of which more later. Ford was a close friend of
Wead's— Ford later said that he had wanted to call the film "The 'Spig'
Wead Story," but the studio was convinced that people would not know
what a "Spig Wead" was— and the film is a lovingly produced, although
sometimes depressing, tribute. In interviews, Ford later went out of his
way to attest to the film's authenticity:

> I tried to tell the story as truthfully as possible, and everything in
> the picture was true. The fight in the club — throwing the cake —
> actually happened. I can verify that as an eye-witness— I ducked it.[111]

The film's credits openly assert that the *Wings of Eagle* is based on fact.
The screenplay credits include the claim, "Based on the Life and Writings

of Commander Frank W. 'Spig' Wead." Before the film begins, the following appears on the screen:

> This motion picture is dedicated to the men who brought air power to the United States Navy. One such man was Commander Frank "Spig" Wead. The flying records he smashed helped win him the lasting respect of his fellow Navy men. The screenplays he wrote helped him win the lasting respect of his fellow writers in Hollywood.

However, also part of the film's opening credits, in small type at the bottom of the screen, is the following disclaimer:

> The characters and incident and films in this photoplay are fictitious and any similarity to actual persons living or dead or to actual films is purely coincidental.

In other words, the film is based on the life of a real human being to whom we owe a great deal, but the characters and events are fictitious. What the filmmakers have done is tell Wead's basic story but also to give themselves the freedom to make things up. Some of the fictionalization, interestingly enough, involves Ford himself. The director in the movie who gives Wead employment as a screenwriter is called "John Dodge," a play on words since both Ford and Dodge are American automobiles. Actor Ward Bond is dressed as Ford — dark glasses and boots. Ford claimed that "everything in the picture is true" — except, obviously, the portrayal of himself.

The reference in the disclaimer to "films" is also interesting in that it refers to a liberty *Wings of Eagles* takes in portraying Wead's first screenplay. Wead and "Dodge" are shown screening the "rushes" — preedited film — of the 1932 *Hell Divers* starring Wallace Beery and Clark Gable — and comment on how the young Gable will become a star, which he did. *Hell Divers* did feature Gable and Berry, but it was directed, not by Ford or even "Dodge," but by George Hill. Ford's first film with Wead was actually *Air Mail* (also 1932) starring Pat O'Brien and Ralph Bellamy — not as potent a combination as Gable and Beery. Just as Ford fictionalized himself, he distorted his whole relationship with Wead — presumably for dramatic effect.

In the year prior to *Wings of Eagles,* another biographical film had a similar incongruity — claiming authenticity upfront while also carrying a traditional disclaimer that it was fictitious. *Somebody Up There Likes Me,*[112] based on the autobiography of middleweight champion boxer Rocky Graziano, has a disclaimer that it is fictitious but also displays at the film's start a message from Graziano himself—"This is the way I remember it—definitely."

This disconnect—claiming fictionalization while at the same time promoting the film as a true story—even resulted in a slight brou-ha-ha at the 1955 Academy Awards when *Interrupted Melody*, based on the life of opera singer Marjorie Lawrence, won the Oscar for "best original story and screenplay." "How can the screenplay qualify as an original story when it is based on someone's life?" asked columnist Army Archerd.[113] Of course, inventing a story while claiming that the film was based on someone else's life had become standard Hollywood practice.

The concept of disclaimers—the film is fictitious—when used with obviously fact-based films basically suggests an alternate universe in which there is a recognizable fact-based figure leading a different existence. It relies on the audiences' "willing suspension of disbelief," using Coleridge's phrase,[114] assuming that they suspect that this is not the way the charge of the Light Brigade or the battle of the Little Big Horn really happened but go along with the entertainment of a movie.

FILM PERSONAS

The same reliance on the audience's suspension of disbelief began to apply to fictional personas that utilize the real names of performers. The slapstick comics The Three Stooges—Moe Howard, Larry Fine, and Curly Howard (and later Shemp Howard)—usually used their own names in their films in which they played wacky, pie-throwing, eye-poking clowns—activities that they evidently did not do in real life. Jack Benny portrayed himself in his radio and television shows and some spin-off movies as a miser who has a vault in his basement protected by a moat filled with alligators and by an ancient guardsman—again, something that he was not. What Benny and the Stooges and others were doing were playing characters that simply had their names. (Under the same argument, this is why with the 1997 film *Contact* the filmmakers could argue that although they used footage of President Clinton in this science fiction film, Clinton's image became an actor playing a president.)

This alternate universe of personas carrying the same names as actors proved too much for actress Ann Sheridan, who was asked to play a character named "Ann Sheridan" in the 1943 Warner Brothers movie *Hollywood Canteen*[115]—based on the "canteens" during World War II in which actual movie stars served coffee and danced with servicemen. In the original screenplay, the character Ann Sheridan was to fall in love and promise to marry one of the servicemen. Sheridan said this was "crazy." Such a thing wouldn't happen, and it especially wouldn't happen with her — that is, the real Ann Sheridan. The studio replaced Sheridan in the film with actress Joan Leslie, who plays a character named Joan Leslie who falls in love with and promises to marry one of the servicemen at the Hollywood canteen. And, of course, *Hollywood Canteen* carries a disclaimer that the characters and events are fictitious.

This alternative universe of actors playing fictionalized versions of themselves could reach dazzling heights. In screenwriter Charles Kaufman and director Spike Jonze's 1999 film *Being John Malkovich*, actor John Malkovich plays John Horatio Malkovich, who finds that a puppeteer has found a way to follow a passageway into Malkovich's mind. Malkovich said that he assumed that people would realize it was only a movie. For Kaufman and Jonze's next film, writer Susan Orlean sold them the film rights to her nonfiction book *The Orchid Thief: A True Story of Beauty* and assumed Kaufman and Jonze would do a traditional adaptation. When she read the script of *Adaptation*,[116] she found that it had become a screenplay about Kaufman's inability to adapt the book. There was a fictionalized version of Kaufman and of Orlean herself, showing a fictitious version of how she had written her book. In the movie, the Orleans character is a pill-popping adulteress who posts nude photos of herself on the Internet. There was also a fictitious character of Kaufman's twin brother Donald. Orlean ultimately decided to approve the script of the film, saying exactly what makers of fact-based films claim the audience understands: "It's a movie. It's not real life."[117] She said as well, "The people who know me know what's true and what's not. The people who know my work can probably guess what's real and not real. The general public? Let's hope they get it."[118] Both films carried disclaimers, by the way.

In a November 19, 1997, episode of the television situation comedy *Ellen,* British actress Emma Thompson played a character named "Emma Thompson" who was an alcoholic, closeted lesbian actress who wasn't even British but had learned her British accent from watching Julie Andrews movies. Emma Thompson is British. (The ownership of film personas will be discussed in Chapter IV).

Post-*Youssoupoff*

Film comedies often poked fun at the disclaimer that they were made to carry. Even the 1951 British film *Green Grow the Rushes*,[119] starring Richard Burton and Robert Livesey in a comedy about whiskey smuggling, begins with the printed legend: "The characters and events depicted in this

film are fictitious. Any resemblance to people living or dead is A MIRACLE."
Charlie Chaplin played with the wording in a mock disclaimer for his 1940
film *The Great Dictator* in which he portrayed both the dictator Hynkel
and a Jewish barber. The disclaimer reads, "Any resemblance between
Hynkel the dictator and the Jewish barber is purely coincidental."[120]

The effectiveness of disclaimers has been much debated. Some have
found them a demonstration of the lack of intent to injure,[121] others have
seen them as "helpful to a finding that the work is not of and concerning
the plaintiff but by no means a bar to identification" since the issue in the
tort of defamation is what a reasonable person might infer and not what
the author intended;[122] and one court discounted them as "nothing more
than tongue-in-cheek."[123] Disclaimers are generally seen as indicators of
the overall concept that films are by nature fictitious.

Relatively few motion picture libel actions in the years since *Youssoupoff* have reached the appellate level or been argued in federal or higher
state court and have, therefore, become matters of record. This suggests
that the circumstances of *Youssoupoff* were "exceptional," just as the contemporary analysis of the case predicted.[124] Still, there has been a ham-
mering out about how much credence the courts will give to the idea that
fact-based films are "fictional" and whether techniques used to establish
identification in fiction work when applied to film. In most cases, while
not usually addressing the issue of the disclaimer, the courts have required
demanding standards of identification and implicitly accepted the concept
that films are fictions.

Two years after *Youssoupoff v. MGM*, a psychic, palmist, and some-
time actress who worked under the name of "Casandra" or "Cassandra"
sued RKO Radio Pictures for both libel, appropriation, and invasion of
privacy[125] in a minor film entitled *Bunker Bean*.[126] The film, which was
based on both a novel and a play of the same name, has a character named
"Countess Casandra" who was a con artist. Confirming that the plaintiff
was not referred to by her real name, that the actress portraying Countess
Casandra did not resemble the plaintiff, that the plaintiff had never advertised herself as *Countess* Casandra, and that Cassandra was a character in
Greek mythology, the court concluded that identification was lacking,
adding, "The defendant had as much right to use the name 'Casandra' in
their motion picture, for a character representing a fortune teller or alleged
psychic, as the plaintiff has to assume the name "as psychic and palmist."[127]

In 1942, Warner Bros. produced the musical film *Yankee Doodle Dandy*
based on the life of George M. Cohan, composer and lyricist of such Broadway songs as "Give My Regards to Broadway" and "You're a Grand Old
Flag." Cohan had been part of a show business family who performed as

"the Four Cohans." In 1899, he married another entertainer, Ethel Levey, who briefly performed with the family as "the fifth Cohan" and also played in a number of Cohan's legendary musicals, including *Little Johnny Jones* and *George Washington, Jr.,* sometimes impersonating men. Cohan and Levey were divorced in 1906, and Cohan married Agnes Harris, the sister of his business partner Sam Harris and a dancer in *Little Johnny Jones.* In 1941, dying of cancer, Cohan, as previously noted, sold the rights to his life story to Warner Bros. in return for approval of characterization, dialogue, and references concerning him and his family. The contract also specified that he would have approval of the actor who would play him — ultimately, James Cagney. As part of the script approval process, Cohan told Robert Bruckner, the principal screenwriter, that there would be no overt love-making and no reference to his first wife. Bruckner, consequently, gave Cohan only one wife in the film, played by Joan Leslie. Her name was Mary — so named so that Cohan could write the song "Mary (Is a Grand Old Name)" in her honor, which the real Cohan did not do since neither of his wives were named Mary — and she was a performer who ultimately stays home and takes care of Cohan. "Mary," then, could be seen as a composite of Ethel Levy and Agnes Harris. In the film, Cohan and his one wife Mary grow old together.

The film was a huge success — especially since it was a patriotic movie that was released in May 1942 after World War II had begun — and was nominated for eight Academy Awards, including Best Picture and Best Original Story, and won awards for sound recording, scoring of a motion picture, and best actor for Cagney as Cohan. Cohan died in December 1942. After the success of the film, Cohan's first wife, Ethel Levey, sued the studio for invasion of privacy (although the case is freely cited in defamation proceedings).[128] The court's decision focused on identification and found that there was no resemblance of the actress playing Mary Cohan to Ethel Levy, that there were incidents in the film that Mrs. Levy had no part in, and that the wife character was minor to the film as a whole. The court concluded, "The reproduction in the picture of songs plaintiff sang and of scenes in which she took part and the introduction of fictional characters and a largely fictional treatment of Cohan's life may hurt plaintiff's feelings but they do not violate her right of privacy."[129] (Levy died in 1955 at the age of 64 in New York City, the same year Cagney reprised his Cohan role for a cameo in the film *The Seven Little Foys*.)[130]

By the time of *Wright v. RKO* (1944),[131] the studios evidently had developed a system with which the courts seemed generally satisfied. The suit was for libel concerning the RKO film *Primrose Path*.[132] The movie was based on a play of the same name by Robert Buckner and Walter Hart, which was adapted from the novel *February Hill* by Virginia Lincoln, although the film's credits do not mention the novel. In the film, Mamie Adams supports her alcoholic husband and two daughters by prostitution, the same profession her own mother had practiced. Mamie's eldest daughter, Ellie May, wants to leave this pathless life, and when she meets and falls in love with Ed Wallace, who works at the hamburger stand on the beach, she feels she has her chance. However, when Ed finds out Ellie May's family secret, the relationship begins to fall apart. She is about to take up her mother and grandmother's profession but is saved by Ed.

After the film's release, the Burdettes, former neighbors of Lincoln, the author of the novel on which the play that was the source of the film was based, sued for libel. The court found that the filmmakers had omitted and changed details from the book that might have connected the Wright/Burdette family with characters in the film, including names and the location of the story. The court took special note that the book, which the plaintiffs claimed was libelous (and that as a result the film was libelous), was not cited as a source for the movie. The only real person whose personality the court felt was retained in the film was the father of the Wright family, who was dead. Based on this analysis, the court held for RKO.

Fighting Father Dunne (1947)[133] concerns the founding and maintenance of a newsboys' home in St. Louis by Father Peter Dunne. Matt Davis had become a resident of the home when he was 13 in 1906 and stayed there for four years. While Davis presented no behavior problems while he was at the home, a character named "Matt Davis" is portrayed in the movie as a juvenile delinquent who kills a police officer. Davis sued for libel, and a jury found for the movie studio. The verdict was upheld on appeal in *Davis v. RKO Pictures.*[134] There was a similar situation in *Aguilar v. Universal City Studios,*[135] concerning the film *Zoot Suit,*[136] which was based a play that was based on the Sleepy Lagoon murder trial of the 1940s. In the film, the character who has the same name as an actual person is part of the gang involved in the murder. In both cases, the courts stated that the issue was whether persons who knew or knew of the plaintiff could reasonably have understood the exhibited picture to refer to [him/her]"[137] and concluded that, given the differences between the actual person and the character in the film, identification had not been proved. The *Aguilar* court added, "In a country of this size, containing all nationalities, it would be truly remarkable if an author used a name which was possessed by no one. Only the creator of "Mork" from Ork would appear to be safe."[138]

The novel and movie *Anatomy of a Murder* was inspired by an actual murder case in which the novelist was actively involved. In 1952, Lieutenant

Peterson shot and killed Maurice Chenowith for the alleged "rape" of Peterson's wife. Peterson was tried in Marquette, Michigan in 1952 and acquitted by a jury on the defense of insanity. His attorney was John Voelker, who later became an associate justice of the Supreme Court of Michigan. On his own time, Voelker, under the pseudonym Robert Traver, wrote the novel *Anatomy of a Murder,* which was inspired by the Peterson case; it was published in 1957. A controversial film version — since it dealt explicitly with the subject of rape — was produced in 1959. In the movie, Lieutenant Manion shoots and kills Barney Quill for the alleged rape of Manion's wife. He is acquitted on a defense of insanity.[139]

Hazel Wheeler, widow of Maurice Chernowith, and Terry Ann Chenowith, his daughter, sued the book's publisher and Columbia Pictures for libel and invasion of privacy. Wheeler claimed she was defamed by the book's portrayal of Janice Quill — Barney Quill's wife — a character not in the movie. Terry Ann claimed that she was defamed by the film's portrayal of Mary Pilant, the illegitimate daughter of Barney Quill, whom his unseen lover had had out of wedlock. In *Wheeler v. Dell Publishing,*[140] concerning the widow's claims, the court found that her situation was comparable, not to Princess Irina Youssoupoff, as Ms. Wheeler had argued, but to Mrs. Levey in *Levey v. Warner Bros. Pictures,* stating that no one who knew Hazel Wheeler could reasonably identify her with the character of Janice Quill.[141] The court gave as its justification the same reasons that Mrs. Wheeler found the characterization to be defamatory — Mrs. Wheeler denied having any of the unsavory characteristics of Janice Quill.[142] As for the child, she was nine at the time of the murder, but her alleged counterpart in the movie is the "romantic lead."[143] The court confirmed the lower court judgment, finding no identification.

The apparent difficulty of establishing "identification" has led plaintiffs to other types of actions such as invasion of privacy[144] and suits involving the right of publicity.[145] The actress Elizabeth Taylor, for example, drew on the right of publicity in 1982 in suing the American Broadcasting Companies (ABC) and David Paradine Productions for their "planned exhibition and broadcast of a fictional, made-for-television movie exploiting" her name, likeness, and public and professional reputation.[146] The production was later abandoned, and the suit dismissed. But twelve years later, Taylor sued the National Broadcasting Company (NBC) in California Superior Court to prevent the network from using her image and likeness or using an actress to play her in a miniseries about her life, again invoking the right of publicity. Unlike the first one, this suit reached court. In the time between the two suits, the California right of publicity statute had been amended and reexamined. The court rejected Taylor's argument, stating that the right of publicity cannot be used to stifle comment on the lives of public people. An injunction against NBC would constitute an unconstitutional prior restraint against First Amendment-protected expression.[147]

As the Elizabeth Taylor situation ultimately illustrates, these other types of actions have usually met with little success. In 1965, 20th Century–Fox released a political satire/farce entitled *John Golfarb, Please Come Home,*[148] which ends with a football game between Notre Dame and a team assembled by an Arab sheik whose son has been refused admission to that school. Notre Dame sued the filmmakers[149] but, pointedly, not for libel.[150] The action was rather for unfair competition, in that the defendants had illegally appropriated the university's name, reputation, and goodwill. The court could find no support for the university's action, stating that "the University's grievance, notwithstanding its disclaimer, sounds in defamation and its remedy, if it can prove libel, is at law."[151] Earlier in the decision, the court provided its opinion as to the claim of libel: "Is there any basis for any inference on the part of rational readers or viewers that the antics engaging their attention are anything more than fiction or that the real Notre Dame is in some way associated with its fabrication or presentation? In our judgment, there is none whatsoever."[152]

There was no chance of a libel suit concerning the 1979 film *Agatha,*[153] a film that fictitiously answered the mystery as to where mystery writer Agatha Christie had been for eleven days in 1926. Mrs. Christie had died in 1976. Her heirs sued both the filmmakers and the publishers of a related book for violation of their right of publicity. The book was labeled a novel, and as such did not qualify for the news or biography exemptions of the New York privacy statute. The court then addressed the question as to whether a novel or film, as fictionalizations, are entitled to any constitutional protection; the answer was yes, and the court cited the *John Golfarb* decision —*Notre Dame Du Lac v. 20th Century–Fox*—for its finding that the viewer of the film would certainly know that the events portrayed were fictitious.[154] The court held that, "the right of publicity does not attach here, where a fictionalized account of an event in the life of a public figure is depicted in a novel or movie, and in such novel or movie, it is evident to the public that the events depicted are fictitious."[155]

A case similar to the Agatha Christie suit involved the 1972 crash of Eastern Flight 401. In 1976, John Fuller wrote a nonfiction account of the crash and its investigation titled *The Ghost of Flight 401,* so called because Fuller discovered that there has been reported sightings of the ghosts of the crew after the crash. The book was made into an NBC television movie in 1978.[156] The movie basically turned the story into a ghost tale, with the pilot's ghost trying to tell the investigators what happened. The movie retained the actual name of the flight and the date of the event but changed the name of the pilot — from Robert Loft to Dom Cimoli — as well as the names of others involved in the incident and its investigation. The family of the flight's pilot sued the book's publisher and the film for invasion of privacy and for violation of a Florida statute that was similar to the New York statute evoked in the Christie suit in that it prevented unauthorized commercial or advertising use of the name or likeness of a person. The Florida circuit court found for the defendant, and on appeal the Florida court of appeals held that the statute was inapplicable since the movie did not qualify as either commercial or advertising use under the statute. The appeals court also affirmed the lower court's decision that the defendant's conduct was not of a sufficiently egregious nature to establish a claim of invasion of privacy but tellingly added:

> We are wary of a blanket rule barring all relatives of a deceased from bringing a common law invasion of privacy action simply because the relatives were not directly involved in the publicity. However, in our view such relatives must shoulder a heavy burden in establishing a cause of action. When there are unusual circumstances, such as those that were involved in most of the cases which have recognized claims by the relatives, it may be that a defendant's conduct towards a decedent will be found to be sufficiently egregious to give rise to an independent cause of action in favor of members of decedent's immediate family.[157]

Plaintiff Victories

Three cases form major exceptions to the courts' trends toward accepting fact-based films as fictions, to requiring exact identification of the plaintiff and the characters in the film, and to according some implicit credit to the disclaimer. The three, however, are limited to their specific situations.

In 1945, MGM produced the World War II drama *They Were Expendable*,[158] based on William L. White's 1942 nonfiction book of the same name. The book was the story of Lt. John Bulkeley who had pioneered the use of the PT boat in combat. The book also described the heroism of Lt. Robert B. Kelly. The film spans in time from December 1941 through April 1942.

Lt. John Bulkeley was the commanding officer of MTB-3 (motor torpedo squadron), which had arrived in Manila Bay on September 28, 1941.

After the attack on Pearl Harbor on December 7, 1941, the six-boat squadron was used to run messages from Corregidor to navy headquarters. On December 17,1941, the squadron rescued more than 300 survivors from the SS Corregidor, which had run into an American minefield and sunk. In January 1942, the boats conducted an attack on a group of transports and sank a 5,000-ton freighter. In addition, under the cover of darkness on March 11–13, 1942, General Douglas MacArthur and many of his staff were evacuated from Corregidor by the remaining boats of MTB-3. They were taken on a voyage of 560 miles to an island where the general could be picked up by a U.S. Army airplane and flown to Australia. After the U.S. Asiatic Fleet left the area, the patrol boats (PT boats) were the last visible signs of a fighting naval force in the Philippines. As the boats were lost, the men from the squadron were sent to work for the Army in defense of the peninsula. Bulkeley was awarded the Congressional Medal of Honor and retired as a vice admiral. Kelly received the Navy Cross for his heroic actions.

The modest Kelly was only persuaded to agree to be portrayed in a motion picture version of the book by a personal request from the secretary of the navy. He gave written permission that he could be depicted by a character corresponding to him but specified that his own name not be used. This was done. Bulkeley's character, renamed "John Brickley," was portrayed by Robert Montgomery; Kelly's became "Rusty Ryan" and was played by John Wayne. Even General MacArthur was fictionalized. While the incident of the evacuation of MacArthur is shown in the film — and the film begins with a quote from General MacArthur shown on the screen — he is never referred to by name. An actor dressed as the general and wearing sunglasses as MacArthur did is shown being evacuated. On leaving the boat, the character makes a point of shaking Lieutenant Brickley's hand, who in turn salutes him. (The evacuation is portrayed — and indeed begins — a later film, MacArthur,[159] in which the general, played by Gregory Peck, openly and frequently refers to Bulkeley by name.)

However, while there were these "fictions," the film was painstakingly and even lovingly made by people who had fought wars. The screenwriter Frank "Spig" Wead was a navy veteran. The director, John Ford, had joined the navy when the war started and had filmed actual battles. He also had known Bulkeley.

Yet in spite of the attempts to fictionalize and therefore distance the film from Lieutenant Kelly — changing his name, making the evacuation that of a MacArthur-like character — and in spite of his signed release, Lieutenant Kelly sued for libel because he felt the movie's portrayal of his counterpart, who was played by Wayne in the same manner he brought to most of his action hero roles, showed him to be heroic but moody and undisciplined. Kelly claimed to have been held up to ridicule by the movie in the Boston military community in which he moved.[160] (Interestingly enough, Bulkeley did not feel that the film's portrayal of Kelly was inaccurate.[161])

The court appears to have been particularly sympathetic to Kelly's embarrassment among his fellow officers. It suggested that the screenwriter's characterization of "Rusty Ryan" was a layman's view of military heroism rather than that of a professional in the military and imagined a motion picture of Mr. Justice Holmes in which he was shown deciding cases in a way laymen would regard as fair but that lawyers would regard as unprofessional.[162]

As for identification, the court pointed out that while the movie had a disclaimer that the characters and events depicted were fictitious, it also carried the credit, "Based on the book *They Were Expendable* by William L. White," apparently to take advantage of the book's popularity. In the book, Kelly's actual name is used in a prologue. The court had little difficulty in concluding that by directing viewers to the book as the source for the movie the filmmakers were forging an identification between Kelly and "Ryan." It is in this context that the court cavalierly dismissed the importance of the disclaimer:

> The disingenuous legend that the persons and events shown in the picture were fictitious and that any similarity to actual persons living or dead was purely coincidental would not have been treated by the average person or naval officer as anything more than a tongue-in-cheek disclaimer in view of the express reference by the movie to Mr. White's book, in view of the statement of Navy cooperation and in view of the unmistakable portrayal of General MacArthur, his family and other historic personages, including both Lt. Buckley [sic] and the plaintiff.[163]

The claim that a movie that portrays recognizable events is fiction is a fabric of fragile weave. The creators of *They Were Expendable* wanted to have their cake and eat it; they wanted to capitalize on the book's success by claiming it as a source and yet fictionalize Kelly as per his request; the court found that they could not do both. The damages that the court awarded were meager compared to those given to the Youssoupoff's — only $3,000 for loss of reputation among naval officers who attended performances in two Boston theaters and for mental disturbance — and yet the court noted that Kelly could take justification in the award as emblem that his reputation was intact.[164] Kelly died in 1989, Bulkeley in 1996.

In the second (and a related) case, another veteran of Bataan and Corregidor in the Philippines also sued the makers of *They Were Expendable*. In his book, White referred to a nurse he named "Peggy." In the film, this nurse, played by Donna Reed and renamed "Sandy," was shown to have a romantic relationship with Lieutenant Ryan. After the book's release in 1942, "Peggy" was identified as Lt. Beulah Greenwalt, who, at the time, was still a prisoner of the Japanese, having been captured in May 1942 and taken to a camp. She and other nurses were liberated by U.S. forces in February 1945, ten months before the movie was released in the U.S. on December 20, 1945. In January 1946, Greenwalt married Bruce Walcher, another prisoner of the Bataan "Death March," whom she had met in a Denver hospital. Beulah Greenwalt Walcher then sued Loewe's, Inc., parent company of MGM, claiming that the portrayal of "Sandy" was "a humiliating invasion of privacy" and "cheapened her character." She had had no such romance with Lieutenant Kelly, she insisted. In its defense, Loewe's, Inc., argued, just as MGM had in *Youssoupoff*, that "Sandy" in the film was a "composite character" rather than a portrayal of White's "Peggy." On December 3, 1948, a federal court jury in Missouri ruled in Walcher's favor, awarding her $290,000, rather than the $400,000 she had asked for.[165] Since it was a jury verdict with no appeal of record, the case did not establish a legal precedent. As was evidently the situation with Lieutenant Kelly, the jury was likely to have been sympathetic to nurse Greenwalt's 33 months of imprisonment and her humiliation of being newly married while a movie was in mass circulation suggesting that she had been romantic with another man — Lieutenant Kelly — whom she claimed to have barely met. (Bulkeley thought that Kelly and Greenwalt had been offended by Ford's subtle suggestion that "Ryan" and "Sandy" had slept together.[166]) Walcher died in 1993 at the age of 81.[167] There was no mention of the lawsuit in her obituaries, and in discussions with a potential ghostwriter of the Walchers' memoir, she and her husband had described the money they received from "John Ford and MGM Studios" as "a relatively paltry settlement."[168]

The third case involved an episode of a television series. On October 15, 1959, the American Broadcasting Company (ABC) Television network premiered the television series *The Untouchables,* based on the nonfiction book by Eliot Ness and Oscar Fraley.[169] It was produced by Desilu Studios. In the first episode, which was later released as a theatrical film entitled *The Scarface Mob,* investigative work by Eliot Ness, a U.S. Treasury agent, and his band of "untouchables"— agents who could not be corrupted — led to the 1931 conviction of Alphonse (Al) Capone, head of the Chicago rackets. Having disposed of Capone, the series then pitted Ness against other gangsters of the period, most of whom the real-life Ness had had no connection with. The series had begun with the disclaimer that it was "based on the book by Eliot Ness and Oscar Fraley, although certain portions have been fictionalized." By the series' end in 1963, the disclaimer read that "the events and characters are fictitious, although some characters are based on the book by Eliot Ness and Oscar Fraley."[170]

Feeling perhaps that it had eliminated Al Capone from the series too quickly, Desilu brought back Al Capone in 1961 in an episode entitled "The Big Train." The episode had a factual basis: on August 19, 1934, Al Capone and other federal prisoners were indeed transferred from the federal penitentiary in Atlanta to the federal penitentiary at Alcatraz in California. But the creators of *The Untouchables,* playing "what if," developed from this the fiction that Capone's gang had tried to free Capone in the course of the transfer with the assistance of a corrupt prison guard and that Ness and his men foiled the attempt. The corrupt guard had long become a stereotype of prison films.

In response to the entire series, Al Capone's son and daughter sued the *Untouchables'* production company for misappropriation of Capone's name, likeness, and personality and for unjust enrichment. They lost, as the court found they had no rights in the matter.[171] But in a concurring opinion, Justice Duffy of the court of appeals stated that "the fictitious products [of Desilu] overstepped the bounds of decency."[172] He specifically cited "The Big Train" as an incident that was "completely fictitious. Nothing like it, so far as Al Capone was concerned, ever occurred."[173] The fictions in "The Big Train" so enraged James V. Bennett, director of the federal Bureau of Prisons, that he publicly protested the broadcast to the Federal Communications Commission.[174] While Capone was dead and could not sue for defamation, and his family had no rights to his image, one of his prison guards was still alive and sued for defamation for the depiction that one of Capone's guards assisted in his fictitious escape.[175]

The defendants argued that the plaintiff's real name was not used, that only one of the two guards was portrayed as corrupt, and that the plaintiff could not show that the corrupt guard was specifically identified as him. But the plaintiff listed all of the things that were done in the show to anchor it in reality: the transfer of Capone did take place on August 19, 1934 — the date shown on the screen in the show; the production used the names of two persons actually associated with the transfer — Capone and Attorney General Homer S. Cummings; Capone's actual prison numbers— 40886 in Atlanta and 85 at Alcatraz — were utilized; authentic film of prisoners was shown as part of the show; and the transference of the prisoners from San Francisco to Alcatraz by barge as depicted in "The Big Train" was the way it was actually done.

The court affirmed the overruling of the defendant's demurrer — basically, a response to a complaint that says, "so what," meaning that even if what the plaintiff is saying is true, there is still, according to the defense, no cause of action. The court held that the issue of identification was a jury matter that could be decided by "the extrinsic fact approach."[176] The court cited *Youssoupoff* as an example that "semi-fictional portrayal of a real life event is fraught with the possibility that the public, or at least that segment of the public that knows the plaintiff, will believe the presentation refers to the plaintiff."[177] The demurrer decision was influenced, perhaps, by the court's admission that "No prior Georgia case appears to have presented the exact question involved here as to whether a dramatic presentation of an incident that actually happened may be defamatory."[178] The court struggled through territory already explored by other courts, including whether defamation in a film or television show was slander or libel, and ultimately turned the matter over to jury deliberation. The suit was settled on February 1, 1963, for an undisclosed amount and so never went to trial.[179]

These three cases, however, stand out as anomalies amid all the unsuccessful suits against filmmakers from people who felt they had been defamed or had their rights or privacy or publicity violated.[180]

The irony of the *Youssoupoff* decision is that it produced the disclaimers that accompanied almost every film made in the United States since *Rasputin and the Empress* and yet, given the relative lack of judicial interest in the issue, fostered no real change in the way filmmakers treated historical events. The personalities and traits of actual people and the details of actual events were routinely altered in favor of more effective or at least conventional dramatic effects. Even if the historical events portrayed were within living memory, the filmmakers took comfort in the presumed safety of the disclaimer.

This distortion of history in television shows — in which the motivation of historical characters and the events of their lives were typically simplified, romanticized, or distorted — was parodied in a humorous episode of the science fiction television series *The Twilight Zone* in "Showdown with Rance McGrew," written by series creator Rod Serling.[181] McGrew, the star of a television western that turns historical western characters like Jesse James and Billy the Kid into stock villains whom McGrew defeats, is visited by the ghost of Jesse James. James tells the star that he and the others have been watching the show from their perch in western heaven and have taken offense in McGrew's misrepresentation of them. James comes back to life as McGrew's agent and forces him to do his stories with accuracy and fairness.

The Effect of *Sullivan*

In *New York Times Co. v. Sullivan*,[182] the U.S. Supreme Court held that falsity of a statement about public officials would no longer be sufficient for libel but, in addition, required a showing of absolute malice — a statement made with either knowledge that it was false or with a reckless disregard as to whether it was false or not.[183] The *Sullivan* actual malice rule was later extended to public figures.[184]

At first blush, the *Sullivan* rule would appear to make recovery for libel in motion pictures more difficult since those found to be appropriate subjects for motion pictures might per se qualify as public figures. In *Gertz v. Robert Welch Inc.*,[185] the court permitted states to define their own standards of liability in libel suits brought by private persons "so long as they do not impose liability without fault."[186] The requirement of "fault" would appear to bring intent to the forefront of defamation cases and to make a film disclaimer notice of lack of intent to identify film characters with actual persons all the more important.

Yet Daniel Smirlock has suggested that the *Sullivan* rule and its offspring pose special risk for fictional works.[187] *Bindrim v. Mitchell*[188] held that the novelist who attended nude marathon sessions of a psychiatrist and then described such events in a novel using a fictionalized psychiatrist showed "actual malice" simply from her knowledge of the difference between the real events and her fictional account.

In cases related to film and television since *Sullivan*, however, there has been no indication that Smirlock's concern is justified. In fact, the effect appears to have been just the opposite. In *Street v. National Broadcasting Co*,[189] the plaintiff was the prosecutrix and main witness in the famous 1931 trial of the Scottsboro Boys — a group of young black men who were accused of raping a young white woman. In 1978, NBC television presented *Judge Horton and the Scottsboro Boys*, a dramatization of the trial in which the plaintiff was portrayed.[190] Release had not been sought of the plaintiff because the producers mistakenly thought her to have died. She sued for defamation, but the court found that the plaintiff was still a public figure for purposes of later discussions of the Scottsboro case and so subject to the higher standard of absolute malice.[191] Further, the court found no evidence of actual malice — that NBC had knowledge or the ability to know that its portrayal of the plaintiff was false — since the movie was based on some historical records and analysis— Judge Horton's findings in the 1931 trial and a book on the trial by Dr. Daniel Carter.

The 1986 film *Missing*[192] was based on the nonfiction book *The Execution of Charles Horman* by Thomas Hauser, which in turn was based on the search for Horman by his father and his wife. Horman was killed in Chile at the time of the Allende coup. Ray Davis sued the director and the studio for libel, claiming that the U.S. State Department official "Ray Tower" in the film was based on him and that the film portrayed him as ordering or approving the order to kill Horman.[193] Among his allegations were that the filmmakers did not contact him for verification and that they relied "unreasonably" on the Hauser book. The film begins with a statement that was similar to and even more emphatic in its linking the film to reality than Bernie Hyman's prologue for *Rasputin and the Empress* in 1932: "The film is based on a true story. The incidents and events are documented. Some of the names have been changed to protect the innocent and also to protect the film."

The court determined Davis to be a public figure and found no actual malice, stating that the record gave no indication that the filmmakers ever questioned Hauser's account.[194] Davis was, the court noted, never mentioned by name. Furthermore, the court acknowledged the filmmakers' need to fictionalize and develop composite characters: "The movie's Ray Tower character is a fictional composite of the American presence operating in Chile at the time. He is a symbolic figure. The artistic input in the scenes questioned is found in perishable syntheses and composite treatment in films."[195]

By the late 1990s, complaints from public figures about how they were being portrayed in movies and television shows seldom developed into court cases. Former Alabama governor George Wallace, on the basis of a script for a film biography with his name as the title and not the finished product, complained publicly that a television movie based on his life was "falsehoods and lies."[196] He and his family specifically complained about scenes that showed a black servant of the governor's contemplating killing him with an ice pick and Wallace's attempted suicide. The filmmakers acknowledged that the two scenes did not describe actual occurrences and were not intended to be taken that way. Instead, they claimed, that the scenes were dramatic vehicles necessary to illustrate broader truths about Wallace.[197]

Wallace took no legal action. Gary Sinese, who played Wallace, received an Emmy award for his portrayal less than an hour before the real George Wallace died in September 1998.

From Modified to No Disclaimers

The incongruity of a disclaimer that states that the characters and events of a story obviously based on fact are "fictitious," and that any similarity with actual people living or dead is purely coincidental, began to rankle even filmmakers. William L. White, who also authored the book *They Were Expendable*, wrote the story of his wartime adoption of a young girl named Margaret and called it, *Journey for Margaret*. For the 1943 film version, also titled *Journey for Margaret*, the newspaperman who adopts Margaret is called "John Davis," and other names and incidents are changed from the book. But the disclaimer reads, "Except for the character of Margaret, the characters and events in this photoplay are fictitious...."[198] Similarly, the 1948 John Ford cavalry film *Fort Apache*[199], which was based on a story by James Warner Bellah that had the American Indian leader Cochise as a character, carried this disclaimer: "With the exception of Cochise, the characters and events in this film are fictitious...."

In the late 1940s and 1950s, filmmakers explored a documentary or cinema vérité style to contemporary dramas. During and right after World War II, *film noir* became the vogue, with hard-boiled detective stories or mysteries in which the lighting was dark, as were the characters' moods and morals. Some of these films were suggested by true-life events and would carry prologues not that dissimilar from the one that caused the trouble for *Rasputin and the Empress*, which would state, "This is a true story." These films would also usually have disclaimers in small print that the characters and events were fictitious.

In 1957, 20th Century–Fox produced *Three Faces of Eve*,[200] which was based on a book by Drs. Corbett H. Thigpen and Harvey M. Cleckley. It is about a real-life Georgia woman with multiple personalities, although the woman's real name is not used. The journalist and television personality Alistair Cooke delivered a prologue to the film that clearly attacked the "true story" prologues and films' fictionalization of actual events. He explicitly debunked fictionalized films based on fact that begin with the statement:

> This is a true story. When we hear that at the beginning of a motion picture, it usually means that there was a man called Napoleon but after that any resemblance between what happened to Napoleon and what is shown on the screen is clearly miraculous.

Cooke — who knowingly or unknowingly was using the same language as mock disclaimers in comic films like *Green Grow the Rushes*— went on to say that *Three Faces of Eve* was based on a doctor's clinical records.[201]

After a while, implicitly admitting that the traditional disclaimer often made no sense, filmmakers began to insert "modified disclaimers" similar to those used in *The Untouchables*. For example, the 1982 film *Hammett*[202], which was an imagined story of the real-life crime author Dashell Hammett, has as its disclaimer, "Although it is acknowledged that Dashell Hammett was a real personage, the characters and events in this film are fictitious...."

Modified disclaimers stated that while the film was suggested by real-life events, "some of the characters and events are fictitious," leaving the audience to guess which characters and which events.

One of the more elaborate disclaimers appeared in closing credits of the 1992–1993 ABC TV-series *The Young Indiana Jones Chronicles*, which was a "prequel" to the popular Indiana Jones feature film series—*Raiders of the Lost Ark* (1981), *Indiana Jones and the Temple of Doom* (1984), and *Indiana Jones and the Last Crusade* (1989).[203] In the series, the younger version of this fictional hero met real-life notables of the twentieth century. Presumably to acknowledge that younger audiences might misunderstand the liberties taken with fact in order to arrange the encounters between young Indiana Jones and Sigmund Freud, William Butler Yeats, and Ernest Hemingway, the disclaimer read:

> This is a work of fiction. While Young Indiana Jones is portrayed as taking part in historical events and meeting real figures in history, many of the characters in the story as well as the situations and scenes have been invented. In addition, where real historical figures and events are described in some scenes, the chronology and historical facts have been altered for dramatic effect.

The step from a modified disclaimer that states that the film was based on actual events and characters with some fictionalization to no disclaimer at all was taken by Oliver Stone and by Robert Redford. Stone's 1991 film *JFK* was based on New Orleans district attorney Jim Garrison's prosecution of Clay Shaw on the charge of conspiring in the assassination of President John F. Kennedy.[204] The film presented the thesis that Kennedy was murdered by a band of right-wing conspirators opposed to his desire to wind down the Cold War and withdraw forces from Vietnam. It also suggested that then-Vice President Lyndon Baines Johnson was at least knowledgeable about the conspiracy and complicit in the coverup.[205]

Some would argue that the thesis was speculative to the point of fantasia. Shaw was, after all, acquitted of the charge. The film was based on Garrison's book *On the Trail of the Assassination*—as well as Jim Marrs's *Crossfire: The Plot that Killed Kennedy*—and so the filmmakers could have retreated to the shelter of *Street vs. National Broadcasting Co.* and claimed that the film was just dramatizing one person's perception of events. But *JFK* also shows flashbacks of the Kennedy assassination as Garrison claimed that it had happened with newly filmed scenes made to blend with the Zapruder film of the actual assassination. Furthermore, the film carries no disclaimer. This could have been because the film was partially based on Garrison's account of the Shaw trial, although, as previously noted, it has him and his staff making discoveries about the Kennedy assassination — that in the Zapruder film of the assassination Kennedy's head rocks back, suggesting that he had been shot from in front and not from behind — that had actually been made by others previous to Garrison. Shaw and most, although not all, of the actual persons portrayed had, however, died by the time the film was released, thus lessening the threat of a defamation suit. Former CIA director Richard Helms reportedly threatened to sue if he was portrayed in the film. Sam Waterson played a CIA director seemingly modeled on Helms, who ultimately did not sue.[206] The film's central premise — that there was a conspiracy to assassinate President Kennedy — had been explored previously in the 1973 film *Executive Action*,[207] which had a screenplay by once-blacklisted writer Dalton Trumbo based on a story by Donald Freed. A major difference between the *JFK* and *Executive Action* is that *Executive Action* shows the conspiracy as it is happening, while *JFK* focuses on the discovery of the existence of the conspiracy from the perspective of a "lone investigator." *Executive Action*, however, did begin with a disclaimer:

> Although much of this film is fiction, much of it is also based on documented historical fact. Did the conspiracy we describe actually exist? We do not know. We merely suggest that it could have existed.[208]

Robert Redford directed *Quiz Show* about the "quiz show" scandals of the 1950s.[209] Based on a chapter of a book by Richard Goodwin and describing the story of Charles Van Doren and his having been given the answers to questions before broadcast of the quiz show *Twenty-One*, the film carried no disclaimer, even though the names of actual persons— Van Doren; his father, the poet Mark Van Doren; Charles Van Doren's TV rival Herbie Stempel; Goodwin; the author Edmund Wilson; and Dan Enright and Al Freedman, the creators of the quiz show "Twenty One"— were attached to characters in the film. Charles Van Doren, Stempel, Goodwin, and Freedman were alive when the film premiered. Goodwin was involved in the production.

There were many claims that the film took liberties with the facts.

Goodwin is shown as the man who cracks the case. This portrayal offended judge Joseph Stone, who had actually been the prime mover in the grand jury investigation — Goodwin having been involved in the congressional hearings only. Freedman was quoted as saying, "The film is fixed. It is even more rigged than the show it portrays."[210]

No suits concerning *Quiz Show* or *JFK* reached a court of law. The standard of *Sullivan* — the need for "public figures" to prove absolute malice — would have applied and may have been a deterrent to those portrayed.

Perhaps reflecting the criticism he received concerning *JFK*, Stone, in his film *Nixon*,[211] which is in some ways a sequel in subject matter and tone to *JFK*, begins it with a modified disclaimer that favors the word "conjectured" over "fictitious":

> This film is an attempt to understand the truth of Richard Nixon, the 37th president of the United States. It is based on numerous public sources and on an incomplete historical record.
>   In consideration of length, events and characters have been condensed, and some scenes among protagonists have been conjectured.[212]

The film's condensation of history and thesis that Nixon's supposed involvement in an attempt to assassinate Cuban leader Fidel Castro inadvertently led to the assassination of President Kennedy were widely criticized.[213] In discussing the film, historian Stephen Ambrose took up the filmmaker's argument that Shakespeare too changed historical events for dramatic purposes by stating, "[But Shakespeare] was not writing about contemporaries to begin with, and he had no political agenda to push. Stone does."[214] Ambrose also compared Orson Welles, whose film *Citizen Kane* was a fictionalized account of the life of newspaper baron William Randolph Hearst, to Stone:

> By changing names, Welles made it clear that the movie was fiction, then took advantage of the inherent right of fiction writers: to make things up. Robert Penn Warren used Huey Long's life as the basis for "All the King's Men"; but like Welles he changed names and never claimed historical accuracy."[215]

Another interesting feature that filmmakers began to employ was the "crawl," a name used to describe writing that "crawls" up the screen, usually at the end of the film. For the historically based film, the crawl describes what happens to characters after the conclusion of the story as portrayed in the film. The device has been used in films that have carried both "based on a true story" claims and "some of the characters are fictionalized" disclaimers as well as films such as *Quiz Story* that have carried no disclaimers. Writer Amy E. Schwartz points to the crawl as yet a further way filmmakers will disown the need to be historically accurate while at the same time clinging to the film's connection to history:

> But consider the specific claims of semi-historic filmmakers that their movies bear no responsibility toward the historical fact.... [T]hen the use of the crawl presents a real problem. The point of the signoff, after all, is that it returns you to the real world. It offers almost exactly that what you've been watching is part of a story about real people, a story that continues into the present.[216]

In many ways, then, the crawl is doing what the prologue of *Rasputin and the Empress,* which started all the trouble, tried to do— indicating that people portrayed in the film are still alive, which means they really existed, while at the same time taking liberties with the historical facts.

First Amendment Issues

Some will argue that litigation against filmmakers on the issue of the depiction of real-life people in films and legislation to curb their activity restrict the filmmakers' First Amendment rights. It comes down to what is protected by the First Amendment and what is truth in the movies.

In the 20th Century–Fox film *Titanic* (1953)[217]— based on the actual event of the sinking of the Titanic in 1912 — everyone is very brave, and the men stand on the ship while it is sinking and sing "Nearer My God to Thee." In the 1958 British movie based on the same event—*A Night to Remember*[218]— some people on the ship are shown as heroic and some as cowardly, while the 1997 film *Titanic*[219] emphasizes chaos and panic with just a few heroic acts. It is not really a question of which depiction of the sinking is true and which is false; it is a question of perspective. The 1953 film concentrates on just the heroic acts. The 1958 and 1997 films take the camera back a bit and show both the heroic and the cowardly. What would have been false is to show heroism where there was none or cowardice where there was none.[220] Similarly, a film that portrays a complex historical character — Napoleon or LBJ — will by necessity concentrate on some aspects and not others.

Complaints about war films with some basis in history have really been about perspective. Steven Spielberg's *Saving Private Ryan,*[221] for example, which begins with a group of U.S. soldiers landing at Omaha Beach in Normandy on June 4, 1944, was denounced by some British veterans and the British press for failing to highlight the role played by British servicemen in the capture of Omaha Beach.[222] Earlier, the 1945 U.S. film *Objective Burma!* [223] had actually been banned in Great Britain (until 1952) for failing to highlight British participation in the Burma campaign.[224] Both of these U.S. films, which use fictional characters in a historical setting, had as their *perspective* U.S. participation in these battles.

Then there is the portrayal of Thomas E. Dewey as a crooked district attorney in the film *Hoodlum*.[225] This is not a question of perspective or taking only certain aspects of a complex character or of being true to the spirit of Thomas E. Dewey. The portrayal is false by anyone's standards. Should the First Amendment protect it? There is a line someplace, the makers of *Hoodlum* crossed it, and they did it because they could. They could have called the character "Thomas E. Dolan." Scripts are vetted by attorneys. It is likely that when the attorneys reviewed the script and saw the portrayal of Dewey they said, "Dewey is dead, and neither he nor his family have any rights that we can violate"—since this is what they told the family when they complained. So a whole generation and future generations—through VHS and DVDs—will be presented with a false picture of Thomas E. Dewey.

The First Amendment does not protect false statements. The problem is that even false statements about the deceased are not libel or slander because the dead cannot sue for these actions by statute—except in Rhode Island for a very short period of time. But the question is, does the principle—that false statements are not protected by the First Amendment—apply to actions where the person portrayed is still alive or in actions where the deceased's family can sue on the grounds of invasion of privacy or invasion of publicity in some states, commercial misappropriation in some states?

In 1955, Paramount Studios made a film version of the Broadway play *The Desperate Hours*,[226] which was based on an actual event. *Life* magazine ran a story and suggested that the play and film portrayed the experiences of the specific family that was held hostage by escaped convicts in the family's home. In truth, the actual events were more benign for the family than what were shown in the play and film. The play and film had changed the family's name, but the article identified them. The family sought damages under a New York statute protecting the right of privacy, and *Life* defended the article as a newsworthy subject that was exempted from the statute and protected by the First Amendment. The Supreme Court ultimately decided the case, *Time v. Hill*, in favor of the plaintiff, stating,

We held in *New York Times [v. Sullivan]* that calculated falsehood enjoyed no immunity in the case of alleged defamation of a public official concerning his official conduct. Similarly, calculated falsehood should enjoy no immunity in the situation here presented us.[227]

So, according to *Time v. Hill,* false statements carry no "immunity."

Actors Against Their Wills

Filmmaking involves editing film that is shot at different times in particular sequences. It has, for example, long been a practice to insert actual footage of crowds or natural disasters in sequence with footage shot on sound stages, thus adding a certain verisimilitude. Sometimes this technique has been employed using historical characters. At the end of the 1968 film *The Extraordinary Seaman,*[228] a modern version of Oscar Wilde's "The Canterville Ghost" set during the World War II and using old newsreels as background, the actors come out for a bow just as if they were doing curtain calls in a theater. The actor David Niven bows, and his name is superimposed over him. Then there is footage of Winston Churchill, British prime minister during most of the war, waving, and his name is superimposed over him. The same is done for Faye Dunaway and the Soviet dictator Joseph Stalin. Thus, Churchill and Stalin are treated as if they were actors in the film.

While *The Extraordinary Seaman* sequence is playful in tone, the same technique could be used to insert historical figures in the action. As mentioned previously, this process allowed the makers of *Hennessy* to use film of Queen Elizabeth II in their fictional story and cause the British government to worry about whether it looked like the Queen was acting in the movie for money.

However, modern technology has brought the concept beyond inserting old film in sequence. Woody Allen's 1983 *Zelig*[229] is a mock documentary about the fictional character of Leonard Zelig that inserts Zelig into actual newsreel footage and also "creates" new newsreels in which Zelig appears with actors impersonating such historical figures as Adolf Hitler. In *Forrest Gump* (1994),[230] Tom Hanks, playing the title character, through a combination of computer technology and editing, interacts with Presidents Kennedy, Johnson, and Nixon, who shake hands with Gump. The dubbing of voices even makes the presidents to seem to be talking to Forrest Gump and commenting on what he is doing. Similarly, President

Clinton became an actor in the previously mentioned 1995 science fiction movie *Contact.*[231]

The technology is advanced enough to allow filmmakers to fabricate larger sequences or even an entire motion picture in which historical figures interact with actors and with people from history whom they never met. Such historical figures could be made to say and do things that they would never do. While the family of Thomas Dewey can object but not sue over an actor playing him in the movie *Hoodlum* and saying things he would never say, film techniques are now such that the actual image of Dewey could be used with a dubbed-in voice.

For the living, the laws of defamation would apply, with the absolute malice standard presumably being met with ease since deliberate falsification would be apparent. The dead, however, cannot sue for libel. The permission of the copyright holders of filmed material would need to be obtained, but usually these are not the people in the footage. The issue of right of publicity would be raised, and, if the right was valid in the particular state, the use could be prevented by families. However, at this writing, only 10 out of 50 states allow that right to pass to descendants.

At the heart of the issue of "falsification" is a distortion of history, the presentation of something that is know to be fictitious as having happened and thus allowing generations to believe, incorrectly, that what they were shown to have happened is true. At this writing, there are few protections to allow these distortions of history. The laws of copyright and privacy were not developed to deal with such things and will have to catch up.

Historical Fact v. Fiction in the Theater

Just as films in the late twentieth century and the beginning of the twenty-first grappled with the tension between fact and fiction, so did plays.

Near the end of the 2002 play *Mr. Goldwyn*, movie mogul Samuel Goldwyn is on the phone with the Danish ambassador and indicates that the ambassador is saying the Danish people are upset because Danny Kaye, who is playing Danish author Hans Christian Andersen in Goldwyn's film of the same name, is Jewish. The playwrights admitted that they have no support for this allegation of Danish anti-Semitism and claimed they invented Goldwyn's telephone conversation with the ambassador as a way to depict his audacity and paranoia. They called it "artistic license, and the play's producer, who knew Goldwyn, said, "Accuracy must yield to dramatic requirements."[232]

Richard Greenberg may have written the shortest disclaimer ever for his 2002 play *The Dazzle:* "The Dazzle" is based on the lives of the Collyer brothers, about whom I know almost nothing."[233] In *The Dazzle*, the brothers, who died in 1948, are joined by a rebellious heiress in a complicated triangle that has no connection to brothers' actual lives. The author claimed that the fictitious elements of the characters names just took over but that he retained the brothers' names because they "stuck" with the play.

Arthur Miller's drama *The Crucible* was revived frequently in the decades after its 1953 debut. (Miller himself wrote the screenplay for a 1996 film version and was nominated for a best screenplay Oscar.) The play was based on the Salem witch trials of the late seventeenth century. Trial records helped Miller to approximate the external actions of both those accused of witchcraft and their accusers. He said in discussing its 2002 Broadway revival:

> What their internal psychology was, was not on any record. That is what I had to create. I suppose it is history, but it's something more. It's an imaginary reconstruction. It wouldn't be a document you would turn to for absolute historical truth, if there is such a thing. If you are writing a work of literature, it's literally impossible to avoid changing what people are like. The story takes over finally. The real question is whether a play casts any light on any human or social situation. If it's simply an exploitation of a historic person, then it's reprehensible."[234]

Anna Deavere Smith, the actress, playwright and professor says: "What's good about turning a historic event or current event into a work of theater is that it allows the audience to reflect on it to respond to the play in a way they didn't when the event happened, because they were too overwhelmed by it.[235]

Edward Albee based his 2002 play *Occupant* on the life of his friend the artist Louise Nevelson. "I didn't distort Nevelson for dramatic effect," Albee said. "She was quite capable of doing that herself. She rewrote facts as she saw fit." In the play, Albee has Nevelson answer the question, "Do facts mean anything to you?" by replying, "They can be useful."[236]

The View Today

A logical question to raise is, how would *Youssoupoff* have been decided if it had been an American case and had come after *Sullivan*? Interestingly enough, the second Youssoupoff case, his invasion of privacy suit against CBS, was tried the year after *Sullivan*. Attorneys for CBS raised a "freedom of the press" defense, citing *Sullivan*. The court rejected it, stating that *Sullivan* had been limited to public officials and that it found no indication that the Supreme Court meant for it to apply to private citizens such as Prince Felix Youssoupoff. This was the year before the Supreme Court extended *Sullivan* to apply to public figures, which Youssoupoff was, as surely as the plaintiff in *Street v. National Broadcasting Co.* As a public figure, Youssoupoff would have had to show "actual malice" as well as identification. As to the former, if it could have shown that Irving Thalberg had been informed by Mercedes de Acosta that Rasputin and Princess Irina had never met, that could have been used to establish that MGM knowingly portrayed a falsehood. But there would still be the question of identification. Natasha and Prince Paul Chegodieff were arguably just as much a composite, just as much a fiction, as Paul Tower, Mary Cohan, and the University of Notre Dame. And without identification, there is no libel.

Six decades after *Youssoupoff v. MGM*, the recognition of a filmmakers' need to fictionalize is fairly well established. *Sullivan* and *Gertz* provided support for the view, long held and expressed by filmmakers, that their stated intention not to depict actual people was important in determining defamation. *Youssoupoff* brought the whole question of fiction in film to the forefront. Even though film creates the illusion of reality before the eyes of an audience, subsequent case law largely established that it is, as the saying goes, only a movie. *Youssoupoff* also taught filmmakers, however, that their expression could not be unbridled, that there is a line where film's ability to convince an audience that what it is seeing is real goes too far. That line is reputation. The most famous and influential crossing of that line was *Rasputin and the Empress*, as litigated in *Youssoupoff v. MGM*.

As for what can be done for families of the deceased who cannot sue for libel, some have suggested extending the "statute of limitations" for libel to a period of time after death, as Rhode Island did — just to set the precedent for some reasonable protection for the deceased's reputation before he or she completely passes into history — or even setting the precedent of applying criminal libel laws for what are regarded as really heinous and false portrayals that are, then, crimes against a state. This would be a legal "neutron bomb," knocking a lot of things over in the process. The fear is that the possibility of prosecution for criminal libel would chill expression. But the reason legislative or court/governmental action would appear to be necessary is because there is a larger picture here. The quote from Zemeckis concerning *Contact* and from the attorneys for MGM/UA concerning *Hoodlum* shows that filmmakers feel they are largely unrestricted.

II

The Perfect Storm

"Free speech doesn't give one the right to cry fire, falsely,
in a crowded theatre.

— Justice Oliver Wendell Holmes,
Schenck v. United States

In late October 1991, the *Andrea Gail*, a swordfish boat, was caught
in a storm of unprecedented strength — called "the perfect storm" because
it was caused by a unique combination of meteorological forces — and lost
at sea. Its captain was Billy Tyne. There were five other crewmembers on
board. The incident received a great deal of media attention, and this
caused Sebastian Junger to write a book called *The Perfect Storm*, which
was published in 1997. That same year, Warner Bros. obtained the movie
rights to the book, and in 2000 the studio released a film of the same name
starring George Clooney as Billy Tyne. The film grossed $150 million in
the United States.

Junger said in his preface that in writing the book he decided that he
would not imagine what happened — which he would have had to do since
the entire crew had died — but instead would discuss the event with family members and those who had been through storms themselves and then
infer what might have happened. He only quoted people who had spoken
to him. Reported conversations — such as the few radio communications
from Tyne — he placed in italics to make it clear that it was a remembered
rather than exact quote.

In a motion picture, however, it is impossible to infer an event. One has to show something happening. It is impossible to place statements in italics to indicate they are not exact quotes. The screenwriter, Bill Witliff, and the director, Wolfgang Petersen, created a plot that shows Billy Tyne being told by the boat's owner, Bob Brown, that Brown will give the boat to someone else unless Tyne's brings in bigger catches than he has been doing. As a result, Tyne goes farther and farther out, gets a big catch, but then is faced with coming back through "the perfect storm." Since his ice machine has broken, Tyne knows that if the boat lays up somewhere until the storm passes, the fish will spoil. He and the crew decide to go back through the storm and are lost at sea.

In contrast to the premises of this plot, Junger's book indicates that the *Andrea Gail* was one of the most successful boats in Gloucester and that for his most recent catch Tyne had personally earned $20,000. Junger wrote that, as a rule, Tyne simply ignored Brown and was not afraid of him. The book states that once the boat was out, Tyne reported that he was having trouble with the ice maker — that it was producing half of its normal share of ice — but there is no indication that it had broken down completely or that the fish would spoil. The film has Tyne's fellow captain, Linda Greenlaw, in frequent radio contact with him. At one point, she tells him that he's going so far out he's off the charts, and at another time she screams that the storm he's caught in is a "bomb" that's going to explode. According to Junger's book, Greenlaw actually went farther out than Tyne and arranged to refuel his boat. They had only one nondescript radio conversation about the storm. The filmmakers created incidents to explain why Tyne went out so far and why he attempted to come back through the storm.

No one knows what happened. The filmmakers decided they had to create a traditional narrative — man decides to do something and either succeeds or fails.

The filmmakers received releases from many who were portrayed in the film or from the family members of those who had died. According to the Tyne and Murphy families, they did not give permission to the filmmakers to portray any of the family members who were living or to portray Tyne and Murphy. Without these permission, the filmmakers had to decide whether or not to rename the captain of the ship. Changing the names of characters in films based on actual events has been commonly done in motion picture history — see *Journey for Margaret*, *Inherit the Wind*, and *Judgment at Nuremberg*. But the makers of *The Perfect Storm*— knowing that the *Andrea Gail* incident had captured national attention — promoted it as being "based on a true story." Since the crew were all dead, and the dead cannot sue for libel, the filmmakers knew that libel was something they did not have to worry about.

After expressing concerns about the film to the filmmakers and not receiving what they felt was a satisfactory response, Erica Tyne and Billie-Jo Francis Tyne, on their own behalf and as surviving children of Billy Tyne; Dale R. Murphy Jr., on his own behalf and as surviving child of crewman Dale R. Murphy; Debra Tigue, on her own behalf and as Murphy's ex-wife; and Douglas Edward Kosko, who had left the crew before it sailed, filed suit again Warner Bros., Baltimore/Spring Creek Pictures LLC, and Radiant Productions, Inc., in U.S. District Court for the Middle District of Florida for commercial misappropriation under Florida Statute 540.08. The children and Jodi Tyne, Billy Tyne's ex-wife, also sued for common law invasion of privacy.

Section 540.08 states, "No person shall publish, print, display or otherwise publicly use for purposes of trade or for any commercial or advertising purpose the name, portrait, photograph, or other likeness of any natural person without the express written or oral consent to such use." The statute provides express post-mortem rights, so the plaintiffs could sue on behalf of their deceased family members as well as on their own behalf since their names and likenesses were used in the movie. Tyne's children and wife were shown in a photograph and at a brief funeral scene at the film's end. Tigue, Koskov, and Murphy Jr. were played by actors and given dialogue.

In the complaint, the defendants claimed that they had not given permission for the use of their own image or that of their deceased family member. They also claimed that in the marketing and promotion of the film worldwide and in the opening titles of the film itself, the defendants advertised the film to be "based on a true story." And yet, the complaint reads,

> [The] said fictionalization is infected with material and substantial falsity. Specifically, decedent Tyne is depicted in the Picture in a false light as emotionally aloof, reckless, excessively risk-taking, self-absorbed, emasculated, despondent, obsessed and maniacal. Said Picture further falsely depicts decedent Tyne as having piloted the Andrea Gail in an unprofessional, unseaworthy, and incompetent manner and as having suffered a self-imposed death, abandoning his crew and any hope of survival. Moreover, the Picture publicly discloses and, alternatively, fictionalizes and falsifies matters of a private and intimate nature concerning decedent Murphy and his family, said private matter having no materiality to any historical narrative of the sinking of the *Andrea Gail.*

> Defendant made no effort to ensure that the incidents, dialogue, portrayals, and chronologies as portrayed in the Picture were factually accurate. To the contrary, Defendants engaged in a knowing and calculated fictionalization of the true or provable facts, while holding the Picture out to the general public as a true story.

The plaintiffs asked for compensatory damages, including but not limited to reasonable royalties for use of their names, images, and likenesses and that of their deceased family member and compensation for personal humiliation, wounded feelings, and emotional harm. They also reserved the right to ask for punitive damages.

The defendants moved to dismiss. They claimed protection under the First Amendment, arguing that the plaintiffs ignored the critical distinction between exploiting a person's likeness in connection with the sale of a commercial product and portraying a person in an expressive work such as a book or movie. The defendant's motion stated,

> Nor does it matter that the film includes fictional elements. Obviously, no one knows exactly happened aboard the ill-fated Andrea Gail during its final days. Like all other so-called "docu-dramas," defendants' film dramatizes the historical events, adding dialogue and characterization. Recognizing that fictional expression is entitled to the same First Amendment protection as fact, the courts have uniformly held that plaintiffs may not use the right of publicity to complain about the way an author or filmmaker chooses to express the story — whether the story consists of fact, fiction, or a combination of both.

The defendants insisted that the Tyne plaintiffs had no cause of action for the alleged portrayal of Billy Tyne in a false light and that the portrayals in the film did not violate Florida's Statute 540.08. In both instances, the defendants relied heavily on the case *Loft v. Fuller*,[1] which involved a widow's suit concerning the portrayal of her late husband in the 1978 television movie *The Ghost of Flight 401*. The court in *Loft* held that the film did not have a "commercial purpose" under the statute.

The defendants also dismissed the plaintiffs' reliance on two "older New York cases"—*Spahn v. Julian Messner Inc.*[2] and *Binns v. Vitagraph Co. of America*,[3] in which the court relied on a theory of falsity to allow the plaintiffs to recover on their misappropriation/invasion of privacy claims, stating that the cases were inconsistent with Florida law and were anomalies, even in New York.

In response to the defendants' motion to dismiss, the plaintiffs argued that "the calculated and undisclosed fictionalizations contained in the Picture constitute culpable falsity and defeat any claim by Warner that such publication is protected under the First Amendment," citing *New York Times Co. v. Sullivan*[4] and *Time Inc. v. Hill*.[5] They also argued that the film, which generated $150 million in U.S. box office revenues and was later released to video, television, and other markets and had related merchandise products for sale "undoubtedly represents an endeavor which has 'a commercial purpose.'"

The plaintiffs also said that the New York and Florida statutes were comparable and noted that in *Messenger v. Gruner + Jahr Publisher*[6] the court in New York had reaffirmed both *Spahn* and *Binns*, stating that a substantially fictionalized use of a person's name or persona, even if not defamatory, may be actionable. They also noted, countering the defendants' claim that the Tyne children could not sue for invasion of privacy on behalf of their father, that in *Loft*, the court had written,

> We are wary of a blanket rule barring all relatives of a deceased from bringing a common law invasion of privacy action simply because the relatives were not involved in the publicity. However, in our view such relatives must shoulder a heavy burden in establishing a cause of action.

The court refused to grant the defendants' motion to dismiss. The case prepared for trial.

On the basis of two articles I had written, my work on this book, my knowledge of the history concerning this cause of action, and cases I have handled, I was hired by the plaintiff's attorney as an expert witness and functioned as an unpaid consultant. As a witness, I was deposed by the defendants' attorney over a four-hour period. The defense then subpoenaed the unfinished manuscript for this book, and the plaintiffs' counsel opposed the subpoena.

The plaintiffs' very able attorneys— Steve Calvacca and Ned McLeod — had already framed the arguments in the complaint. At best, my "consultant capacity" was meant to "fill in." They asked my advice on two matters: support for the claim of "fictionalization" in the privacy claim and for the issue of the applicability of the film under the statute — specifically dealing with the *Loft* precedent.

As to the former, I saw immediate comparisons with the *Kelly v. Loewe*[7] case involving the film *They Were Expendable* — one of the few successful libel cases involving a film portrayal. Even though the *Tyne* case was not for libel, the court's decisions concerning the damage done to Lieutenant Kelly's reputation were relevant to the issue of falsity raised in the privacy complaint. I argued that, like *They Were Expendable*, *The Perfect Storm's* roots in both an actual event and a nonfiction book were promoted in marketing the film. The *Kelly* court had held that the defendants could not claim lack of identification due to their fictionalizations and also promote the film as a true story. Like Lieutenant Kelly in *They Were Expendable*, Captain Tyne was presented as a stereotypical action hero—brave but reckless, he sacrifices his men's lives for the ship's catch of fish.

The Perfect Storm begins with the printed claim that it is "based on a true story." In its ending disclaimer, it repeats the claim and does so in a way that is actually much different from other films cited here that were based on fact. Most films based on fact carry a disclaimer—derived from the *Rasputin* case. Some may modify it to state, "While based on a true story, some of the events and characters are fictitious...." *The Perfect Storm* carries this disclaimer at the end of the film's closing credits: "This film is based on actual historical events contained in *The Perfect Storm* by Sebastian Junger. Dialogue and certain events and characters in the film were created for the purpose of dramatization."

I stressed that it is important to notice the difference. Other "based on fact" films claim to be either wholly or partly "fictitious." *The Perfect Storm's* disclaimer states that it is based on "actual events" with changes made for the purposes of "dramatization." Since the word "fictitious" has been in use in disclaimers for more than sixty years, the change must have been deliberate. There is a difference between fictionalizing something and dramatizing it. For example, if a writer takes a transcript of a debate between two senators in Congress, retypes the debate, and hands it to two actors to recite on stage, he has not fictionalized it, he has dramatized it. He may need to trim some of the duller moments. He may need to create a narrator to fill in the background. But these are changes made for the purposes of dramatization. The two characters are not fictitious. By claiming that the film is based on "actual events" with changes made for the purposes of "dramatization," the makers of *The Perfect Storm* are consciously veering from the path of other fact-based films and indicating that they are presenting the "actual" truth with some changes made to facilitate putting the story on screen.

Since after the boat leaves the dock the screenwriters had to make up all the incidents and dialogue—since everyone died, no one knows what happened—one could argue that if any film ever made should have had a disclaimer that some of its events were fictitious, *The Perfect Storm* should have. Instead, the filmmakers claimed that its portrayal of what happened on the *Andrea Gail* was "actual."

As to the Florida statute, I noted that the defendants claimed that the statute was not applicable and had cited *Loft v. John G. Fuller*, 408 So. 2d 619 (1982), which concerned a TV movie based on the nonfiction book *The Ghost of Flight 401*. The book described an actual air crash and subsequent reports of sightings of the ghosts of crew members. The *Loft* court found the statute — which applies to actions in which a person's name or likeness is used for commercial trade or advertising purposes— did not apply to the book and the film.

Like *They Were Expendable* and *The Perfect Storm*, the film *The Ghost of Flight 401* was based on a nonfiction book and then fictionalized portions of it.[8] *Ghost* expanded on the ghost sightings, making it more of a horror movie. So, both films promoted and capitalized on the fact that they were based on actual events, even though they fictionalized them.

But it is important to cite the differences between *Ghost* and *The Perfect Storm*. This goes to the applicability of the statute: the *Ghost of Flight 401* was a TV movie made 20 years before *The Perfect Storm*. There were no box office receipts— U.S. or international — because the movie was made for television. There was no direct advertising income. There were commercials aired at breaks in the viewing, but they were not necessarily particular to the movie — everything broadcast the day of viewing was broken up for commercials, even older movies such as *Casablanca*. There was no related merchandise. The film was not released on videotape as part of a marketing plan — that wasn't being done in 1978. (It was not available on video during the initial *Tyne* proceedings.) Lacking these things, the *Loft* court concluded that the *Ghost of Flight 401* was not "commercial" under the statute.

In contrast, *The Perfect Storm* generated both domestic and international box office receipts, merchandise sales, and video sales— all much more "commercial" than the *Ghost of Flight 401*. Perhaps more important is that it has paid "product placements" within the film itself. Product placements have become common in movies, and the income they generate is substantial. For example, Julia Roberts hops aboard a Federal Express truck in *Runaway Bride*,[9] and Hector Elizondo has a line, "Wherever she's going, she'll be there by 10:30 tomorrow"— promoting the ad slogan of Federal Express. A Federal Express plane crashes in *Cast Away*[10] and Federal Express packages wash to shore to sustain the Fed Ex executive who is stranded on a deserted island.

I argued that there was blatant product placement in the *Perfect Storm*. Linda Greenlaw, portrayed by Mary Elizabeth Mastrantonio, and Captain Tyne, played by George Clooney, have a discussion about suntan lotion — specifically whether she is wearing Coppertone or Hawaiian Tropic and which one he is wearing. In a lecture on mass communication, Professor Gerald J. Baldasty describes the product placement in the film:

> *Perfect Storm.* Local bar the Crow's Nest features three neon Bud Light signs, a Budweiser metal sign and a big Bud Light sticker on the pool lamp, while the customers are seen drinking only one kind of beer. The kids, however, are drinking Pepsi.[11]

These are paid commercial spots. In the years since *The Ghost of Flight 401* was telecast, commercial product placement in films has become big business.[12] These spots are in the film forever. The character representing Billy Tyne is hawking suntan lotion, and the whole movie is advertising products. The depiction of Billy Tyne and of all real-life characters portrayed in the movie are being used for commercial and advertising purposes. I argued that the commercial and advertising purposes of *The Perfect Storm* make the statute applicable in a way *The Ghost of Flight 401* did not.

I also tried to distinguish the *Ghost of 401* from *The Perfect Storm* in another way. It was always strange to me that the *Loft* court decisions spoke mostly about the nonfiction book, even though the plaintiffs had sued both the book publisher and the film producers. I soon found out why. In researching the TV movie, which was not available on video, I saw a cast list in which the name of the ghost, played by Ernest Borgnine, was "Dom Camino"—not "Loft." So, they had changed the names in the movie. This is why the court had focused on the book and did not really deal with the movie on the issue of commercial misappropriation—the filmmakers had not appropriated Loft's name or likeness. This made the cases distinguishable. *The Perfect Storm* had used Tyne and Murphy's names and likenesses and those of their children and ex-wives. (The plaintiffs' arguments had already been framed, and, at best, my research might have been used at trial. If only because of the disposition of the trial, none of my arguments were ever utilized.)

As the trial date inched closer, the topic acquired some more momentum because of the release of the films *A Beautiful Mind*[13] and *Black Hawk Down*.[14] *Black Hawk Down* told the story of U.S. soldiers fighting their way through the streets of Mogadishu in 1993. It makes a greater effort toward accuracy than some fact-based movies. It even had the cooperation of the Pentagon. But, as the disclaimer at the end of the film admits, some characters are composites, some are fictitious. A character based on real-life ranger Stebbins had his name changed to Grimes at the request of the Pentagon because Stebbins was serving 30 years in prison for rape. When interviewed on television about specific scenes in the movie, actual participants in the 1993 event said the spirit might have been right but that some of the scenes just didn't happen. Somali-American community leaders called for a boycott of the film, saying the movie depicted their people as savages.

A Beautiful Mind was based on the life of mathematician John Nash. The film took a nonfiction biography — the screenplay won the Oscar for best *adapted* screenplay — and turned it into a typical Hollywood film scenario— hero overcomes adversity through willpower and love. The Nashes themselves did not contemplate a lawsuit. They had, in fact, cooperated with the filming. However, some mental health professionals were concerned that the film would give people with family members suffering from schizophrenia false hopes about what they can expect in the future. Rumors were spread, supposedly by those who hoped that films other than *A Beautiful Mind* would win the best picture Oscar, that the film ignored Nash's homosexuality and child out of wedlock. (It didn't matter. The film won the Oscar as best film.)

I raised the issue of fictional and composite characters in a question to Ridley Scott, the director of *Black Hawk Down*, during a January 15, 2002, National Press Club conference about the film. He responded — somewhat coldly — by beginning his statement with an annoyed, "Look!" This type of question had evidently been coming up a great deal. Scott answered that "there are 100 characters in the book and you can't tell a film about a 100 characters," and "in normal drama, in simplistic terms, there is a good guy and a bad guy and a woman and a man." He and the screenwriter had, for the purpose of audience comprehension, "got it down to 37." But rather than lose some of what happened to the other 63, they took bits and pieces of these people and gave them to composite or fictitious characters. "We put it into the fundamental rules of drama," Scott said, "otherwise we'd be watching this massive documentary, and the cause and effect process [would get] very confusing."[15]

The topic received a great deal of press. I was interviewed by *USA Today* (January 8, 2002), WABC-radio, New York (January 8, 2002), and MSNBC (March 22, 2002).

In phone conversations during this period, the plaintiffs' attorneys told me they looked forward to using deposed statements of Warner executives in the trial, statements that repeated the implicit claim in the film's disclaimer that events had been "dramatized" rather than "fictionalized," along with the film director's statement that much of the film had indeed been fictionalized.

The *Tyne v. Warner* trial was set for June 3, 2002, but on May 9, Judge Anne C. Conway surprisingly granted the defendants' motion for summary judgment, stating that the film was protected by the First Amendment and that the studio was well within its rights to fictionalize the account of the ill-fated sword-fishing boat *Andrea Gail* and its crew.

In her ruling, the court, in its analysis of the §540.08 complaint, came down strongly and conclusively on the side of the plaintiff's argument that the likenesses of Tyne and the plaintiffs were not used for trade, commercial, or advertising purposes, finding the *Loft* decision "squarely on point." The court did not address any of the issues raised as to the differences between *Tyne* and *Loft*.

Having adopted *Loft* wholeheartedly, the court did not address the First Amendment issue, except to quote *Burstyn v. Wilson*, 343 U.S. 495 (1952) that motion pictures are entitled to First Amendment protection. "This provides another basis for the Court's conclusion that the Defendants are entitled to summary judgment on these claims," the court wrote.

Burstyn was a landmark case in that it rejected the New York censorship board's ban on the movie *The Miracle* on the ground of sacrilege — the 1948 Italian film tells the story of a woman who is seduced by a vagabond she believes is St. Joseph and who, when she finds she is pregnant, feels she has conceived the son of God.[16] By 2002, *Burstyn* was a quaint, fifty-year-old historic case. The *Tyne* plaintiffs had not contended that films were not protected by the First Amendment but that the protection was not absolute and that it did not extend to false statements.

As to the issue of the falsity of the depiction in the movie, the court quoted the defendants' motion to dismiss, claiming that the plaintiffs had "confused the statutory action of unauthorized publication with the common law action of false light invasion of privacy. The Court, however, has no such problem distinguishing those two causes of action. Consequently, the Court determines that the truth or falsity of the events depicted in the Picture is of no import to the issue of whether there was an unauthorized publication of the Plaintiffs' and decedents' likenesses."

The plaintiffs' attorneys expressed surprise that the court had refused to dismiss the case, let it proceed over an eight-month discovery period, and then granted summary judgment to the defendants on issues raised in the original motion to dismiss.

Warner Bros. trumpeted its victory in a press release. "We are extremely pleased," the studio said. "The plaintiffs' theory that Warner Bros. needed their permission to make *The Perfect Storm* ... profoundly threatened free speech.... The court's ruling is a huge victory not only for Warner Bros. but for all writers, artists and filmmakers who may now continue to find inspiration in historical events without having their creative visions censored and controlled by anyone with a connection to those events."

But then the plaintiffs appealed to the U.S. Court of Appeals for the 11th Circuit , By this point, I was not personally involved in the case.

On July 9, 2003, the appeals court upheld the district court's summary judgment decision for Warner Bros. on the claim of invasion of privacy, holding that a movie's fictionalized portrayal of Tyne was not outrageous enough to allow his survivors to pursue an invasion of privacy claim against the movie's producer. The plaintiffs had asked the court to recognize a relational-right exception and allow the cause of action to survive their father's death because the depiction was "egregious," quoting the *Loft* decision's allowance that a claim for a decedent's family could be allowable if the defendant's actions were "egregious." The court declined, stating, "The Florida courts have made it plain that this exception was not crafted to provide a derivative cause of action for minor technical inaccuracies, or even major ones."[17]

The appeals court also asked the Florida Supreme Court to clarify whether the state's law for unauthorized use of a person's likeness for commercial purposes extends to use in a motion picture. In the appeal, the plaintiffs had worked to distinguish *Loft*, arguing that newspapers had reported Loft sightings. The court acknowledged the plaintiffs' arguments, quoting that "the [*Perfect Storm*] depiction of the events at sea, and the relationships between the crew members and their children, had never been reported in the press and were intentionally fabricated ... and ... not protected by the First Amendment." In addition, the plaintiffs submitted that the inclusion of both terms "advertising" and "commercial" in the statute constitutes "surplusage" if they are both read to refer to the promotion of a product or service. Further, the plaintiffs argued, if the statute only protects against unauthorized uses for promotion, then the two exception provisions appear to be unnecessary. The court summarized the plaintiffs' point: "[I]f §540.08(1) applies only to advertising or promotional purposes in all cases, then there would be no reason for §540.08(3)(a) to limit the statute's applicability to uses that involve news media 'for advertising purposes,'" the court explained. The exemption for resale of artistic works appears superfluous as well if subsection (1) relates solely to promotional situations, the court said. Due to the "uncertain[ty] as to the scope of §540.08 and the applicability of the *Loft* decision in the circumstances presented," the court certified to the Florida Supreme Court the following question: "To what extent does Section 540.08 of the Florida Statutes apply to the facts of this case?"

The plaintiff's initial brief to the Florida Supreme Court argued that

1. structural analysis supports a broader interpretation of the term "any commercial purpose" in the statute;

2. Florida's adoption of New York's right of privacy statute requires adoption of New York's construction statute;

3. culpably false publication is not immune under Section 540.08;

4. the remedial nature of Section 540.08 supports a broader interpretation of its scope;

5. Section 540.08 does not require extraneous product endorsement; and

6. the case does not involve "avowed fiction which would be protected under the First Amendment."

In addition to these arguments, the appeal allowed the plaintiffs to get on the record statements from the depositions of the filmmakers they had taken. The film's director, Wolfgang Petersen, admitted when he was deposed,

> Q: You fictionalized the events and dialogue which took place on board ship after it left port, correct?
>
> A: Yes.
>
> Q: Did you fictionalize the character portrayals as they were revealed during that voyage?
>
> A: … I mean the way characters speak defines the character, so yes.
>
> Q: So, if you fictionalized dialogue, then you fictionalized character portrayals, correct?
>
> A: Yes.

At another point, Petersen said what Warner Bros. did not admit in its disclaimer and subsequent statements about the nature of what the film shows after the boat leaves the harbor.

> Q: Now in doing some of the fictionalization you've acknowledged you did, did you fictionalize, amongst other things, some of the motivations that shaped the actions as it unfolds on the screen?
>
> A: Yeah. For example, a very, very important thing for me was the decision when … they were forced to face the fact shall they now stay out there when the big storm is, so to speak, in their back or shall they really turn around and go through the storm, what they obviously did because they all died — and went for it. Nobody knows what happened. So again, I had to fictionalize that.

Petersen referred to a "greater truth," and the plaintiffs' attorneys picked up on it:

Q: So we tell a greater truth if we exaggerate or distort the actual facts?

A: Absolutely, absolutely.

Q: History becomes just what you, as a filmmaker, choose it to be...?

A: This is not a documentary. This is a motion picture, largely fictionalized, to tell a story about fishermen in Gloucester, Massachusetts ... and how their life is, and not an accurate recreation and retelling of every single element of the story. Because if you do that — right? — you might have a story that is accurate but not very dramatic.... If you just go with the facts, very often — very, very often, you get a film that just doesn't really get into your heart. Is it correct in every detail? Of course not, because we had to — made up a lot of things.

Having obtained this admission, the plaintiffs' attorney zeroed in on the difference between what the studio was claiming and what Petersen had just testified.

Q: And would it surprise you, given that testimony, that Warner Bros., in this lawsuit, has denied that there was any fictionalization in the movie?

A: If that is the case, it would surprise me.[18]

In a separate deposition, coproducer Paula Weinstein wrestled with the question of fictionalization, trying to use the same language as the film's disclaimer — that some events were "dramatized" rather than "fictionalized":

Q: Is it fair for me to assume that in shaping these various motivations and developing the scene, you weren't interested in telling an historically accurate story as much as creating a very dramatic effect for the audiences.

A: We were interested in creating a dramatic story that represented in spirit the book that we bought from Sebastian [Junger].

Q: You were not interested in telling a factually historic account, were you?

A: It was impossible — half of the story — once they're at sea, nobody knows what happened.

Q: So therefore you made things up, correct.

A: We dramatized.

Q: You fictionalized.

A: As I said earlier, Sebastian hypothesized what might have happened, and we dramatized that.

Q: You wouldn't say you fictionalized a good deal of those events?

A: I would say they're fictionalized.

As to how the film was marketed and what the audience was led to believe, Bradley Ball, Warner's president of marketing, testified,

A: It was very important to us to market the film as based on a true story and based on the history that took place relative to the magnitude of the storm and the people involved and not as fiction or something that was, you know, in the mind-set of a great screenwriter....

Q: And 90 percent of the people [in the audience] would have no way of knowing whatever deviations may have existed between what's portrayed in the film versus what was portrayed in the book.

A: Probably 90 percent of the audience would have no way of knowing anything about the story, deviations or not.

The discovery process had revealed an internal Warner's memo expressing concern about the film's infidelity to the facts. The depositions also showed that most of those deposed could not remember what had been fictionalized in the movie and what had not.

In its answer, Time Warner reiterated that the Florida statute did not apply to films and that films are protected by the First Amendment. It concluded,

As recognized by Judge Conway in her district court opinion in this matter, Plaintiffs are trying to achieve precisely what [courts] have refused to allow — an end run around the law of defamation and the use of the commercial misappropriation tort where it was not meant to apply.... Plaintiff's essential assertion has always been that Warner Bros. falsely portrayed decedent Bill Tyne and did so with "actual malice." If Tyne were alive, those allegations might state a claim for defamation. But they do not state a claim under Section 540.08, a statute which has nothing to do with defamation and in which falsity (and hence "malice") is not even an element.[19]

In its reply to the answer, the plaintiffs argued that the Court must reject Warner's interpretation of Section 540.08 because it avoids the statute's plain language and nullifies the statute and that the First Amendment does not require "commercial purpose" to be given an unduly restrictive interpretation in view of the newsworthy exemption. The reply concluded that the statute applies to the facts of this case subject only to the statutory newsworthiness and legitimate public interest exemption.[20]

The entertainment, arts and sports section of the Florida Bar filed an amicus brief in support of the plaintiffs,[21] and a number of film and publishing organizations— the Motion Picture Association of America, the Freedom to Read Foundation, the American Booksellers Foundation for Free Expression, the Publishers Marketing Association, the Video Software Dealers Association, the Magazine Publishers Association, and the Comic Book Legal Defense Fund —filed a joint amicus brief in support of the defendants.[22]

Oral arguments were presented to the supreme court of Florida on February 4, 2004. As of this writing, the Supreme Court of Florida has not issued a decision, and so the fate of this particular case is uncertain. The details of the case have been presented in this chapter to illustrate the types of strategies the families of decedents portrayed in a fact-based film must employ since the dead cannot sue for libel.

III

Courtroom Movies
Based on Fact

In normal drama, in simplistic terms, there is a good
guy and a bad guy and a woman and a man.... We put
[*Black Hawk Down*] into the fundamental rules of
drama, otherwise we'd be watching this massive documentary, and the cause and effect process [would get]
very confusing.

— Ridley Scott, director

The fictionalization of factual events in film has raised numerous legal
issues. It is especially interesting, then, to see how films based on factual
courtroom dramas have been treated. Trials are usually well documented,
and so have a record against which deviations can be ascertained. One
could assume that, if only through the help of technical advisors hired
concerning the legal content of the film, the legal issues concerning accuracy would have been called into focus. Also, since this group of films
focuses on one type of incident, the filmmakers' decisions concerning
issues of truth and fiction may be easier to see.

The trials are presented chronologically. For the oldest trials, there
was little possibility of defamation as a result of the film, but the larger
issue of promulgating false history is always there.

Trial of Thomas More (1535)
Film: *A Man for All Seasons* (1966)

THE FACTS

Thomas More was born in 1477.[1] He studied for the bar and became a lawyer. Patrons supported him because of his keen intelligence. In 1501, he was elected a member of Parliament. Thomas More married Jane Colte, oldest daughter of his new friend John Colte, a gentleman of Newhall, Essex, in 1505. She bore him three daughters and died in 1511. Very quickly, More married Alice Middleton, a widow seven years his senior.

Both Cardinal Wolsey and the young King Henry VIII were anxious to secure More's services at court. In 1516 he was granted a pension of 100 pounds for life. In 1521, he was knighted and made subtreasurer to the king. In 1523, he was elected Speaker of the House of Commons on Wolsey's recommendation; he became high steward of Cambridge University in 1525, and in the same year was made chancellor of the Duchy of Lancaster. He built himself a mansion about a hundred yards from the north bank of the Thames, with a large garden stretching along the river, where he and the king would often walk.

In October 1529, More succeeded Wolsey as chancellor of England. He was the first nonprelate to hold the office — perhaps signaling the start of Henry VIII's loosening of his country's ties with the Catholic Church. The chancellor was the equivalent to the chief justice of the U.S. Supreme Court and a cabinet member.

In this time of Reformation, More burned heretics — those whose views were contrary to the Catholic Church — and wrote scatological letters about the German priest and reformer Martin Luther.

Wolsey fell from power partly because of his inability to manage the church's response to the king's plan to marry Anne Boleyn, whom King Henry began courting in 1526, even though he was already married to Queen Catherine, who could not provide him with a son. Henry felt he had a right — for his own satisfaction and for the good of his kingdom — to marry Anne. More was well aware when he became chancellor that the king was asking the Church to annul his marriage to Queen Catherine so that he could marry Anne. The king had asked More for his support soon after his appointment as chancellor, and More told him that he believed that the original papal dispensation — allowing Henry to marry Catherine, his late brother's wife — had been valid and, consequently, so was the marriage. A few months after More's appointment as chancellor, the king issued a royal proclamation ordering the clergy to acknowledge Henry as

"Supreme Head" of the Church "as far as the law of God will permit." More immediately offered to resign his chancellorship, an offer the king refused to accept. But More's firm opposition to Henry's plans to divorce Queen Catherine and deny papal authority quickly lost him the royal favor, and in May 1532, he resigned his post of lord chancellor after holding it less than three years. As a result, he lost all of his income except his pension of 100 pounds a year and the rent of some properties.

For the next eighteen months More lived in seclusion and gave much time to writing. In March 1534, the Act of Succession was passed, which required all who should be called upon to take an oath acknowledging the issue of Henry and Anne as legitimate heirs to the throne, and to this was added a clause repudiating "any foreign authority, prince or potentate." On April 14, 1534, More was summoned to Lambeth to take the oath and, on his refusal, was committed to the custody of the abbot of Westminster. Four days later, he was removed to the Tower of London and in November was charged with treason.

In April and May 1535, Thomas Cromwell, the king's secretary, visited More in person to demand his opinion of the new statutes conferring on Henry the title of Supreme Head of the Church. More refused to give any answer beyond declaring himself a faithful subject of the king. On June 12, Sir Richard Rich, the solicitor-general, while two other men were taking away More's books, held a conversation with More.

On July 1, More was indicted for high treason at Westminster Hall before a panel of 18 judges, one of whom was Cromwell. More faced four counts of treason:

1. that when interrogated on May 7, 1535, he had refused to accept the royal supremacy over the Church of England;

2. that he had engaged in treasonous correspondence with Bishop Fisher, who had been executed the week before;

3. that he had referred to the Act of Supremacy as a two-edge sword so that by accepting it one saved the body and killed the soul and by rejecting it one saved the soul but killed the body; and

4. that he had spoken against the Act of Supremacy in his conversation with Rich.

More responded that he had been silent during the May 7 interrogation and that under common law silence was regarded as affirmation and not denial of what was being said. He noted that there was no evidence of treasonous correspondence against him since the letters to and from Bishop

Fisher had been burned and concluded that the "two-edge sword" statement was mere hypothetical rhetoric.

More's defense was so effective that the government dropped the first three charges and relied solely on Rich's testimony. Rich testified that in their June 12 conversation More had denied Parliament's power to confer ecclesiastical supremacy on Henry. More said that Rich's account was a lie. Rich asked that the two other men in the room be called to confirm his account, but both men testified that they were too busy binding up More's books and did not pay attention to what was being said.

The jury found More guilty. The defendant was convicted on the testimony of one person. (Twelve years later, the requirement that there must be two witnesses testifying against the defendant for him or her to be put to death was enacted.) More then responded publicly to the verdict, saying that the Act of Supremacy contradicted a higher law and was therefore invalid. He was sentenced to be hanged at Tyburn, but some days later this was changed by King Henry to beheading on Tower Hill. The execution took place "before nine of the clock" on July 6, 1535. The king was so mindful of the effect of More's eloquence that he sent Sir Thomas Pope to More's cell before he was brought out to the block to tell More, "The king's pleasure is ... that at your execution you not use many words." More complied. He met his death with calm and dignity, joking that those with him would have to get him up the scaffold and that, as for getting down, he would have to fend for himself. The body was buried in the Church of St. Peter ad Vincula.

More was canonized on May 20,1935 by Pope Pius XI.

THE FILM

The film *A Man for All Seasons*[2] is based on the play of the same name by Robert Bolt, which premiered in London in 1960 and on Broadway in 1962.[3] Both the London and Broadway productions starred Paul Scofield as Thomas More. The play focuses on the end of More's life — his refusal to take the oath required by the Act of Succession, trial, and execution.

The play was in the line of dramas about medieval and Renaissance history. Irish playwright George Bernard Shaw dramatized the life of Joan of Arc in 1922 in his *St. Joan*, and in 1935 T.S. Eliot wrote *Murder in the Cathedral*, a verse drama about the martyrdom of St. Thomas Becket in the reign of King Henry II. American dramatist Maxwell Anderson composed three free-verse plays about Tudor/Elizabethan monarchs: *Elizabeth the Queen* (1930), *Mary of Scotland* (1933), and *Anne of the Thousand Days* (1948). French playwright Jean Anouilh's 1953 play about Joan of Arc was translated by American playwright Lillian Hellman and performed on Broadway in 1955 as *The Lark*. In 1959, *Becket,* also on the martyrdom of Thomas Becket and also by Anouilh, was produced at the Théâtre Montparnasse; it was performed on Broadway in 1960 in a translation by Lucienne Hill starring Sir Laurence Olivier and Anthony Quinn.[4] Christopher Fry's verse play about Henry II, *Curtmantle,* which also touched on the death of Thomas Becket, debuted in 1961.

Shaw, while following the basic aspects of Joan of Arc's life and adhering fairly closely to the trial transcript, turned her life into an examination of the birth of nationalism. Eliot, Fry, and Anderson used their history-based stories to fly to poetic heights but sometimes twisted the plots for dramatic purposes. Anderson, for example, in *Elizabeth the Queen*, which was filmed in 1939 *as The Private Lives of Elizabeth and Essex*,[5] has the earl of Essex seize Elizabeth's court but then removes his troops when she promises to share the throne with him; she then doublecrosses him. In reality, Essex never came close to seizing the throne; he brought his troops to London in hope of rallying the populace, but the citizens closed their windows and barred their shutters, leaving Essex to be arrested and later executed.

Bolt, however, rather than following Eliot and Fry in writing a verse drama, used as his model the work of the German playwright Bertolt Brecht. Brecht's style utilized overtly theatrical devices to achieve an effect known as "alienation." The audience is constantly reminded that the play is a play and is told what morals or lessons they are to draw from it.[6] Bolt employed a character referred to as "the Common Man," who speaks directly to the audience and assumes a number of roles, including More's servants and ultimately More's executioner. Eliot had explored the technique of having characters speak to the audience in *Murder in the Cathedral* when he had the three murderers of Becket step forward and justify their action. In its didacticism and its subject of a Catholic saint, *A Man for All Seasons* also resembles the Medieval saints plays, which presented unblemished portraits of its subjects for didactic purposes.

In 1966, Columbia Pictures filmed Bolt's play with a screenplay credited to the playwright and direction by Fred Zinnemann, whose credits included such movies as *High Noon* (1952), *From Here to Eternity* (1953), *Oklahoma* (1955), *The Nun's Story* (1959) and *The Sundowners* (1960). Scofield, who had made only a few films, was called on to repeat his stage role, and an all-star cast was assembled to support him, including the noted director and actor Orson Welles in the small but showy role of Cardinal Wolsey; Robert Shaw as King Henry VIII; Leo McKern, who had played both the Common Man and Cromwell on stage, as Cromwell;

Wendy Hiller as Alice More; Susannah York as More's daughter; and Vanessa Redgrave in a silent cameo as Anne Boleyn. One major change in the film was the elimination of the character of the Common Man — such a theatrical device evidently being viewed as uncinematic. His lines were taken over by different actors playing the executioner and servants.

A Man for All Seasons was tremendously successful at the box office — the character of More who is willing to die for his convictions provided a sense of stability in the upheaval of the 1960s with the United States still reeling from the Kennedy assassination and finding itself more and more tied to a war in Vietnam — and achieved the unique distinction of winning Oscars, Golden Globe Awards, and New York Film Critics Circle Awards for best picture, best actor, best direction, and best adapted screenplay.

In 1988, actor Charlton Heston directed a new film version of the play with himself as More, Sir John Gielgud as Wolsey, and Vanessa Redgrave as Alice More. Heston had frequently played More in stage revivals. There was some criticism that Heston — who had won an Oscar for his performance as Ben Hur in 1959 and had starred in a number of action dramas including El Cid and the Planet of the Apes— was somewhat robust to play More and the 87-year old Gielgud somewhat frail to play the corpulent and self-indulgent Wolsey.

Like Bolt's play, the 1966 film follows the outlines of More's life closely and borrows extensively from the trial transcript. An oft-quoted line of More's to Robert Rich on seeing that Rich, who has testified against More, has been appointed chancellor of Wales— More says, paraphrasing the Bible, "It profits a man nothing to give his soul for the whole world. But for Wales?"— is, however, entirely of Bolt's invention.

Bolt compresses the timeline — making it seem like it covers months rather than six years. Unlike Maxwell Anderson, Bolt sticks fairly closely to the historical facts. The events portrayed are mostly the events that happened, although there are inaccuracies. Richard Marius has pointed out that, although Cromwell was More's interrogator while More was in the Tower, he was not his prosecutor, as both the movie and play show, but rather just one of 18 judges at the trial. More's family did not appear to regard Cromwell as More's nemesis since soon after More's death Roper asked Cromwell to be godfather to a child born to Roper and More's daughter Margaret — although having a godfather who was the vicar general was undoubtedly to the child's and family's advantage.[7]

Where Bolt veers most from historical accuracy, however, is in his characterizations. Robert Rich is portrayed as a craven and shallow sycophant, courting More's favor, and ultimately siding with Cromwell. Rich was a politically savvy man who achieved a feat that Wolsey, More, and Cromwell could not — he survived the turbulent reigns of Henry VIII, Edward VI, Lady Jane Grey, and Queen Mary, and lived thirty years after More's death into the early days of Queen Elizabeth I's reign.

Of greater importance, the film presents a picture of More as incredibly heroic, noble, honest, and even spotless. Bolt and the filmmakers admittedly had to deal with the fact that More is a Roman Catholic saint. The real More, however, had his flaws— his refusal to bend from his convictions that led to his martyrdom also led to his burning heretics. More's stand against heretics was part of his defense of his faith for which he ultimately and heroically died. But "when heretics burned," as Marius notes, "More gloated." And More was a political animal. Although the film shows him standing up to Wolsey, he instead stayed on Wolsey's good side until Wolsey's fall from grace, at which point he criticized Wolsey for his own political advancement, most notably in his maiden speech as lord chancellor. In the film, More brings up the defense that if his silence can legally be inferred to mean anything it must mean that he *consents* to the Act of Supremacy only in response to Cromwell's assertion otherwise. In reality, More himself brought up the argument as the main part in his defense.

Part of the reasons for the unquestioning portrayal of More is the original Brechtian concept of the play. The play is presented in blacks and whites. It offers a didactic message and is not meant to be taken realistically. In that context, More becomes an almost allegorical figure. Marius refers to the portrayal of More in the film as that of a "Catholic Abraham Lincoln, an icon of purity who provoked reverence and affection." Retaining the prime alienation technique of the play — the Common Man, who spoke to the audience and who played numerous roles— would have been overly theatrical and unrealistic in the realistic medium of film. However, simply excising the Common Man and retaining the didactic, simplified, and uncritical portrayal of More, makes More, and perhaps the film, unrealistic.

There is no question that More died heroically for his convictions, but he was a complicated human being in a complicated time, more complex than the portrayal in this historical pageant. More was caught on the wrong side of a political and religious reformation.

Overall, the one-sided portrait of Thomas More is problematic. The teaching website teachwiththemovies.com notes that because of *A Man for All Season*'s historical inaccuracies it was on the website's "not recommended for teaching" list for several years.

> However, a number of people, including a biographer of Thomas More and college professors, prevailed upon us to recommend the

film. They argued that Thomas More was an important historical figure, a man to be greatly admired, and a leader of the Renaissance at the same time that he was a proponent of many medieval beliefs. We also became aware that many teachers were using the film, both in the U.S. and in England. And so, we figured out ways to turn the inaccuracies of the film into strengths in discussions in the classroom and at home.[8]

It is odd, then, that a film as earnest, well-intentioned, and well-known as A *Man for All Seasons* must still be taken — historically speaking — with a proverbial grain of salt.

Litigation. Since the people portrayed in this movie had been dead more than 400 years by the time it was released, and, as noted, the dead cannot sue for libel, there were no lawsuits from the people portrayed or their families. But the distance of time alone does not prevent anyone living from claiming that they were portrayed in an historical movie. The disclaimer about a movie being fictitious is used for both historical and nonhistorical films. In a film that is, say, a romantic comedy, the screenwriters' dentist could sue and claim that he was obviously being portrayed on the screen as the movie's drunken and lecherous dentist. For historical movies, a living human being could conceivably claim that his or her character had ended up in the movie. For example, Sir Laurence Olivier claimed in a 1986 book that he had based his makeup for the evil king Richard in his stage production and 1955 film version of Shakespeare's *Richard III* on the theatrical producer Jed Harris, the most "loathsome person I have ever met."[9] If Harris, who lived until 1979, had known this, and had felt that others had known this (identification) and that it had caused him damage, he could conceivably have sued. But as far as the people portrayed, the further removed the events portrayed in a movie are from the present day, the less likely is the prospect of litigation.

While not litigation, there was some settlement involving the authorship of the screenplay. Robert Bolt won Academy Award nominations for best screenplay from adapted material for *Lawrence of Arabia* (1962), *Doctor Zhivago* (1965), and *A Man for All Seasons* and won the Oscar for the last two. But for the first film Bolt was working from an existing script written by blacklisted writer Michael Wilson. Among its actions on a number of disputed credits, the Writers Guild of America later restored Wilson as coauthor of the screenplay for *Lawrence of Arabia*.

The credits for *A Man for All Season* were similarly changed to cite Constance Willis, who is listed as "continuity" in the film's original credits, as the screenplay's coauthor. Bolt died in 1995.

Amistad Trial (1840)
Film: *Amistad* (1997)

THE FACTS

In 1839, five or six hundred African men were purchased by a Portuguese slave trader. They were shipped to Havana, Cuba, then a Spanish colony. Slavery was legal in many countries, including the United States, although the international slave trade had been banned by laws and treaties in nations such as Great Britain, Spain, the Netherlands, and the United States. However, the trade still continued, and the Africans were landed near Havana and sold openly in the slave market. Fifty-two members of the Mendi tribe, from present-day Nigeria, were sold to Jos Ruiz and Pedro Montez, two Cubans who planned to sell the Mendians to a Cuban sugar plantation. The Mendians were given Spanish names and designated as "black ladinos," indicating that they were long-term slaves who had lived in Cuba long enough to know the language and customs. Ruiz and Montez placed them on board the schooner *Amistad*, which means "friendship," and set sail on June 28, 1839, for a port down the Cuban coast.

On the fourth night out, the Mendians broke free of their chains, seized machetes, and, at dawn, attacked the captain and his three-man crew. Their leader, Sengbe Pieh, given the Spanish name Cinque, killed the captain. Two members of the crew escaped in the ship's boat; the cabin boy, an actual ladino, was not harmed. The two Cuban slavers, spared on the promise that they would take the ship back to Africa, steered east to Africa by day but turned the vessel toward the United States by night, hoping to make some friendly southern port. On August 26, the *Amistad*, its provisions exhausted, was apprehended off Long Island by a U.S. coastal survey brig and taken to New London, Connecticut.

Ruiz and Montez immediately insisted that the Mendians were escaped slaves, pirates, and murderers and claimed them as their property. The Mendians did not speak English or Spanish and so could not communicate with anyone. They were brought before a federal judge, who set a trial date. The Spanish ambassador demanded that President Martin Van Buren return the ship and the Mendians to Ruiz and Montez and that the whole matter be dealt with under Spanish law, as treaty obligations stipulated. Van Buren personally preferred to return the Mendians and in so doing not alienate his southern pro-slavery support, but the matter had already been placed under court jurisdiction.

Three prominent abolitionists intervened — Lewis Tappan, a merchant and industrialist who had raised funds to defend and care for the

Mendians; Reverend Joshua Leavitt, editor of the antislavery journal, *Emancipator*; and Simeon S. Jocelyn, an engraver active in the antislavery movement. They obtained legal counsel and a translator to take testimony from the Mendians, which became the basis of the defense's case.

On January 7, 1840, the Mendians' trial began in the district court in Hartford, Connecticut. Tappan, aided by a British commissioner stationed in Havana to help suppress the illegal slave trade, uncovered evidence to support the Mendians' story: proof that the documents establishing them as ladinos were forged. The judge, persuaded by this evidence, concluded that even under Spanish law, the Mendians were free men and ordered President Van Buren to have them transported back to Africa.

Van Buren, worried that this case would damage his standing in the south, ordered the government's lawyers to appeal the case to the U.S. Supreme Court. Tappan approached John Quincy Adams, who was a luke-warm supporter of abolitionism, for help, and Adams finally agreed.

The case went before the Supreme Court on February 22, 1841. Adams' argument, extending over two days and lasting seven hours, centered on what he considered to be the cornerstone of Anglo-American rights and liberties, the principle of habeas corpus. By Spain's own laws, he argued, the Mendians were illegally enslaved. If the president could hand over free men on the demand of a foreign government, how could anyone in the United States ever be sure of their "blessing of freedom"? The Court, with one dissent, agreed.

By the time the Court rendered its decision, however, John Tyler, a southern pro-slavery Whig, was president; he refused to provide a war-ship for the Mendians' return. In December 1841, Tappan and his fellow abolitionists obtained a ship and missionaries who would accompany the Africans home. Cinque went home to become a chief of his people. In 1878, near death, Cinque returned to the mission and died a Christian.

THE FILM

Amistad[10] was released in 1997, directed by Steven Spielberg, the direc-tor of two other well-received, fact-based films—*Saving Private Ryan* (1998) and *Schindler's List* (1994) as well as more-fanciful films such as *E.T. the Extra-Terrestrial* (1982) and the Indiana Jones series (1981–89).

Amistad begins by recounting the slave revolt and the slavers' trick of bringing the ship to Long Island. The *Amistad* is boarded by U.S. sailors and taken to Connecticut, where Cinque and the others are jailed. The real-life abolitionist Tappan and a fictional, African-American one, Theodore Joadson, promote the cause of the Amistad captives, assisted by the young lawyer Roger Baldwin, who mainly tries property cases and who sees the slaves as a different form of property dispute. Through the course of the trials, Baldwin's attitudes change toward Cinque and the Africans.

The initial trial is before a Connecticut judge and jury with claims presented by the Spanish slavers, the American sailors, who claim salvage on the high seas, and the U.S. government, honoring its 1795 treaty obligations to return the ship and slaves to the Spanish government. In addition, a Spanish diplomat intends to see the slaves returned to Cuba to be executed for murder. Unable to communicate with the slaves due to the bumbling translation work of an incompetent linguist, Baldwin and Joadson — rather than Tappan and the British ambassador — search the *Amistad* for and find documents that show that the ship came from Africa and that, consequently, prove the slaves were not born on plantations and therefore were not Spanish slaves whose ship had strayed into American waters. President Van Buren is campaigning for reelection from the back of a railroad car and gets the first trial judge to recuse himself so that Van Buren can handpick the judge's successor, a young judge named Coughlin, whom the president can influence.

The abolitionists seek the help of former president John Quincy Adams, but he turns them down. Queen Isabella II writes numerous letters to the United States protesting that the slaves must be returned, and John C. Calhoun threatens that civil war may be the outcome if the case is not resolved in a pro-slavery fashion. Adams does, however, encourage, the Mendi attorney and supporters to find out their client's story.

Baldwin and Joadson find a British/Mendi sailor who speaks both English and Mendi to serve as a translator for Cinque and the other *Amistad* slaves. Through this interpreter, Cinque describes how he was taken captive near his village, brought to the slave fortress Lomboko in Sierre Leone, and then put on a slave ship for Cuba. He describes the systematic brutalization of the slaves, including the casual murder of fifty slaves who were tossed overboard when the Spaniards discovered they would not have enough food to keep all their captives alive for the entire Atlantic journey.

The prosecutor openly questions Cinque's claims and gets him to admit that the Mendi also keep slaves and that slavery has been known in Africa for generations. However, as a result Cinque's horrific testimony, Judge Coughlin rules that the *Amistad* survivors should be given their freedom and returned to Africa, while the slavers should be jailed for murder.

Van Buren requests that the United States appeal the case to the Supreme Court. Adams finally agrees to assist Baldwin and Joadson. He

meets and bonds with Cinque, who accompanies Adams and Baldwin to
the Supreme Court trial. Adams presents the case as one of Cinque's heroism in the face of disastrous odds. Pointing to Cinque, Adams claims that

> [H]e is the only true hero in this room.... If he were white, he
> wouldn't be standing [here] fighting for his life. If he were white ...
> songs would be written about him; ... his story would be told and
> retold in our classrooms; our children ... would know his name as
> well as they know Patrick Henry's!

Adams also speaks about how the independence of the judiciary is
threatened if the court caves in to political pressure brought by Van Buren,
and indirectly by the queen of Spain. The Supreme Court's decision grants
the *Amistad* survivors their freedom. Cinque returns to find his family
missing, village empty, and his country in civil war.

• ***Analysis.*** Although John Quincy Adams and Cinque did meet once, in
New Haven, they never had the long and complex series of personal
exchanges and dialogues that the film provides.[11] Cinque and the other
African captives never attended arguments in the Supreme Court, which
is still the case with most parties in Supreme Court actions. Roger Baldwin was not a young, hungry attorney who threw in his lot with the abolitionists but was forty-six years old, and one of the most highly respected
attorneys in the state of Connecticut in 1839; he was already an abolitionist
himself. (The film's portrayal of Baldwin gives him the dramatic action of
"seeing the light.") In the film, President Van Buren replaces Judge Andrew
T. Judson with a new younger judge, Judge Coughlin. Judge Coughlin never
existed, and Judge Judson did actually finish out the case. The irony—and
probably the better story—is that Judson was initially opposed to the abolitionists and overcame these feelings in rendering his verdict. African-
American historians have complained about the creation of a fictional
Theodore Joadson when historic black abolitionists such as the Reverend
James W.C. Pennington actually did participate in the *Amistad* affair.

John Quincy Adams' argument was pretty much as the movie presented it.

In short, the film creates numerous distortions of facts in order to
work in a number of minor "dramas"—Baldwin's "seeing the light" and
Adams' bonding with Cinque. It is, however, generally true to the basic
facts of the story and to the spirit of what happened.

A film about a trial, *Amistad* includes a scene that presents a mini-
textbook in case preparation for attorneys. The fictional Joadson, after
Adams again refuses to take the case, asks at least for Adams' advice on

the case. The old man says that he has always found that the attorneys who win cases tell the best stories. Joadson visibly dismisses this as a bromide from a dottering old lawyer and starts to leave when Adams suddenly asks him, "What is your client's story?" Joadson begins, "They are black slaves from East Africa—" Adams shakes his head and asks, "Where are you from?" Joadson replies, "Georgia," and Adams asks whether that is Joadson's story, that he is a man from Georgia or is it not, rather, that he is a former slave who has fought to make other slaves free. "You and young Baldwin," Adams says, "have struggled and struggled and finally found out that their clients are black. Congratulations. You've determined what they are but you haven't figured out who they are. And when you do that, you'll know their story." The scene is the invention of the screenwriter but is in keeping with the events and the spirit of what happened. The Effective Lawyer Communications Project of Georgia State University obtained a license from the makers of *Amistad* to use clips from the movie for an instructional video entitled "What Is Their Story?"

There were also critical denunciations of *Amistad*. History professor Warren Goldstein, writing in the *Chronicle of Higher Education*, insisted, "The picture is profoundly false," especially in its superficial portrayal of the abolitionist movement—Baldwin was an experienced lawyer who devoted his life and risked his reputation for the cause—and its decision not to depict the church folk throughout the North who raised money for the cause as anything but irrelevant and ineffectual. This was more than a story about individuals, Goldstein wrote, but about institutions, organizations, and movements. He added,

> Historians needn't object to dramatic license. The trial of *Amistad* captives, for example, actually employed two translators of the Africans' Mende language, instead of the one shown in the film. That detail is unimportant. Dramatic misrepresentation is something else again, and when it occurs, historians should not hide.[12]

• **Litigation.** There were, of course, no lawsuits from those who were portrayed in *Amistad,* all of them having died. However, there was relevant litigation involving at least one of the fictionalizations that the filmmakers added to the historical events. Novelist Barbara Chase-Riboud sued the filmmakers for copyright infringement, claiming that elements from her novel about the *Amistad* incident, *Echo of Lions,* had been borrowed without permission or attribution in the film.[13] In her complaint, Chase-Riboud alleged 40 similarities between fictional elements of her book and the film. Most significantly, she pointed out the presence of a rich black abolitionist as a central character in both the book and film when no such character existed in the events surrounding the actual *Amistad* incident. Chase-Riboud also noted that both the book and film indicate that Adams and Cinque became friends, although evidence is that they only met once. The court denied her request for an injunction, claiming that the similarities Chase-Riboud noted in her suit were due to the fact that both the film and her novel were based on the same historical incident. The court did find similarity between the fictional Theodore Joadson character in the film and a character in her novel, but this alone was insufficient for the court to grant an injunction. Chase-Riboud later settled the suit for an undisclosed amount.

Trial of William "Duff" Armstrong (1858)
Film: *Young Mr. Lincoln* (1939)

THE FACTS

In 1858, William "Duff" Armstrong, whose father had been a friend of Abraham Lincoln, was tried for the murder of James Preston "Pres" Metzker. According to Armstrong's account, he had been friends with Metzker, but a drunken Metzker attacked him.[14] A James Norris joined in the fight. The three were separated, and Armstrong saw Metzker the next day and thought he was fine. A few days later, Metzker died, and Armstrong and Norris were arrested and jailed. Norris, who had killed another man, was convicted of manslaughter. Armstrong was tried separately at the Bearstown, Illinois, courthouse. His parent's friend, "Uncle Abe," agreed to defend Armstrong, even though Lincoln was running for the U.S. Senate and preparing for his debates with his rival Stephen Douglas.

Lincoln produced a doctor as a witness who testified that Metzker might have suffered the injuries that killed him by falling off his horse. However, one prosecution witness, Charles Allen, testified that, aided by the light of a full moon, he had seen Armstrong strike Metzker with a "slungshot"—a sack with a weight that is used as a weapon, much like a blackjack. Lincoln was unable to shake Allen on cross-examination, but during his summation he declared to the jury that Allen had been lying about what he said he had seen and, to prove it, he passed around an almanac that indicated that on the day of the murder the moon had been near the horizon at the time and could not have produced enough light for Allen to see what he claimed to have seen. According to Armstrong's recollections, five minutes after the jury entered the room, he heard laughter. The jury returned an acquittal for Armstrong after the judge and the lawyers got back from supper. Armstrong lived another 40 years. Lincoln lost the Senate race to Douglas in 1858 but was elected president of the United States in 1860 and in 1864. He was assassinated in 1865.

THE FILM

The year 1939 is widely considered to have been the finest year for Hollywood filmmaking. Films produced that year included *Gone with the Wind, the Wizard of Oz, Mr. Smith Goes to Washington, Goodbye Mr. Chips, The Hunchback of Notre Dame, Of Mice and Men, Wuthering Heights, Love Affair, Dark Victory, The Women, Stagecoach, Ninotchka, Gunga Din, Drums Along the Mohawk,* and *Beau Geste.* That year, in addition to *Stagecoach* and *Drums Along the Mohawk,* John Ford directed *Young Mr. Lincoln,*[15] based on the early life of the sixteenth president of the United States, Abraham Lincoln, for 20th Century–Fox.

Ford had formerly explored this period of U.S. history with his 1936 film *Prisoner of Shark Island,* about Dr. Samuel Mudd, who was imprisoned as one of the conspirators who assassinated Lincoln in 1865, in spite of his claim that he set the broken leg of principal assassin John Wilkes Booth without knowing who he was. (The character of Lincoln also appears briefly in Ford's 1924 silent film *The Iron Horse.*) The subject of Lincoln was then "hot" in literature and film. Carl Sandburg had published the first volume of his six-volume biography of Lincoln in 1928 — *Abraham Lincoln: The Prairie Years;* the final four volumes, *Abraham Lincoln: The War Years,* were published in 1939, the same year as the film *Young Mr. Lincoln.* In 1928, poet Steven Vincent Benét had produced the poem "John Brown's Body" about the Civil War. In 1930, Benét wrote the screenplay for D.W. Griffith's *Abraham Lincoln,* the first sound biography of Lincoln. And the year before *Young Mr. Lincoln,* Robert Sherwood's *Abe Lincoln in Illinois* was produced on Broadway and won the Pulitzer Prize for drama — it was filmed in 1940.

Ford was a Civil War buff and had a special affection for Lincoln. In a series of interviews thirty years later, he referred to a cut scene in *Young Mr. Lincoln* in which Lincoln prophetically sees a poster for a performance by actor Edwin Booth, his future assassin's brother, which he can't afford to see; Ford referred to Lincoln affectionately as that "poor ape." Before publication, he asked the interviewer to change the word "ape," fearful that readers might think he had been insulting Lincoln's memory.

The screenplay for *Young Mr. Lincoln* was written by Lamar Trotti, who had also scripted Ford's *Drums Along the Mohawk;* he based his screenplay on Sandburg's and other biographies, as well as on a story he remembered from his days as a reporter in the 1920s in which a mother would not confirm which of her two sons was the murderer. Trotti's screenplay was nominated for an Academy Award but lost, as did most other nominees, to *Gone with the Wind*. (Trotti went on to write the classic *Ox Bow Incident* in 1942, won an Oscar for his screenplay for the film biography *Wilson* in 1944, and died in 1952 at the age of 52. Ford made classic after classic and died in 1973.)

In the movie, young Abe Lincoln loses his love, Ann Rutledge, to sickness. He trades the Clay family a flannel cloth for the contents of a barrel, and inside the barrel is a copy of *Blackstone's Commentaries*. Shortly thereafter, evidently in 1838, having apprenticed in the law, Lincoln settles his first case between Messrs. Hawthorne and Woolridge. That evening, during the Fourth of July fireworks celebration, Matt and Adam Clay defend their sister's honor against the harassment of Scrub White and his friend Jack Cass. White is found to have been stabbed to death. Mrs. Clay, who saw what happened, refuses to testify so that her testimony will not implicate one of her two sons.

Mrs. Clay asks Lincoln to defend her boys, and, even though it is only his second case and his first trial, Lincoln agrees. He borrows an almanac from the Clays to take notes on, lacking any paper.

The prosecution calls Mrs. Clay to testify, and she refuses to implicate either of her sons. Seeing her anguish, Lincoln begs the court to let her step down.

Jack Cass testifies that the "taller of the two" stabbed White. On cross-examination, when Lincoln asks how Cass could have seen the murder in the dark, Cass says that he saw the killing in the light of the full moon. Lincoln excuses the witness and, as Cass walks away, then produces the almanac that shows that the moon was not full. Lincoln accuses Cass of the murder. Cass breaks down and confesses. The movie ends with Lincoln walking up a hill with thunder in the sky. The final image is of the statue of a seated Lincoln at the Lincoln Memorial.

• *Analysis.* The screenwriter Lamar Trotti combined the story of the 1858 Armstrong trial with a tale of a 1920s murder. He also provided an answer to the question, why did Charles Allen/Jack Cass say he saw the murder. Trotti went for the typical melodramatic, "Perry Mason" solution: Cass lies to implicate the Clays for a murder he committed, and he confesses his guilt under Lincoln's cross-examination. What really happened in the Armstrong case was what happens in most of the murder cases in which the defense is successful — the murderer did not confess but, rather, by impeaching the eyewitness, Lincoln created reasonable doubt in the mind of the jury.

The more important act of juggling Trotti committed was moving the date of the trial from 1858 to 1838. In doing so, Trotti endowed the young Mr. Lincoln with the 20-years' worth of trial lawyer experience the real Lincoln had when he pulled out the almanac at Armstrong's trial. Trotti also inserted Douglas into the plot by showing him to be a rival for the affections of Mary Todd, whom Lincoln would later marry, and as an advisor to the prosecutor — thereby prefiguring their later opposition in the Senate race.

More recent assessment of Lincoln has questioned the importance of Ann Rutledge — she died at 19 and left no writings behind — and the accuracy of stories such as Lincoln reading *Blackstone* by firelight. But these stories were in Sandburg and were considered authoritative at the time of the film.

Some legal analysts, especially Bergman and Asimov,[16] in looking at the film have scoffed at the Lincoln's loose handling of legal procedures during the trial. But what Ford does do, and very well, is capture the period atmosphere. It should be remembered that the date of the actual trial was 1858, three years before the Civil War. The last surviving Civil War veteran died in 1949, ten years after this film was made, so there were people around in 1939 who had lived through the period. Ford used the same attention to deal with his westerns. He claimed to have known the real Wyatt Earp. Earp died in 1929, and in the decade before his death he visited old friends on film sets that Ford worked on and told stories of the Old West. The late 1880s were just forty to fifty years removed from when Ford was making his classic westerns, including *My Darling Clementine*, his version of the Wyatt Earp story. The time span is the same as World War II veterans telling stories about the war in the year 2000. Ford had access to survivors of the period and was also a great reader of history. Consequently, his recreations of the period in such film as *Young Mr. Lincoln* has more validity than many.

In his analysis of the film, Norman Rosenberg puts the film in a broader anti-lawyer and anti-law context, stating that "*Young Mr. Lincoln* marks its hero as someone who works within but is not really of the legal machinery; he uses common sense and his humanity rather than, as Lincoln calls it in the film, 'lawyer talk.'"[17] Rosenberg notes that Ford has Lincoln roam the periphery of the courtroom, sometimes barely in the shot, sometimes visibly only as a shadow.[18] Marsha Kinder argues that the film demonstrates Lincoln's patriarchal and phallic power as he abruptly rises— sometimes "popping up"—from a sitting position and untangles himself "into a visual erection."[19] While I am personally uncomfortable with Kinder's imagery, Ford does have Lincoln tower above everyone in the film, especially Douglas, Cass, and the opposing counsel, except in the scene when the judge visits Lincoln at night and advises him to turn the case over to a more experienced lawyer like Douglas. Then Lincoln, as Rosenberg observes, violates professional courtesy and remains seated in front of the judge, leaning back to show that he works with the legal system but is "not quite of" it.[20]

The film makes the younger Lincoln a better lawyer than he could have been at that time of his life and makes the trial more dramatic. The real Lincoln could not break the witness on the stand and left the almanac for his summation; in real life, the eyewitness was not the murderer, lying to hide his own guilt. Consequently, while one could conceivably argue that the film evokes Lincoln's spirit in an entertaining way, the shifts in time and other historical distortions make the film an inaccurate one.

• *Litigation.* None known.

Andersonville Trial (1865)
The Andersonville Trial (1970)

THE FACTS

Andersonville in Sumter County, Georgia, near the town of Americus, was the largest Confederate prisoner of war camp.[21] Of the nearly 50,000 prisoners who were confined there during the war, 13,000 died of disease or malnutrition. Its commandant was Major Henry Wirz. Wirz had been born in Zurich, Switzerland, and studied at the University of Zurich. After earning medical degrees in Berlin and Paris, he emigrated to Louisiana, where he practiced medicine. He joined the Confederate Army and was wounded in the Battle of Seven Pines in May 1862, losing the use of his right arm. When the Union and Confederate armies stopped exchanging prisoners in 1863, the Confederate Army established Andersonville as a prisoner of war camp. General John Henry Winder, impressed by Wirz, who had been his clerk, appointed him commandant of the new camp.

After the Confederate surrender and the assassination of President Lincoln on April 15, 1865, President Andrew Johnson ordered the formation of a military commission of the War Department to try the alleged conspirators. Major General Lee Wallace was second officer of the court. The first tried before the military tribunal were those accused of the presidential assassination. Although the defendants could produce witnesses, they were not allowed to testify on their own behalf. Of those convicted of the assassination, four, including Mary E. Surratt, were hanged in the yard of the old jail in Washington, D.C., on July 7, 1865. Three were sentenced to life, and one to six years.

Wirz was arrested, and on August 23, 1865, the commission filed two charges against him. The first count alleged that Wirz had conspired with Confederate president Jefferson Davis, General Winder, and various other high ranking Confederate officials to "impair the health and destroy the lives" of Union prisoners of war. The second charge had 13 specifications, alleging that Wirz had murdered thirteen Union prisoners of war at Andersonville by shooting, stomping, subjecting such prisoners to the mauling of bloodhounds, and various other mistreatment, although the count listed no individual names. General Wallace now served as president of the military court. The original plan was to try not only Wirz but Davis, General Robert E. Lee, and other Confederate generals and officials. President Johnson eliminated all charges but those against Wirz. General Winder would likely have faced charges as well had he not died of a heart attack in February 1865. Of all the "conspirators," only Wirz was tried.

At first, Wirz had five attorneys, chief among them Louis Schade, who, like Wirz, had immigrated to America from Switzerland. Schade's colleague, O.S. Baker, was one of the five. Schade and Baker did the work pro bono since Wirz was penniless. Schade had been a close friend and supporter of Illinois senator Stephen Douglas in the Lincoln-Douglas campaign, which revolved around issues of slavery. After moving to Washington, Schade was known to support the South as the United States inched toward Civil War.

The defense filed for dismissal of the charges against Wirz on the grounds that a military tribunal had no jurisdiction to try a civilian; that the charges were vague as to time, place, and manner of offense; and that as a Confederate officer Wirz was entitled to the terms agreed to between Generals Sherman and Johnston upon the latter's surrender. The court overruled the motions, and Wirz then pleaded not guilty to all charges. When the defense motions were defeated, the other three attorneys abandoned the case, leaving only Schade and Baker.

Wirz's trial began on August 25, 1865. Colonel N. P. Chipman, U.S. Judge Advocate, headed the prosecution. The government presented 160 witnesses. The prosecution's key witness, however, was Felix de la Baume, who testified concerning most of the thirteen killings of which Wirz was accused. Some questioned his testimony as reflecting an unrealistic omnipresence. De la Baume was reportedly rewarded for his testimony on the government's behalf and given a position in the Department of the Interior. After Wirz's execution, some Union soldiers of German ancestry reportedly identified "de la Baume" as a deserter from the 7th New York Infantry whose real name was Felix Oeser.

Of the 160 witnesses called by the prosecution, 10 testified to alleged cruelty on the part of the defendant. Approximately 145 of the government's own witnesses, almost all of whom were former inmates of Andersonville, testified that they had no knowledge of Wirz ever murdering or killing a prisoner with his own hands or otherwise. Some testified that Wirz inspected the prison every day and often warned them that if any man escaped he would "starve every damn Yankee for it."

Under the court's rules, the defense had to have its witnesses approved in advance by the prosecution. Chipman interviewed the defense witnesses and decided, on his own discretion, who would testify and who would not. In his 1911 book on the trial, Chipman claimed that of the 106 witnesses subpoenaed, 68 had reported, and 39 had been dismissed by the defense itself.[22] Chipman's book critiques and dismisses the statements of the twelve defense witnesses who testified. They recounted Wirz's efforts to improve camp conditions and his anguish at his failure to do so. During the trial, a letter from Wirz was presented that showed that he had complained to his superiors about the shortage of food being provided for the prisoners. When Wirz fell ill during the trial, Wallace forced him to attend, and he was brought into court on a stretcher. He did not testify.

By the end of the trial, even Schade and Baker, evidently disgusted by the proceedings, resigned as Wirz's attorneys. Chipman delivered the prosecution's closing statements and also summarized the defense's case. Wirz did read his own closing statement, which concluded:

> Every respectable and reliable witness, either for the government or for myself, who was in a position to know anything about the history of Andersonville, has stated before this court in the most positive and unequivocal terms that all the stories about my cruelty were entirely new to them when they came to Washington and had never reached their ears before.

The trial ended on October 24, 1865, and the verdict was announced one week later. Henry Wirz was found guilty on the first charge of conspiring with other Confederate officials to murder the prisoners. On the second charge, Wirz was found guilty of eleven of the thirteen alleged murders of Union prisoners. The sentence was that he be "hanged by the neck til he be dead."

Wirz was remanded to his cell to await execution. He reportedly rejected an offer to avoid execution if he implicated Jefferson Davis in a plot to kill the prisoners. Wirz told the Irish priest who was there to give him the last rites, "I will not purchase my liberty by perjury and a crime."

Wirz personally wrote President Andrew Johnson asking for either an executive pardon or a swift execution. The request for a pardon was rejected. Wirz also wrote Schade, thanking him for all he had done and asking that Schade and the people of the South care for his family.

On November 10, 1865, Wirz received the last rites of his church from Father R. E. Boyle. Surrounded by soldiers shouting "Andersonville, Andersonville," Wirz mounted the scaffold in the prison yard with the priest. He said, "I die innocent." A Major Russell read the death warrant to Wirz and then whispered to him that he deplored the duty. Wirz replied, "I know what orders are, Major. And I am being hanged for obeying them."

The trap door was sprung, but Wirz did not die immediately. To the shouts and taunts of the mob, he choked to death over a two-minute period.

The U.S. government refused the request of Wirz's widow to return the body to his family for a Christian burial. Wirz's body was buried "without ceremony" in the Old Capitol Prison yard next to Mary Surratt, who, along with the others who were sentenced to death in the military tribunal's first trial, had been executed in the same yard as Wirz. Schade petitioned the government on behalf of Wirz's family. The body was reburied at Mt. Olivet Catholic Cemetery in Washington, D.C., in 1869. The service at the gravesite was offered by Father Boyle, with Schade and members of Wirz's family and friends attending. The inscription on the flat grave marker is "Captain Henry Wirz C.S.A./Confederate Hero Martyr/ Died November 11, 1865."

Eleven days after Wirz's execution, de la Baume was fired from his position at the Department of the Interior.

In 1908, amid a great deal of controversy, the Georgia division of the United Daughters of the Confederacy erected an obelisk monument in Wirz's memory at Andersonville. One of the inscriptions claims that "this shaft is erected" in order "to secure his name from the stigma attached to it by embittered prejudice...."

In 1868, as adjutant general of the Grand Army of the Republic (GAR), Chipman, working from a suggestion from a Union soldier from Ohio, initiated the creation of Memorial Day and cosigned with GAR commander-in-chief General John Logan General Order No. 11 that proclaimed the holiday. When he became president, Ulysses S. Grant appointed Chipman secretary of the District of Columbia. Chipman was later elected to Congress from that district in 1871 and served two terms. His speech on the relationship between the federal government and the District of Columbia was later published.[23] In 1876, Chipman moved to Red Bluff, California, where he practiced law, farmed, and for 15 years served on the state board of trade. In 1897, he was appointed commissioner of the Supreme Court, a position he held until the commission was disbanded and replaced by the District Court of Appeal. He was appointed presiding justice of the newly created appellate court, a position he held until his retirement in 1921.

Chipman's account of the trial was published in 1911 under the title *The Tragedy of Andersonville: Trial of Captain Henry Wirz, the Prison Keeper.* The book was prompted, according to Chipman, by the 1908 erection of the monument to Wirz in Andersonville and its inscriptions indicating that Wirz's trial was tainted by "prejudice." He was also responding to statements by Jefferson Davis in articles published in 1890 that Wirz was an "unhappy victim of a misdirected popular clamor."[24] Forty-six years after the event, the 75-year-old Chipman did not write a memoir of the trial so much as re-argue it as, by his own admission, an advocate. The more than 500-page book picked from the more than 2,000-page trial transcript and presented selections and excerpts in a form accessible to the general public. "The most important feature of the record of the trial," Chipman wrote, "is its exposure of the policy of the Confederate government and its guilty participation in the crimes of Andersonville."[25] The trial, Chipman claimed, was an indictment against the "conspiracy" of the Confederate leadership, and he viewed Wirz as a "willing sharer" in the conspiracy.[26] Acknowledging defense testimony of Wirz's acts of kindness, Chipman wrote, "These things showed that there was some human kindness in his nature, but they are not wholly incompatible with guilt and are themselves insufficient to raise a reasonable doubt that he committed the crimes charged against him."[27] Chipman concluded,

> As an illustration of the horrors of war, [Andersonville] will always stand unparalleled. As furnishing a study of human suffering upon a stupendous scale and as showing that modern civilization has not mitigated the cruelties to which a professedly Christian people may resort, the past century has exhibited nothing like it.[28]

Chipman died in his home in San Francisco on February 1, 1924, at the age of 88.

Wallace went on to serve as governor of New Mexico and was in office when Billy the Kid was captured and shot by Pat Garrett in 1881. In 1880, he wrote *Ben Hur: A Story of Christ,* which became a best seller and later a stage play and two major motion pictures (MGM, 1926 and 1959). Wallace died in Indiana in 1905.

Schade continued to practice law in Washington, D.C. In April 1867, he published "A Defense of Captain Henry Wirz," arguing that Wirz had been made a scapegoat. In 1873, Schade became publisher of *The Washington Sentinel.* Ironically, Schade purchased the house at 516 Tenth Street where President Lincoln had died after he was shot at Ford's Theater and brought to this house across the street. Schade published his newspaper from the house's basement. He opposed the corruption of Boss Shepherd, who was the last mayor of Washington, D.C., until 1964. Schade died in 1903 at the age of 74. His fellow attorney on the case, Baker, had died in 1889 at the age of 61.[29]

There were no subsequent war crimes trials after Wirz's execution. He remains the only person executed for war crimes in the United States. The precedent of his trial was cited in the war crimes trials at Nuremberg after World War II.

The Film

The Andersonville Trial was written by Saul Levitt using the official record of the trial of Henry Wirz as its basic source material.[30] Levitt, who was also writing for the TV series *The Untouchables* while *Andersonville* was in rehearsals, had first explored the subject in his 1954 teleplay "The Trial of Captain Wirz" for the TV anthology series *Climax.* The play debuted on Broadway on December 29, 1959, starring George C. Scott as Captain Chipman, Albert Dekker as Otis Baker, and Herbert Berghoff as Wirz. It ran for six months. Levitt said he attempted to stay as close to the facts as possible while injecting his own concepts of the personalities involved. The play is set in the time and place of the trial, formal names and roles of characters reflect those of historical participants, and some of the dialogue is derived from the original trial record.

The play was published by Random House Publishing in 1960 and was presented as a television movie in 1970 with a teleplay by Levitt. Scott, the year after his Oscar-winning performance as General George Patton, directed, with William Shatner as Chipman and Richard Basehart as Wirz. Both Shatner and Basehart were classically trained actors who had just finished stints in television science fiction shows— Shatner in *Star Trek* and Basehart in *Voyage to the Bottom of the Sea.* Cameron Mitchell played

General Wallace, and Jack Cassidy portrayed the defense attorney named Otis Baker. Buddy Ebsen, who was still playing Jedd Clampett in the *Beverly Hillbillies* on television, portrayed the camp's doctor, Dr. John Bates. Also in the cast as witnesses were John Anderson as Seymour Ambrose, Harry Townes as Colonel Chandler, Whit Bissell as a doctor testifying on Wirz's condition, and Albert Salmi as Sergeant Gray. A young Martin Sheen was cast as Captain Williams, one of Wirz's guards. Woodrow Parfrey played Louis Schade. Baker is clearly Wirz's attorney, and Schade has just a few lines and speaks to Wirz in an unspecified advisory capacity. The production was thought to be so prestigious that many recognizable character actors — Alan Hale Jr., Ford Rainey, Charles McGraw, Ian Keith, Bert Freed — took silent roles as the judges of the military tribunal.

The movie was widely praised and won the Emmy as outstanding single program of the year. Levitt also won an Emmy for best writing. The movie has been released on videotape. (Two years later, Levitt cowrote, with Daniel Berrigan, the play *The Trial of the Catonsville Nine* about a trial that took place 100 years after the Wirz trial and again used trial transcripts as its basis. The play was later filmed.[31] Levitt died in 1977 at the age of 66. *Andersonville* and *Catonsville* are his major works.)

The setting of the play is, as in the original trial, in the U.S. Court of Claims, Washington, D.C., a courtroom borrowed by the military commission to provide space for the public and press. When the film begins, Wallace is told that Wirz had tried to kill himself. He insists that the trial has been delayed long enough and that his Baltimore-born attorney Otis Baker must enter the plea. Chipman reads the charges and speaks to Baker in an angry and contemptuous manner. Chipman alludes to Baker's "political" motives, indicating that Baker had supported the South in the war. Baker's motions to dismiss are rejected. Wirz is brought in and physically portrayed as an ill and frail man who can hardly lift his arms. As in the actual trial, he is given permission to lie down on a chaise lounge during the course of the trial. Wirz begs the court for help in getting letters to his wife and family, and Wallace promises they will be sent in a military packet.

Wirz tells Baker the trial is simply a formality of which the outcome is already decided. He resigns himself to accept that he will be convicted because he was on the wrong side in the war.

Chipman presents witnesses who describe the hellish conditions in the camp — the only source of water was a stream where all the camp waste was dumped, on both sides of the stream was a swamp where the marsh would go up to a man's waist. There was a dead line which, if the prisoners cross it, would result in their being shot. Witnesses also describe Wirz's own actions — he sent away well-intentioned local citizens who tried to bring food to the prisoners, although on cross-examination Baker points out that Wirz did this while General Winder, his commanding officer, was standing by. Chipman presents dozens of witnesses who testify that escaping prisoners were mauled by dogs. But under cross-examination, a shell-shocked young soldier, who had testified on direct examination that a fellow prisoner was mauled by dogs and that he saw Wirz standing by, allows that the man could also have been torn by thorns of bushes. Baker suggests that another witness who testifies that Wirz ordered that an escaping prisoner be shot has embellished the story over time.

Chipman keeps inquiring of witnesses whether any humane person could have let these things happen, and Baker keeps asking Chipman if he is suggesting that Wirz should have disobeyed his rigid orders from General Winder, which included stopping all prisoner escapes and not diverting food and supplies from the Confederate war effort. Wallace tells Chipman that, as a military court, the tribunal is not interested in pursuing the issue of a soldier disobeying an unjust order. Baker says to Chipman privately that he is just like Wirz, since in backing down from pursuing the issue he, too, is only following orders. Chipman is shocked at the comparison.

Chipman reluctantly puts on a witness—Sergeant Gray, modeled on de la Baume—whom he thinks is untrustworthy but who testifies that he saw Wirz shoot a prisoner named Stuart. This testimony is important since there is finally a name of someone Wirz is accused of murdering. Wirz insists to Baker that the prisoner did not exist, and Baker proposes to Gray in his cross-examination that Gray is a good soldier who knows what the army requires of him and will even lie if the army needs his lie.

In presenting the case for the defense, Baker tells the court that he will not call any of his other witnesses and will instead focus on the testimony of Wirz's in-court physician. The doctor testifies that Wirz is able to raise his arms only with difficulty and that he does not see how Wirz could have pulled the trigger and suffered the recoil in shooting Stuart as Gray described. Wirz insists on testifying so that there will be a record for his children, showing that he is not a "monster."

In his direct testimony, Wirz emphasizes that he was following orders and did what he had to do under the circumstances. Wirz insists he could not have killed the prisoner the way Gray testified because he cannot raise his arms. He keeps repeating the story about his kindness to sixty or seventy drummer boys who were prisoners—he let them live outside the camp and pick berries for the prisoners, although he acknowledges with a father's smile that, hungry, the boys ate the berries themselves.

On cross-examination, Chipman finds contradictions in Wirz's

testimony. In one heated exchange, he even pulls up Wirz's arms to show
that he could have raised them to shoot Gray—and Wirz confesses that
he can lift them some of the time. But in his cross-examination, Chipman
continues to bring up the issue of why Wirz did not disobey orders that
were resulting in the needless deaths of the prisoners—why, for example,
didn't he take the food the local women had brought? Wallace is obviously
uncomfortable with a line of questioning about officers disobeying orders
and tells Chipman that he is pursuing it at his peril. If nothing else, he
says, Chipman is risking being ostracized by his fellow officers. Chipman
responds simply that he must pursue the line of questioning, that it is
important, he feels, for the court to be "human." Admiring Chipman's
courage, Wallace lets him continue over Baker's objection. Chipman asks
Wirz directly, why did you not disobey these orders that were leading to
cruelty and death? When Wirz responds that he was following the orders
of his military superior, General Winder, Chipman interrupts and insists
that General Winder was not Wirz's "moral superior." Wirz breaks down—
as Chipman almost cradles him in his arms—and says that he did not have
the courage to disobey the orders.

Wirz is convicted and led off. As they prepare to leave the courtroom,
Baker concedes that Chipman at least tried to raise the issues but insists
that the outcome was predetermined. Baker wonders why people keep trying to change humans and ignore their bestial instincts. Chipman can only
say, "We try. We try."

The film does not show Wirz's execution.

• *Analysis.* The controversies related to the way in which defense witnesses were excluded from testifying by the prosecution are downplayed
in the movie. Baker alludes to the need to have the prosecution approve
his witnesses but later dismisses all of his witnesses but one. In a depar-
ture from the actual trial, the only defense witnesses are Wirz's in-court
physician and Wirz. Levitt borrows from the testimony of the actual
defense witnesses and gives the details to Wirz to present. In reality, Wirz
did not testify, and there was no cross-examination and breakdown of the
defendant as shown in the play. Chipman did not ask Wirz why he did not
disobey General Winder's orders.

Levitt gives Wirz one attorney, Baker, and relegates Schade to a minor
role as an advisor. The playwright concentrates, then, not on Wirz's fellow immigrant but a more conventional blend of southern sympathizer
and hired gun. The film calls Baker "Otis," its estimation of a "southern"
name, although the real-life Baker's name was "Orrin" and had originally
been "Obadiah." While the film's Baker is from Baltimore, Orrin Smith

Baker was actually born in Massachusetts and practiced law in New York before changing his name to "Orrin" and moving to Virginia in 1862. The film's Baker says he is being paid by a group of southerners, while both Baker and Schade worked pro bono. "Otis Baker" is something of a composite character, taking on Baker's name and Schade's southern sympathies.

The film presents Wirz sympathetically but also suggests that he might have done some of the things of which he was accused. The trustworthiness of Gray's testimony is questioned, but then it is also shown that Wirz can raise his arms.

The film deals with many of the same issues as the soon-to-be discussed *Judgment at Nuremberg*— is a soldier bound to obey any order and a judge to enforce any law, or is there a higher law? Unlike *Nuremberg*, *Andersonville Trial*'s presentation of the issues is clear. It actually builds to the end and does not waffle. It is extremely compelling. It presents the facts of this historical case in a straightforward fashion. Unlike other films based on legal cases, it keeps the names of most of the real-life persons involved in the trial and stays focused on the trial — there is one setting — and not on their imagined private lives. Yet, there is another major fictionalization in the private thoughts of the prosecutor.

The play was written in 1959 when the question of moral responsibility for others was much in people's minds. The Nuremberg trials had begun just 14 years before. Also in recent memory were hearings and blacklists concerning reported communists that sometimes resulted in people falsely informing on others to protect themselves or for their own benefit. The play and film followed in theme the path of Arthur Miller's *The Crucible* (1953) and the 1954 film *On the Waterfront*. These works were full of questions. Do the characters have the courage not to sign their names to lies? To stand up for what they believe? To not harm another person by action or inaction? What, films and plays of this period asked, is our responsibility for others? In depicting Chipman as insisting on raising the issue of an officer's moral responsibility to disobey unjust orders, Levitt far exceeds even Chipman's own account of the trial and does, as Levitt says he did, add the playwright's own ideas of motivation to the real-life characters.

In his account of the trial, Chipman shows no indication of having grappled with these moral issues and instead simply labels Wirz a "willing conspirator" in the deaths of Union soldiers. Chipman reprints the damaging testimony against Wirz, dismisses the defense witnesses as unreliable, and deals with criticism such as his screening of defense witnesses. In short, Chipman presents himself as an unhesitant backer of the prosecution's case, including its motives and results.

In imposing a twentieth-century sensibility on an actual nineteenth-century individual, Levitt is fictionalizing. There is a sense in which he prefigured the Oliver Stone films and the argument of post-modern historical films in *rewriting* history.

Since Chipman's angst and dilemma are at the heart of Levitt's play and screenplay and have little or no foundation in the historical record, this fictionalization mitigates against the play's otherwise close attention to historical details.

• **Litigation.** None know.

• **Author's Personal Note.** As a college student and would-be actor, I adored this film, especially the portrayal of Chipman as a prosecutor who puts his career on the line to raise moral issues. I remember after the 1970 broadcast bumping into the noted philosopher Paul Weiss at the Catholic University of America, where he was teaching and I was studying, and telling him excitedly how I had loved the film and its dealing with these issues. The diminutive Weiss smiled up at me and said he had seen the broadcast and regarded its portrayal of the prosecutor's moral dilemma as "uncooked." He was referring to Levitt's articulation of the moral issues and not to the historical accuracy, although on investigation the same charge may well be leveled against the play on that count.

When I began writing this book, I turned to this favorite film thinking it would prove as an example of something slightly fictionalized but true to the spirit of the actual events. My investigation proved me wrong.

And so, for thirty years I did believe that what I saw was what happened and did not know that it was "only a movie." Most viewers will not have access to the trial transcripts or Chipman's 1911 book, and so they will be in the same boat as I was.

Trials of Oscar Wilde (1895)
The Trials of Oscar Wilde (1960)

THE FACTS

In 1891, Oscar Wilde, then 38 years old and already a noted playwright, poet, and public figure, met the handsome, 22-year-old Lord Alfred Douglas ("Bosie") at a tea party. The two became extremely close. They stayed together in each other's houses and in hotels and went on trips together.

Their relationship — since homosexuality was illegal at the time in England — brought out blackmailers. Douglas, still a student in Oxford, gave an old suit to a down-on-his-luck friend named Wood, who discovered letters written by Wilde to his friend in one of the pockets. Wood extorted £35 (around $150) from Wilde for return of most of the compromising letters. Two other would-be blackmailers were given smaller amounts of money after returning the remaining letters.

Bosie's father was John Sholto Douglas, the Marquis of Queensberry, an angry and perhaps even mentally unbalanced Scottish nobleman best known for promoting and taking credit for rules for amateur boxing (the "Marquis of Queensberry rules"). By early 1894. Queensberry concluded that Wilde was most likely a homosexual and demanded that his son stop seeing Wilde. He threatened restaurant and hotel managers with beatings if he ever discovered Wilde and his son together on their premises.

Wilde learned that Queensberry planned to disrupt the opening night performance of Wilde's new play *The Importance of Being Earnest* on February 14, 1895, and arranged to have the theater surrounded by police.

Four days later at the Albemarle Club — a club to which both Wilde and his wife belonged — Queensberry left a card with a porter: "To Oscar Wilde posing as a somdomite [*sic*]." Wilde did not pick up the card for two weeks but then immediately decided that he must sue Queensberry for libel. Homosexuality was a serious crime, and Wilde presumably thought he had no choice but to sue for the sake of his reputation and that of his wife and family. The drama and music critic — and later to be famous playwright — George Bernard Shaw and the writer and publisher Frank Harris told Wilde that Queensberry was laying a trap for him and urged him to withdraw his suit, but Wilde persisted. On March 2, Queensberry was arrested.

A noted barrister, Edward Clarke, was asked to prosecute Wilde's case. Before accepting the case, Clarke asked Wilde if there was any foundation to Queensberry's charges. Wilde said there was not.

On April 3, 1895, the first trial of Oscar Wilde — the libel action with Wilde as plaintiff — began at the court at the Old Bailey.[32] After Clarke's opening statement and testimony from the porter at the Albemarle Club, Wilde took the stand. Under questioning from Clarke, he denied Queensberry's charges. Queensberry's attorney, Edward Carson — who had gone to Oxford College with Wilde — then cross-examined Wilde. The playwright defended his *The Picture of Dorian Gray* and *Phrases and Philosophies for Use of the Young* against Carson's suggestions that they were immoral or touched on homosexual themes.

Carson then asked Wilde about his relationships with certain young men — newspaper peddlers, valets, or the unemployed — and produced items ranging from fine clothes to silver-mounted walking sticks that Wilde admitted giving them. Suspiciously, the recipients of the gifts were not, in Carson's words, "intellectual treats" and in some cases were barely literate.

Carson asked Wilde whether he had kissed the sixteen-year old Walter Grainger. "Oh, dear no!" Wilde replied, "He was a peculiarly plain boy." Carson zeroed in on this. Was that the reason he didn't kiss him? Why then did he mention his ugliness? "Why, why, why, did you add that?" Wilde stammered and wilted under the questioning.

When Carson announced that he intended to call to the witness box a procession of young men with whom Wilde had been sexually associated, Clarke understood that Wilde faced prosecution from the 1895 Criminal Amendment Act, which had made it a crime for any person to commit an act of "gross indecency." At Clarke's urging, Wilde withdrew the complaint. Queensberry was released.

But Douglas' father was either very vindictive or, as Shaw and Harris had suspected, had planned for this all along. Queensberry's solicitor forwarded to the director of public prosecutions copies of statements by the young men Carson had planned to produce as witnesses. Within hours, an inspector from Scotland Yard appeared before a magistrate to request a warrant for the arrest of Oscar Wilde. Wilde had an opportunity to flee the country but refused.

He was arrested on twenty-five counts of gross indecencies and conspiracy to commit gross indecencies. His first criminal trial (there would be two) of Oscar Wilde began at Old Bailey on April 26, 1895. The chief crown prosecutor was Charles Gill. A parade of young men testified for the prosecution regarding their roles in helping Wilde to act out his sexual fantasies. Charles Parker, a 21-year-old valet, testified that Wilde's friend (and procurer) Alfred Taylor had escorted Parker and his brother to a restaurant where Wilde had inspected them and finally exclaimed, "This is the boy for me!" Parker then claimed that Wilde took him to the Savoy Hotel and sodomized him. Wilde paid Parker £2 ($10). Parker also testified that in a subsequent visit to Parker's lodgings, Wilde asked him to imagine that he was a woman and Wilde was his lover. On the fourth day of trial, Wilde took the stand. His arrogance of the first trial was gone, and he denied all allegations of indecent behavior. But, when asked by Gill what Douglas had meant by the phrase "the Love that dare not speak its name" in his poem "Two Loves," Wilde eloquently responded:

> "The Love that dare not speak its name in this century" is such
> a great affection of an elder for a younger man as there was

between David and Jonathan, such as Plato made the very basis
of his philosophy, and such as you might find in the sonnets of
Michelangelo and Shakespeare.... It is beautiful, it is fine, it is the
noblest form of affection.

Wilde's remarks produced a standing ovation and evidently diluted
the effect of the parade of Wilde's young men. The jury deliberated for over
three hours before concluding that it could not reach a verdict on most of
the charges. Wilde was released, re-arrested, and charged with an additional 15 counts of impropriety.

In the second criminal trial, the prosecution relied only on its
strongest witnesses. Gill, who had failed to achieve a conviction in the first
trial, took the equivalent of second chair while Sir Frank Lockwood,
queen's counsel, solicitor general, assumed the prosecution's helm. Wood
testified in detail of his blackmail of Wilde. After three hours of deliberation, the jury returned its verdict: guilty on all counts except one.

Wilde was sentenced to two years in prison. Queensberry was not
merciful at all and sued Wilde for his court costs for the libel trial. Wilde
was brought out of prison in manacles and told the court he was unable
to pay Queensberry anything because he was bankrupt. Wilde served his
full sentence, the last eighteen months at Reading Gaol, where Wilde wrote
"The Ballad of Reading Gaol," which contains the line, "And all men kill
the thing they love." He came out ill and chastened. Sensing that he could
no longer live in England, Wilde went to Paris, where he died on November 30, 1900, with Boise by his side.

THE FILM

In 1960, with sodomy still illegal in England — and it would remain
so until 1967 — but with frankness in films increasing, United Artists and
Warwick Productions released *The Trials of Oscar Wilde*[33] about the legal
proceedings involving charges regarding the homosexuality of the noted
Irish writer.

That filmmakers felt free to finally film the once-shocking story of
Oscar Wilde in 1960 is evidenced by the fact that there were two Oscar
Wilde films released that year: *The Trials of Oscar Wilde* and *Oscar Wilde*,[34]
the latter from a 1938 play by Leslie and Sewell Stokes that had starred
Robert Morley. After 22 years, Morley was finally able to repeat his stage
performance on film; the most common criticism was that at 52 — and
looking, because of his weight, much older — he appeared too old to play
the 40-year-old Wilde.[35]

The Trials of Oscar Wilde starred Peter Finch, whose role was a change of pace from his previous matinee idol turns—the year before he had played the doctor who was secretly and silently in love with the nun in *The Nun's Story*. Two leading men—James Mason as Edward Carson and Nigel Patrick as Sir Edward Clarke—took supporting roles, signifying that this was felt to be an important film. The movie was based on a book of the same name by H. Montgomery Hyde and on the play *The Stringed Lute* by John Furnell. It was written and directed by Ken Hughes. The Finch film strove to assert its accuracy by obtaining as advisors for the film Lord Cecil Douglas, the then–Marquis of Queensberry, and Vyvyan Holand, Oscar Wilde's son.

Of the two films, as the titles indicate, *The Trials* accurately indicated that there was more than one trial; the film *Oscar Wilde* fudged on that matter. However, in release, distributors sometimes labeled the film "The Trial of Oscar Wilde." Presumably because of the shock value that Wilde's name still brought forth, *The Trials of Oscar Wilde* was released in some areas as *The Man with the Green Carnation*—a reference to an affectation of Wilde's that is noted in the film. (The Morley film was also released under a different title: *Forbidden Passion*.)

The Trials of Oscar Wilde was critically praised. It was nominated for an Oscar as best foreign film and won Finch the British Academy Award as best actor. Unfortunately, its U.S. release was limited due to its theme of homosexuality, which reduced the film's potential income and caused financial problems for its producer Albert "Cubby" Broccoli. Fortunately, two years later Broccoli would produce the first of the highly successful James Bond series. (Director and screenwriter Hughes died in 2001 at the age of 79.)

The film begins with a statement that it takes place in "London in the 1890s," although it shows the opening night of Wilde's play *Lady Windemere's Fan*, which occurred on February 22, 1892. (The film presumably does not specify this because, as part of its compression of time, it does not want to suggest that the events shown cover a three- year period.) The *Trials of Oscar Wilde* follows the basic facts closely, moving from the opening scene to a scene of Wilde with his wife and children being interrupted by the arrival of Mr. Wood, who produces the letter from Douglas. The film depicts several actual confrontations between Queensberry and Wilde, as well as one in which Queensberry charges into Wilde's home accompanied by a boxer as a bodyguard. Wilde throws them both out, easily overcoming the boxer. The film also compresses the time sequences. While Queensberry is stopped by the police when he tried to enter the theater on the opening night of *The Importance of Being Earnest* carrying a cabbage-bouquet as was the case, in the film he does get into the theater after the play is over and presents Wilde with the bouquet. Wilde wittily humiliates Queensberry, who immediately — rather than four days later — rushes to the Albemarle Club and writes the note for Wilde which he gives to the porter. Wilde then comes to the club, not two weeks later, but the next day, reads the note, and rushes to his solicitor.

The film depicts the trials and follows the transcript with accuracy, although in an edited fashion. While *Young Mr. Lincoln* invented its Perry Mason moment in which the murderer is exposed on the witness stand, *The Trials of Oscar Wilde* faithfully presents how Sir Edward Carson, in cross-examining Wilde during the first trial, asked question after question until Wilde, who had been amusing the court and himself with his wit, flippantly says that he had not kissed Walter Grainger because he was "a peculiarly plain boy"— implying that he would have kissed him otherwise. Carson, as played by an unusually thin James Mason with just the trace of an Irish brogue, can barely contain his surprise followed by his joy as he then proceeds to exploit Wilde's slip. The usually glib Wilde begins to stammer in response.

• *Analysis.* The compressions of time can be seen as necessary in a two-hour film covering three-plus years. If there any deficiency in the film, it is in the characterization by Finch. Finch, a fine actor, who later would play to great acclaim a contemporary bisexual man in *Sunday, Bloody, Sunday* (1971), makes a great effort at portraying Wilde as a man effortlessly witty and yet weak. However, this is a Wilde who is physically able to eject a professional boxer from his home. Finch is simply too virile for Wilde. Morley, in his youth, presumably was better cast.

All in all, though, acknowledging its compressions of time, *The Trials of Oscar Wilde* is an accurate depiction of events and the trial. As noted, it uses the trial transcripts extensively. The domestic scenes between Wilde and his wife employ dialogue from Furness' play. The trial scenes benefit from the use of actors as skilled as Finch, Mason, and Patrick and, even if one knows the outcome, become suspenseful as Mason probes and probes to crack Wilde's pretense. This is the way it really happened. Contemporary viewers, however, may find the pace slow, but this is more a factor of the pace of the 1960s.

• *Litigation.* Given the pains the filmmakers took to gain the support and approval of both Wilde's and Douglas' heirs, it is not surprising that there was no litigation concerning this film.

Leopold-Loeb Trial (1924)
Compulsion (1959)

The Facts

Eighteen-year-old Richard Loeb was the handsome and privileged son of a retired Sears & Roebuck vice president and the youngest graduate ever of the University of Michigan, and yet he was obsessed with crime and read mostly detective stories.[36] Loeb's 19-year-old friend, Nathan Leopold, the son of a millionaire box manufacturer, was a law student at the University of Chicago and read, not detective stories, but the German philosopher Nietzsche. He believed that legal obligations did not apply to those who approached the level of Nietzsche's "superman." Leopold's idea of the superman was his friend and lover, Loeb. Leopold's attraction to Loeb was his primary reason for participating in the crime. Leopold wrote that his motive "to the extent that I had one, was to please Dick." For Loeb, however, the crime was basically an interesting intellectual exercise, the chance to actually do what he had been reading about.

The two teenagers spent hours discussing and refining a plan to kidnap the child of wealthy parents, demand a ransom, and collect the ransom after it was thrown off a moving train as it passed a designated point. They decided that, while regrettable, it was necessary to kill the child to minimize the likelihood of being identified as the kidnappers. Their victim was an acquaintance, Bobby Franks. On May 21, 1924, at about five o'clock in the afternoon, Franks was walking home from school when a gray Winton automobile pulled up near him. Loeb called Franks over to the car and asked him to get in to discuss a tennis racquet. Once Franks was in the car he was killed with a chisel. Leopold and Loeb drove to a marshland near the Indiana line, where they stripped Franks naked, poured hydrochloric acid over his body to make identification more difficult, and then stuffed the body in a concrete drainage culvert. The boys returned to Loeb's home, where they burned Franks' clothing in a basement fire.

That evening Mrs. Franks received a phone call from Leopold, who identified himself as "George Johnson." Leopold told Mrs. Franks that her boy had been kidnapped but was unharmed and that she should expect a ransom note soon. The next morning, the Franks family received a special delivery letter demanding $10,000 in old, unmarked bills. The letter instructed that the Franks secure the money and expect further instructions that afternoon. Leopold called Jacob Franks, Bobby's father, at three o'clock to tell him a taxi cab was about to arrive at his home and that he should take it to a specified drugstore in South Chicago. Just as Franks headed out to the Yellow Cab, the police called to say that the body of Bobby Franks had been identified — a laborer happened to see a flash of what turned out to be a foot through the shrubbery covering the open culvert where the body had been placed.

A pair of horn-rimmed glasses were discovered with the body of Bobby Franks. They were Leopold's glasses that had slipped out of his pocket as he struggled to hide the body. They had an unusual hinge and could be traced to a single Chicago optometrist, who had written only three such prescriptions, including the one to Leopold. When the police questioned him about the glasses, Leopold said that he must have lost them. When asked, however, he could not demonstrate how they could have fallen out of his pocket. For his alibi, Leopold said that he spent the day picking up girls in his car with Loeb and driving out to Lincoln Park. Loeb, when questioned separately, confirmed Leopold's alibi. Prosecutors were on the verge of releasing the two suspects when two additional pieces of evidence surfaced. First, typewritten notes taken from a member of Leopold's law school study group were found to match the type from the ransom note. Then, the Leopold family's chauffeur made a statement, in the hope of establishing Nathan Leopold's innocence, that the family car had not left the garage on the day of the murder.

Loeb confessed first, then Leopold. Their confessions differed only on the point of who did the actual killing, with each accusing the other. Leopold later pleaded with Loeb to admit to killing Franks but, according to Leopold, Loeb said, "Mompsie feels less terrible than she might, thinking you did it and I'm not going to take that shred of comfort away from her."

The Loeb and Leopold families hired Clarence Darrow and Benjamin Bachrach to represent the two boys.

Clarence Seward Darrow was born in Kinsman, Ohio, in 1857 and died in 1938 after becoming the most famous lawyer of his day. He had an early lucrative career in private and corporate law, but with his defense of Eugene V. Debs and others in connection with the 1894 Pullman strike he turned to representing the underdog. He became famous as an opponent of capital punishment. None of his more than 100 clients was sentenced to death. Darrow's writings include *Crime: Its Cause and Treatment (1922)*.

Darrow decided to change the boys' initial pleas to the charges of murder and kidnapping from "not guilty" — suggesting a traditional insanity defense — to "guilty." The decision was made primarily to prevent the state from getting two opportunities at a death sentence. The plea meant that the sentencing decision would be made by a judge and not a jury. If the defendants had pleaded "not guilty," the state had planned to try the boys first on one of the two charges, both of which carried the death penalty in Illinois, and if it failed to win on the first charge, try again on the second. Darrow believed that the judge who would hear their case, John R. Caverly, was a "kindly and discerning" man.

The defense hoped to build its case against the death penalty around the testimony of four "alienists," now called psychiatrists. Sigmund Freud was asked to come to Chicago for the trial, but his poor health at the time prevented the visit. The prosecution argued that psychiatric testimony was only admissible if the defendants claimed insanity, while the defense insisted that evidence of mental disease should be considered as a mitigating factor in consideration of the sentence. In the most critical ruling of the trial, Judge Caverly overruled the state's objection and allowed the psychiatric evidence to be introduced.

The hearing of Leopold and Loeb lasted just over one month. The state presented more than a hundred witnesses proving every element of the crime. The defense presented extensive psychiatric evidence describing the defendants' emotional immaturity, obsessions with crime and Nietzschean philosophy, alcohol abuse, glandular abnormalities, and sexual longings and insecurities. The state offered in rebuttal psychiatrists who saw normal emotional responses in the boys and no physical basis for a finding of mental abnormality.

On August 22, 1924, Darrow began his summation for the defense in a crowded courtroom. For over twelve hours, Darrow reminded Judge Caverly of the defendants' youth, genetic inheritance, sexual impulses, and the many external influences that had led them to the commission of their crime.

> How insane they are I care not, whether medically or legally. They did not reason; they could not reason; they committed the most foolish, most unprovoked, most purposeless, most causeless act that any two boys ever committed, and they put themselves where the rope is dangling above their heads.... Why did they kill little Bobby Franks? Not for money, not for spite, not for hate. They killed him as they might kill a spider or a fly, for the experience. They killed him because they were made that way. Because somewhere in the infinite processes that go to the making up of the boy or the man something slipped, and those unfortunate lads sit here hated, despised, outcasts, with the community shouting for their blood. Are they to blame for it? There is no man on earth who can mention any purpose for it all or any reason for it all. It is one of those things that happened; that happened, and it calls not for hate but for kindness, for charity, for consideration.

Darrow attacked the death penalty as atavistic, saying it "roots back to the beast and the jungle."

> Kill them? Will that prevent other senseless boys or other vicious men or vicious women from killing? No! It will simply call upon every weak-minded person to do as they have done.... If the state in which I live is not kinder, more humane, more considerate, more intelligent than the mad act of these two boys, I am sorry that I have lived so long ...

When Darrow finally ended his appeal, tears were streaming down the face of Judge Caverly and of many other courtroom spectators. (Darrow's closing argument was later released as a long-playing record.)

State's Attorney Robert Crowe closed for the prosecution. He sarcastically attacked the arguments of "the distinguished gentlemen whose profession it is to protect murder in Cook County, and concerning whose health thieves inquire before they go out and commit a crime." Addressing Leopold, Crowe said,

> I wonder now, Nathan, whether you think there is a God or not. I wonder whether you think it is pure accident that this disciple of Nietzsche's philosophy dropped his glasses or whether it was an act of Divine Providence to visit upon your miserable carcasses the wrath of God.

He ridiculed Darrow's attempt to blame the crime on anyone and anything but the defendants. "My God, if one of them had a harelip I suppose Darrow would want me to apologize for having them indicted." He reserved his strongest language for the two defendants, whom he referred to as "cowardly perverts," "snakes," "atheists," "spoiled smart alecs," and "mad dogs." Crowe closed by asking Judge Caverly to "execute justice and righteousness in the land."

Two weeks later Caverly announced his decision. He called the murder "a crime of singular atrocity." Caverly said that his "judgment cannot be affected" by the causes of crime and that it was "beyond the province of this court" to "predicate ultimate responsibility for human acts." Nonetheless, Caverly said that "the consideration of the age of the defendants" and the possible benefits to criminology that might come from future study of them persuaded him that life in prison, not death, was the better punishment. He said that he was doing them no favor: "To the offenders, particularly of the type they are, the prolonged years of confinement may well be the severest form of retribution and expiation."

Richard Loeb and Nathan Leopold were moved to the Joliet penitentiary. In 1936, Loeb was slashed and killed with a razor in a fight with
James Day, another inmate. Leopold was rushed to the prison hospital to
be at his old friend's bedside as he died. Day claimed that he was resisting
Loeb's sexual advances, while prison officials called it a deliberate and
unprovoked attack. Day was acquitted by a jury.

In the 1950s, an elderly and now retired Robert Crowe reportedly
offered to write a letter to the Illinois parole board urging Leopold's release.
In 1958, after thirty-four years of confinement, Leopold walked out of
prison. Leopold ultimately went to live in Puerto Rico. He earned a master's degree, taught mathematics, and worked in hospitals and church mis-
sions. He wrote a book entitled *The Birds of Puerto Rico*. Despite saying
in a 1960 interview that he was still deeply in love with Richard Loeb, he
married. Leopold died following ten days of hospitalization on August 30,
1971.

THE FILM

Compulsion[37] was the title of a 1956 fictionalized account of the
Leopold and Loeb trial written by Meyer Levin. Levin was a contemporary of Leopold and Loeb and a journalist covering the case. The story concerns two wealthy Chicago teenagers, Judd Steiner (based on Leopold)
and Artie Straus (based on Loeb), who kidnap and murder a young boy,
become suspects because of glasses found with the boy's body, confess,
and are defended by the brilliant lawyer, Jonathan Wilk.

Like Leopold, Steiner is obsessed with the philosophy of Nietzsche.
Other fact-based parallels are the boys' theft of a typewriter used to type
the ransom note and the inadvertent destruction of the boys' alibi by the
Steiner family chauffeur. Portions of Darrow's final summation are used
in Wilk's summation.

Leopold said that reading *Compulsion* made him "physically sick,"
caused him to feel "terrific shame," and induced a "mild melancholia." He
felt as "if he were exposed stark-naked under the strong spotlight before
a large audience." He also complained that the book depicted the murder
in sexual terms—Steiner saw the murder as a way to kill the girl within
himself—and dismissed such a motive in his own case as preposterous.

The success of the book reportedly caused the recently released
Leopold to move to Puerto Rico. It also led to a Broadway play and acqui-
sition of screen rights by Darryl F. Zanuck. Director Richard Fleischer cast
Dean Stockwell as Steiner, Bradford Dillman as Straus, E. G. Marshall as
District Attorney Horn, Diane Varsi as Ruth, Martin Milner as Sid Brooks,

and Orson Welles as Wilk The film had a screenplay by Richard Murphy, adapted from Levin's novel. (Murphy also wrote the screenplay for *Boomerang,* which is discussed later. After *Compulsion,* he focused on television writing and created the TV series *Felony Squad* in 1966. He died in 1993.)

Compulsion received mostly positive reviews and was a modest financial success, finishing forty-eighth on *Variety's* box-office charts for 1959. Stockwell, Dillman, and Welles together received the best actor award from the Cannes Film Festival.

In the plot of the movie, Straus and Steiner rob their own fraternity house in Chicago in 1924. Driving away, Straus tries to run down a drunk and is furious when Steiner stops him. They are much younger than their classmates— evidence of their brilliance. The two discuss their agreement to carry out dangerous acts as a test of their "superior intellects." Soon afterwards, Paulie Kessler, a local boy, disappears, and his parents receive a ransom note. Then, the boy's dead body is found. Sid Brooks, a college friend of Straus and Steiner also works as a reporter. At the morgue, Brooks finds a pair of glasses with the boy's body. He—bravely—puts them on the corpse and finds that they do not fit. When existence of the glasses is revealed, knowing they belong to Steiner, Straus threatens to deny being with Steiner at the time of the killing. Straus begins to ingratiate himself with the police, amusing himself by starting false leads. When Steiner becomes attracted to Brook's girlfriend Ruth, Straus is angry at first, then suggests that Steiner indulges in another "experience" by raping her. Steiner tries to rape her but physically cannot go through with it. The police trace the dropped glasses to Steiner. He repeats the alibi that he and Straus agreed to, and Straus backs him up. When the police trap them in other lies, Straus confesses.

The two are arrested and charged, and the boys' families hire the famous criminal attorney, Jonathan Wilk to save them from the death penalty. Wilk has always fought against the "ruling class" in America, of which Straus and Steiner's parents are charter members, but he feels that even the rich are entitled to a good defense. He also needs the money. He is shocked, however, to learn that they have already confessed.

After Prosecutor Horn's damning opening statement, Wilk changes the plea to guilty—much to the shock of the boys' parents, who are paying him, and to the seeming surprise of the defendants, who are his clients. He reasons that the jury is certain to sentence the boys to death while a judge may be more merciful.

Wilk presents psychiatric testimony, and Ruth testifies as to Steiner's gentleness. As a result of Wilk's spell-binding closing argument, the judge sentences Straus and Steiner to life plus 99 years. When the boys show no gratitude and in fact are contemptuous of Wilk, he suggests that the hand of God made Steiner drop his glasses— quoting Crowe's actual line in his closing statement.

• *Analysis.* Although the film deals with a brutal murder, the killing is not shown. Rather, it is presented through the medical examiner's description of the boy's body and the reading of Straus' confession. Although Leopold and Loeb were lovers, *Compulsion*— the movie was, after all, made in 1959 —concentrates on their psychological — master and slave — relationship.

The character of Brooks is based on Levin. Although Levin covered the case, Brooks' discovery that the glasses do not belong to the murdered boy is Levin's self-aggrandizing fictionalization.

As noted, some of Darrow's closing argument made its way into the book and film, but it has been compressed from twelve hours to ten minutes. Like the novel and play, the film is an admitted fictionalization that still sticks close to the facts and, some would say, the spirit of the actual case and trial.

• *Litigation.* In 1959, Leopold filed suit against the producers of the movie for $1.5 million. His suit was dismissed eleven years later.[38] The court noted that while the book and movie were "suggested" by Leopold's crime, they were evidently fictional works. The novel and film depicted portions of Leopold's life that he had caused to be placed in public view. The court did not consider the fictionalized aspects highly offensive, which is the standard for determining invasion of privacy.

State of Connecticut v. Harold Israel (1924)
Boomerang (1947)

THE FACTS

In 1924, Father Hubert Dahme, a popular parish priest, was murdered on a street corner in Bridgeport, Connecticut, shot from behind with a .32 caliber bullet. He died in front of the New Lyric Theatre where the noted actress Ethel Barrymore was about to perform in a play entitled *The Laughing Lady.*

A $1,000 reward was offered, and 30 detectives were assigned to the case full time. There were no leads, and panic spread among the Bridgeport populace. Then, a week after the murder, a police officer in Stamford, Connecticut, encountered a man on the streets at 1:20 A.M., searched him, and found a five-shot, .32 caliber revolver with one chamber empty.[39] This jobless and possibly mentally retarded drifter, Harold Israel, was charged with carrying a concealed weapon and vagrancy. Because Israel said he was from Bridgeport, the Bridgeport police were alerted. Witnesses identified Israel as the murderer. During interrogation, Israel delivered conflicting stories and finally confessed. Later, Israel denied that he had committed the murder. A public defender was appointed, and, after a coroner's inquest, the case was sent to the criminal court system.

Harold S. Cummings had been mayor and corporation counsel for Stamford, Connecticut, and was state's attorney for Fairfield County from 1914 to 1924. He was in his last year in office and became convinced of Israel's innocence. In his opening statement as prosecutor of the trial, after describing the facts of the case, Cummings began to take his own case apart. The witnesses could not have seen what they said they had seen, Cummings illustrated. Finally, Cummings recommended that the charge of murder be *nolle prosequi* (a prosecutor's decision to abandon the case). His recommendation was due, in large part, to the opinion of six expert witnesses he had hired who had concluded that the fatal murder bullet could not have been fired from the pistol of the defendant. The experts had found that the suspect's gun was rusty and dulled the "lands and grooves" that the rifling of the barrel gave to a bullet. In contrast, the bullet taken from Father Dahme's brain had sharp markings. The suspect's gun also used ammunition with a "grease groove," traces of which could be seen on any bullet. There were no such traces on the bullet taken from Father Dahme. Most telling, Israel's gun could not fire at a 45-degree upward angle, which is how the bullet that killed Father Dahme would have had to have been fired by Harold Israel. The case is often cited for its pioneering use of ballistics experts.[40]

Although the charges against Israel were dismissed, the murder was never solved. Cummings went on to become attorney general during the Roosevelt administration. He was portrayed in another film cited in this book, "The Big Train" (see Chapter 1). He died in 1956.

The transcript of the trial was published by the Government Printing Office in 1937 as something all U.S. attorneys should read, since, according to the small book's preface, "The primary duty of a lawyer exercising the office of public prosecutor is not to convict but to see that justice is done."

What was little emphasized in the reporting of the trial were two factors: anti-Semitism and greed. One witness said that the killer ran like a

Jew. Another described him as having a large, beaked nose, which the defendant did not. Although the defendant's name was "Israel," he was not Jewish, but rather Pennsylvania Dutch. What definitely influenced the witnesses' identifications was money. Three of the key witnesses against Israel applied for the reward. The legal representative of one of the witnesses claiming the award was also Israel's court-appointed attorney.

THE FILM

The film *Boomerang*,[41] based on the Harold Israel case, was produced in 1947 by Louis de Rochemont, who in 1934 initiated the "March of Time" films — a series of news films that Orson Welles affectionately lampoons and uses as the reasons for the investigation of the meaning of "Rosebud" in his 1941 film *Citizen Kane*. *Boomerang* was directed by Elia Kazan. The city fathers of Bridgeport feared adverse publicity, so *Boomerang* was shot entirely in nearby Stamford — where Cummings had been mayor and Israel had been arrested. Many local citizens appeared in bit parts and as extras. Even the playwright Arthur Miller, who was visiting the set for a conference with Kazan — Kazan would later direct Miller's *Death of a Salesman* — was cast as one of the men in a lineup.

The screenplay was written by Richard Murphy from a 1945 *Reader's Digest* article "The Perfect Case" by Anthony Abbot. Abbott was the pseudonym of Fulton Oursler, an editor for *Reader's Digest* who in 1949 would publish *The Greatest Story Ever Told*, a life of Christ. Dana Andrews played Henry L. Harvey, based on Cummings; Jane Wyatt, Harvey's wife, Madge; Lee J. Cobb, Chief Robinson; Arthur Kennedy, defendant John Waldron; Sam Levene, reporter Dave Woods; Karl Malden, Lieutenant White; and Ed Begley, Paul Harris. Murphy, who would later write the screenplay for *Compulsion*, won an Oscar nomination for his screenplay.

As in the "March of Time" series, a narrator describes many of the events to the viewer. One evening, a lone gunman wearing a light-colored fedora and a dark coat walks up to Father Lambert on the small-town Main Street, raises his 32-calibre pistol, and fires. There are seven witnesses, but none can provide an exact description.

Political pressure for an arrest mounts although the police have no clues. Reporter Dave Woods writes stories about the police being amateurs. The owner of the newspaper hopes to win the election with a campaign to get an arrest, wanting to get back into power any way he can.

A drifter — John Waldron, an ex-serviceman — is picked up in Ohio. He matches the general description of Father Lambert's killer and is armed with the same type of pistol that killed the pastor. All of the witnesses identify him. After being grilled by the police chief and his lead detective for long hours, Waldron confesses.

Young district attorney Henry L. Harvey is told by a nervous party official, Paul Harris, that he better convict Waldron, that the party must win the next election and stay in power or else his life is ruined and he will take everyone else down with him. Harris had invested all his money in a corrupt land deal and needs his administration to buy that land from him or else he will lose his life savings. Harris had tricked Harvey's wife, Madge, into lending him money for the deal to make it look like she is in on the corruption. However, Harvey is sure that Waldron is innocent. His investigation finds that Waldron's gun could not have been the one used in the crime because of a gun pin that malfunctions when the gun is placed at the angle where it must have been if the taller Waldron had shot the smaller Father Lambert.

In court, Harvey takes the place of Father Lambert and has his colleague aim the loaded gun at him from the prescribed angle and then fire. The gun malfunctions, proving that Waldron's gun was not the murder weapon. However, there is a gun shot — Harris shoots himself in his seat in the courtroom and falls dead. Waldron is acquitted.

The closing narration states that the Harvey character was based on Homer S. Cummings, who went on to become the attorney general under FDR from 1933 to 1939.

• **Analysis.** The film closely follows the details of the actual crime. Except for the character of Harvey, who is acknowledged to be based on Cummings at the film's end, the rest of the characters appear to be composites. The locale is described as only "a small city in Connecticut."

Rochemont and screenwriter Richard Murphy took at least one major liberty in making Harvey a young and unheralded attorney, while Cummings was at the time of the trial 54 years old and a nationally known public figure. In this, they followed the approach of screenwriter Trotti in *Young Mr. Lincoln* who had made Lincoln younger than he had been when he tried the case that the film is based on. The reduction in age and stature creates some tension as the young attorney puts his career on the line, while in reality Cummings was an established attorney who had nothing to prove. On the other hand, Cummings still had a great deal to lose if public opinion had risen against him. The defendant is played by the handsome Arthur Kennedy and is portrayed as a decorated serviceman down on his luck — in contrast to what is known of the real-life defendant. By changing Israel's name, the filmmakers obtained more freedom to embroider on the events but abandoned the anti-Semitism that underlay some of the case.

The filmmakers also add some melodramatic features—the hero is blackmailed concerning actions of his wife by a corrupt politician; the defense attorney is inept and wants to plead that Waldron was insane. There is no indication that Cummings demonstrated the deficiency of the pistol on himself or that anyone killed himself in the courtroom. The film is faithful to the mood of the incident and to the heroism of the district attorney's act of putting himself on the line in the name of justice.

• **Litigation.** None known.

Scopes "Monkey Trial" (1925)
Inherit the Wind (1960)

THE FACTS

In 1925, the American Civil Liberties Union (ACLU) advertised for a teacher to challenge Tennessee's Butler Act, a measure passed earlier that year to restrict the teaching of evolution in state-funded schools.[42] Several Dayton citizens, hoping the publicity would benefit their town, approached John Scopes as a possible candidate. Scopes was actually a mathematics teacher and athletic coach who had briefly substituted as a biology teacher. He did not remember teaching evolution, but he had used the standard textbook, Hunter's *Civic Biology*, which contained a short section on the subject. He actually knew little about evolution beyond the basics.

Scopes was charged and remained free after his indictment—there was no prison sentence connected with the Butler Act. He continued to live in his boarding house and even traveled to New York to meet the ACLU executive board that included Norman Thomas and Felix Frankfurter. Nationally known orator and three-times presidential candidate William Jennings Bryan was hired to represent Dayton. When he came to town, the Dayton Progressive Club gave a dinner in Bryan's honor, and Scopes attended. Bryan even recognized Scopes as one of the graduates he had addressed at a high school commencement six years earlier. Also at the prosecution table were Arthur Garfield Hays of the ACLU, the famed international divorce lawyer Dudley Field Malone, who had served as Bryan's undersecretary of state in the Wilson administration, and constitutional expert John Randolph Neal.

The ACLU and various interested parties hired Clarence Darrow to represent Scopes. When he arrived, the celebrity-loving town greeted him as warmly as it had Bryan. Darrow was also feted by the Progressive Club.

Nearly two hundred reporters descended upon the town, including H. L. Mencken of the Baltimore *Evening Sun*, which helped underwrite Scopes' defense. Newspapers and magazines carried articles and cartoons on the case, and telegraph operators wired stories to Europe and Australia. For the first time, news of an American trial was nationally broadcast by radio.

Mencken ridiculed Bryan in print as "a tinpot pope in the Coca-Cola belt," and the rest of the press generally followed his lead.

Restricted in his use of scientific experts, Darrow instead called Bryan as an expert witness on the Bible. Darrow did embarrass Bryan a number of times over his ninety minutes of testimony. A review of the actual transcript, however, reveals that Bryan frequently held his own. Bryan was not a biblical literalist. If his supporters felt disappointment over Bryan's testimony, it was because he did occasionally acknowledge the other side of the argument and was, therefore, a less-than-staunch fundamentalist. If Bryan made a mistake, it was in testifying at all, but he believed, as he said on the stand, "These gentlemen came here to reveal religion. I am here to defend it, and they can ask me any questions they please." Darrow, on the other hand, said that his goal was "preventing bigots and ignoramuses from controlling the education of the United States."

Both sides agreed to a directed verdict, and, consequently, although Bryan did prepare one, there were no closing arguments. Scopes was found guilty and fined $100. Five days after the trial, on Sunday, Bryan went to church services, came back to his rooms, lay down in bed, and died. His death may have been due partly to exhaustion and stress, but he also suffered from a diabetic condition that he did not carefully watch.

On appeal, the Tennessee Supreme Court reversed Scopes' conviction — because fines over $50 had to be imposed by a jury and not a judge — but upheld the validity of the statute. The court recommended that the case not be retried in the interest of the "peace and dignity of the state." The Butler Act remained on the books until it was repealed in 1967.

Scopes left Dayton soon after the trial, returning only once, 35 years later, to promote the film based on the trial. Darrow died in 1938, Mencken in 1956, and Scopes in 1970.

THE FILM

Inherit the Wind[43] was originally a 1955 Broadway play, written by Jerome Lawrence and Robert E. Lee. The play changed the names of the trial participants— Bryan became Brady, Darrow became Drummond, Mencken was Hornbeck, and Scopes was Cates— and created some completely fictitious characters— Jeremiah Brown and his daughter Rachel. Paul Muni played Drummond, Ed Begley played Brady, and Tony Randall, Hornbeck. The published version of the play includes an introduction by the authors, which begins,

> Inherit the Wind is not history. The events which took place in Dayton, Tennessee, during the scorching July of 1925 are clearly the genesis of this play. It has, however, an exodus of its own. Only a handful of phrases have been taken from the actual transcript of the famous Scopes Trial. Some of the characters of the play are related to the colorful figures in that battle of giants; but they have life and language of their own — and, therefore, names of their own.[44]

In the introduction, Lawrence and Lee express their gratitude to Arthur Garfield Hays, who had prosecuted the case with Bryan and who, before his death, shared his memories of the trial with them. Some have commented that Hays may well have offered a portrait of Bryan as well past his prime to play up Hays' own contribution to the trial victory. The character of Davenport in the play is based on Hays.

The play was made into a movie in 1960 by producer/director Stanley Kramer— who would later direct Judgment at Nuremberg, to be discussed later. The screenplay from Lawrence and Lee's play was originally credited to Nathan E. Douglas and Harold Jacob Smith. Kramer later recalled telling the screenwriters to go back to the trial transcript and said he could have changed the title and ignored the screenplay if he had wanted to since "our main source for the screenplay was the trial transcript."[45] Frederic March, playing Brady, was made up to look like Bryan, and photographs of March in makeup as Brady and of Bryan were released side by side by the studio in promoting the film. March modeled his performance on Bryan, studying motion pictures of him and listening to recordings of his voice.[46]

The screenplay mainly "opened the play up"—for example, showing Cates' arrest. It also softened up the role of Hornbeck, modeled on Mencken, for Gene Kelly, the legendary song and dance man who was attempting a serious role as the cynical reporter. At the end of the play, Hornbeck storms out, angry that Drummond is not as cynical as he is. In the film, Hornbeck lingers after Drummond tells him that Hornbeck, who believes in nothing, will die alone. Hornbeck responds quietly that he knows that Drummond will defend his right to be lonely.

In addition to Kelly and March, the movie starred Spencer Tracy as Drummond; March's wife, Florence Eldridge, as Mrs. Brady, and Dick York as Cates. The film was nominated for Oscars for best screenplay, cinematography, editing, and actor — Tracy. It did not win any, although it was very profitable.[47] Lee died in 1994, Kramer in 2001, and Lawrence in 2004.

Bertram Cates, based on Scopes, is teaching evolution to his high school biology class in Hillsboro, Tennessee — subbing for Dayton. The authorities invade the class and arrest Cates for violating the Butler Act. Cates is imprisoned pending trial. Matthew Harrison Brady, based on Bryan and also a three-time Democratic presidential candidate, arrives in Hillsboro to prosecute the case, where he is greeted by the mayor and a large, enthusiastic crowd singing "Give me that old-time religion." Only the story of creation in the Bible is to be taught in schools, the crowd insists.

E. K. Hornbeck of the *Baltimore Herald*, based on Mencken, also arrives in Hillsboro. He has championed Cates in his columns, claiming that Hillsboro is the epitome of ignorance and bigotry. He tells Brady that Cates will have a defender, courtesy of the *Herald*—the great Henry Drummond, based on Darrow. Drummond arrives in town later that evening with little notice.

Cates' image is burned in effigy by the townspeople. Jeremiah Brown, the local minister, holds a town meeting in which he says that Cates' soul is damned. Rachel, Jeremiah's daughter and Cates' sweetheart, begs him to take it back, and Brady interrupts the meeting, quoting for the minister from Proverbs 11:29 — "He that troubleth his own house shall inherit the wind and the fool shall be servant to the wise of heart"—from which the play and film take their title.

In the course of the trial, Brady starts out confidently, full of self-righteousness and ready rhetoric about "the Revealed Word." Drummond complains that the town has given Brady the honorary title of "Colonel" and that everyone is calling him "Colonel Brady," which gives him an unfair advantage over Drummond in the mind of the jurors. When the judge asks Drummond what an appropriate remedy would be, Drummond answers, "Break him. Make him a private. I have no objection to the honorary title of 'Private Brady.'" The judge and the town council quickly confer the "temporary honorary title" of "Colonel" on Drummond. Brady even calls Rachel, who thinks Brady and his wife have befriended her, to the stand and bullies her into giving damaging testimony about Cates.

The judge excludes Drummond's scientific witnesses on the grounds that evolution itself is not on trial. Desperate for some way to challenge

the law under which Cates stands accused, Drummond decides to put
Brady on the stand as an expert on the Bible, and Brady accepts the challenge with gusto. Drummond exposes Brady's untenable literal acceptance
of the Bible. He urges that what is at issue is what makes humanity human:

> In a child's power to master the multiplication table there is more
> sanctity than in all your shouted "Amens!", "Holy, Holies," and
> "Hosannahs." An idea is a greater monument than a cathedral.
> And the advance of man's knowledge is more of a miracle than any
> sticks turned into snakes, or the parting of the waters. But are we
> now to halt the march of progress because Mr. Brady frightens us
> with a fable?

The crowd begins to laugh at Brady, and public opinion as well as the
momentum of the case seems to turn. After the courtroom empties, Brady
buries his head in his wife's bosom as if he were a child, telling her that
they had laughed at him.

The jury brings in the inevitable guilty verdict, but the town fathers
persuade the judge that, with the bad publicity the trial has produced, it
is best for him to go lightly on Cates. The judge imposes a fine of only
$100. Brady protests the light punishment, but Drummond cuts him off,
telling the judge that regardless of the amount of the fine, Cates will appeal
the verdict. Brady tries to make what he considers an all-important closing speech, but with the trial over, people start to leave and talk. The radio
technicians take the microphone away. Trying to shout over the din, Brady
collapses and shortly dies.

Hornbeck says that Brady "died of a busted belly." When Hornbeck
ridicules Brady, Drummond upbraids him. He says that Brady was a once-
great man who had ceased to move forward. Hornbeck reaches for the
Bible, saying that Brady had given his own epitaph at the prayer meeting,
and Drummond quotes the passage from *Proverbs* from memory. Hornbeck charges him with being even more religious than Brady was. Alone
in the courtroom, Drummond picks up Darwin's *On the Origin of Species*
and the Bible, weighs them thoughtfully in his hands, and exits confidently
with both books in his briefcase.

• *Analysis.* While *Inherit the Wind* remains faithful to the broad outlines
of the historical events it portrays, it distorts the factual details. For
example:

Scopes was neither arrested in the act of teaching nor imprisoned.

Bryan was indeed not able to deliver the lengthy closing statement he considered his life's "mountain peak," but not because the judge cut the trial

short but rather because Darrow stated his willingness to accept a guilty verdict in order to move to appeal, and this obviated the need for closing statements.

In the film Mrs. Brady takes care of her husband; in reality Mrs. Bryan was a semi-invalid, and Bryan took care of her.

The phrase of Hornbeck/Mencken —"He died of a busted belly"— was actually uttered about Bryan, not by Mencken but by Darrow; Mencken's actual reported reaction to Bryan's death was, "We killed the son of a bitch."

While Drummond complains that Brady is being called "Colonel," "Colonel" was a customary honorary title used in the courtroom and was extended to all of the legal counsel in the Scopes case, including Darrow.

Although Drummond says that he is not aware of Brady's military record, Bryan had actually been a colonel in the U.S. Army.

The film has Drummond and Brady debating about Darwin's *On the Origin of the Species* and Drummond walking out with both Darwin's book and the Bible, but the book in question at the trial was *Hunter's Civic Biology* that was used in the classroom, not Darwin's.

Although the film has Cates' sweetheart testifying against him, no women participated in the trial, and Scopes did not have a special girlfriend or fiancé at this time, although he dated several Dayton girls.

Darrow did indeed not present his scientific experts, but he did not put them on the stand because he refused to allow Bryan to cross-examine them, not because the judge would not approve them.

While the film suggests that $100 was a token fine, violation of the Butler Act was punishable by a fine of no less than $100 and no greater than $500; imprisonment was not a provision of the law.

There is no mention in the film of the ACLU or its advertisement.

What the film does is perpetuate the myth of what happened in Dayton, Tennessee, during the summer of 1925 as it was spread by Darrow, Mencken, and Hays. What actually happened was easy to discover, but Lawrence and Lee and the filmmakers preferred the myth. Darrow/Drummond is the guardian of free speech and thought, while Bryan/Brady is halting progress by, as Drummond puts it, clinging to the truth of the "pleasant poetry of Genesis."

• **Litigation.** None known concerning characterization. Scopes evidently had no objection to his portrayal since he returned to Dayton in 1960 for the first time in 35 years to promote the film. Bryan and Darrow were long dead, and Mencken had passed away in 1956, shortly after the play debuted. While not litigation, there was some settlement involving the authorship of the screenplay. The original screenplay credits were for Harold Jacob Smith and Nathan Douglas, the latter being a pseudonym for the black-listed writer Nedrick Young. Upon the request of Young's widow and the recommendation of the Academy's Writers Executive Committee, the record of the Oscar nomination for best screenplay was changed on 1993 to "Nedrick Young and Harold Jacob Smith." The Writer's Guild of America similarly changed the official credits for the film.

Court Martial of Billy Mitchell (1925)
The Court Martial of Billy Mitchell (1955)

THE FACTS

Billy Mitchell, the son of a U.S. senator, was born in Nice, France, in 1879.[48] At the start of the Spanish-American War, when he was 18, Mitchell enlisted in the Army and served in the Army Signal Corps in Cuba, the Philippines, and Alaska. In 1903, the Wright Brothers invented the airplane, and Mitchell soon became interested in aviation. Mitchell was assigned to the Army General Staff in Washington in 1912 as a captain. He prepared a report on the needs of American aviation and argued that, with the advances then being made in aeronautics, the United States was being drawn ever closer to its potential enemies and that distance would soon have to be measured in time, not miles. He paid for his own flying lessons— the army thought he was too old and his rank too high for flight training.

A lieutenant colonel during World War I, at the battle of Saint-Mihiel Mitchell coordinated a force of 1,481 British, French, and Italian planes to support American ground forces. He was promoted to brigadier general. His flamboyance made him one of the best-known Americans in Europe, but he quickly earned the enmity of his nonflying contemporaries for his aggressiveness in building airfields, hangars, and other facilities. He was appointed assistant chief of the U.S. Army Air Service in 1919 and was appalled at how quickly the organization he had helped to build in war had disintegrated in peacetime. He proposed a number of innovations for the Air Service — a special corps of mechanics, troop-carrying aircraft, a civilian pilot pool for wartime availability, long-range bombers capable of flying the Atlantic, and armor-piercing bombs as well as the development of bombsights, ski-equipped aircraft, engine superchargers, and aerial tor-pedoes. The press, including the *New York Times*, advocated testing of planes in attacks against actual German ships captured during the war. Traditionalists in the navy fought the idea, but permission to demonstrate his theories was finally granted.

The tests were held in June and July 1921. The bombers sank a Ger-man destroyer first, followed by an armored light cruiser and then one of the world's largest war vessels, the German battleship *Ostfriesland*, fol-lowed by the U.S. battleship *Alabama*—and later the battleships *New Jer-sey* and *Virginia*.

To get Mitchell off the front pages, his superiors sent him to Hawaii. However, he returned with a scathing report on the inadequate defenses he saw there. He also went to Europe and the Far East to study the advances being made in aviation. After returning in 1924, he wrote a 323-page report that stressed that, when making estimates of Japanese air power, "care must be taken that it is not underestimated." Mitchell believed that Japan was the dominant nation in Asia and was preparing to do battle with the United States. He predicted that air attacks would be made by the Japa-nese on Pearl Harbor and the Philippines and described how they would be conducted.

When his term with the air service expired in April 1925, Mitchell was not reappointed. He reverted to his permanent rank of colonel and was transferred to Fort Sam Houston, Texas, as air officer for the VIII Corps.

On September 1, 1925, a naval seaplane was lost on a nonstop flight from San Francisco to Hawaii. Two days later, the U.S. Navy dirigible *Shenandoah* was destroyed while on a goodwill flight, killing all on board including Commander Landsdowne. Mitchell released a scathing denun-ciation of the navy and war department, saying that these and other acci-dents were

> the result of incompetency [*sic*], criminal negligence, and the
> almost treasonable negligence of our national defense by the
> War and Navy departments.... [A]ll aviation policies, schemes
> and systems are dictated by the non-flying officers of the Army
> and Navy, who know practically nothing about it.... can stand
> by no longer and see these disgusting performances ... at the
> expense of the lives of our people, and the delusions of the
> American public.[49]

Secretary of War Dwight F. Davis announced that Mitchell would be disciplined and implied that it would be by court-martial. Mitchell was put under technical arrest, and a court-martial began in Washington, D.C., on October 28, 1925, for insubordination under the catch-all 96th Article of War. Twelve generals and a colonel were appointed to sit in judgment.

The court martial lasted seven weeks. Mrs. Landsdowne testified in Mitchell's defense. Major Allen Gullion took over the prosecution to cross-examine Mitchell, demanding that Mitchell describe for the court what "almost treasonable" meant. Mitchell replied that there were two types of treason: the textbook definition and the definition that had to do with duty and loyalty. Gullion demonstrated a savage style in cross-examination, and there was a suggestion he was after higher things. When the trial was over, Gullion distributed copies of his final summation to the press.

The board deliberated for about half an hour and rendered its verdict — guilty of the charge and all eight specifications. The vote did not have to be unanimous. One of the board members — Douglas MacArthur, later General MacArthur — is thought to have voted for acquittal. The sentence was suspension from rank, command, and duty, with forfeiture of pay and allowances for five years.

The verdict was widely debated on Capitol Hill, and veterans groups passed resolutions condemning the outcome. President Calvin Coolidge approved the sentence handed down by the court but altered the court's verdict by granting Mitchell full subsistence and half pay because Mitchell would not be able to obtain private employment while still in uniform. Mitchell said he would not accept the modified sentence because it would make him "an object of government charity."

Mitchell resigned effective February 1, 1926. He immediately embarked on a four-month, coast-to-coast lecture tour, showing films of the ship bombings and continually expressing his by-now familiar theme of the necessity for military preparedness in the air. His sweeping charges appeared in major American magazines and aviation journals.

Mitchell died in a New York hospital on February 19, 1936, at the age of 56. He had elected to be buried in Milwaukee, his hometown, where he had enlisted in 1898, rather than at Arlington National Cemetery.

Major Gullion went on to become the judge advocate general of the U.S. Army and was instrumental in the internment of Japanese-Americans at the start of World War II. He died in 1944.

In 1955, the Air Force Association passed a resolution to void Billy Mitchell's court martial, but in 1958 the secretary of the Air Force refused to reverse the conviction because Mitchell had attacked his superiors in public.

Although the conviction was not removed, Billy Mitchell had already received a measure of official recognition from a grateful nation when President Harry S. Truman signed legislation in 1946 bestowing a special medal posthumously on Mitchell "in recognition of his outstanding pioneer service and foresight in the field of American military aviation."

THE FILM

The Court Martial of Billy Mitchell[50] was released in 1955, directed by Otto Preminger, with a screenplay by Milton Sperling and Emmet Lavery. It starred Gary Cooper as Mitchell, Charles Bickford as General Guthrie, Rod Steiger as Major Allan Gullion, Ralph Bellamy as Representative Frank Reed, Jack Lord as Commander Landsdowne, Fred Clark as Colonel Moreland, and Elizabeth Montgomery as Mrs. Landsdowne. The movie was nominated for an Academy Award for best screenplay. Used to being his own producer, Preminger often clashed with the film's producer and later expressed little satisfaction with the movie. Lavery and Preminger both died in 1986, Sperling in 1988.

The film picks up General Mitchell's story in 1925 and focuses on his frustration at the treatment of air power by the U.S. Army and Navy and how planes left over from World War I have become death traps. Mitchell's friend Landsdowne dies when his dirigible is lost in a storm, and six of his pilots are killed in crashes. Mitchell denounces the army forces as negligent and is court martialed.

General Guthrie and the other judges are clearly biased against Mitchell. The hearing is held in an old warehouse in an effort to hide the hearing from the press, which favors Mitchell.

Since Mitchell admits making the statement, his only defense is justification. The court, however, refuses to hear evidence of justification — saying it was irrelevant to the charge of insubordination — except for the testimony of Mrs. Landsdowne, which it reluctantly but gallantly hears. Her testimony about her late husbands' concern about the safety of his plane prompts the court to hear other testimony — including that of legendary pilot Eddie Rickenbacker.

Mitchell, although he is ill, testifies. A special prosecutor — Major Gullion — is brought in to cross-examine him. Sardonically, he goads Mitchell into predicting that the United States will one day be attacked by air by the Japanese. General Guthrie says the U.S. government will have to apologize to the Japanese government — which, ironically, although the film does not show this, requested a copy of Mitchell's testimony, presumably as part of its preparation to its act of war at Pearl Harbor in 1941.

Mitchell is convicted and suspended from rank and pay for five years. His later career and death are not shown, although he looks up and seems to see military jets in the sky, suggesting his ultimate justification.

• *Analysis.* The movie is extremely faithful to the historical facts. The names of real-life personages are mostly used, and the events are portrayed in a timeline that reasonably reflects reality. Some of the actual transcript is included in the courtroom dialogue. A problem with the film is that it is so accurate that it is a little dull and stodgy, although some of that may be due to the film reflecting the slower pace of the 1950s.

Another problem is that it is one-sided. That is understandable in that Mitchell was proved right — superior air power led to superiority in combat, as demonstrated in World War II, which was caused when Japan did, indeed, attack the United States. But, except for Gullion — whose sardonic, savage approach and ambition are well and concisely established, General Guthrie and the other prosecutors are cardboard figures. Either by mistake or to fictionalize, Gullion's first name is spelled "Allan" in released credits and not "Allen."

The cast is excellent, and the courtroom scenes between Mitchell and Gullion (Cooper and Steiger) are extremely well played. Cooper, with his carefully honed, exterior-dominant portrayal, is set against Steiger, portly, interior-trained by the Actor's Studio in New York, looming over Cooper — both because he is standing and because Cooper's Mitchell is ill. Like James Mason's Carson in *The Trials of Oscar Wilde*, Gullion probes for an opening in Mitchell's defense by reading from Mitchell's reports and other writings. At one point, Steiger takes a sheaf of papers and says, "I was reading your report...." Cooper, fighting back the pain, says offhandedly, "I'm glad somebody did." The courtroom laughs. Steiger laughs too, a short, burst, without humor, his eyes never leaving the page from which he is reading, and then he continues. He knows that Mitchell is on trial for what he wants him to do publicly — speak out against the U.S. military's approach to air power. So he alternately disarms and then browbeats Mitchell into admitting that he is convinced that the United States will be attacked by Japan, accurately predicting the 1941 Japanese attack on Pearl Harbor but in conflict with U.S.–Japanese relations in 1925. The 1955 audience knew and subsequent viewers know that as soon as Mitchell says "the Japanese," he is right and the U.S. military is wrong.

Cooper was, however, criticized for being too old to play Mitchell — Mitchell was forty-six during the trial, Cooper was fifty-four during filming, although he is very similar to Mitchell in features and in presence.

• *Litigation:* None known.

Nuremberg Judges' Trials (1948)
Judgment at Nuremberg (1961)

THE FACTS

Many judges appointed before the Nazi rise to power — because of the economic and social circles that judges were drawn from — had views that were quite compatible with the Nazi party.[51] A few Jewish judges were sitting on the bench when the Nazis assumed power, but they were removed from their positions by a 1933 law.

In 1938, laws were adopted that imposed different levels of punishment for the same crime — a harsh one for Jews, a lighter one for other Germans. By 1940, sterilization pogroms were underway. By 1942, the "Final Solution," the wholesale extermination of Jews and other persons deemed undesirable, was in full swing.

Two features of German law combined to facilitate Nazism. First, German law, unlike the law of the United States and many other nations, lacked "higher law" on which a judge could base a decision that overrode the discriminatory laws adopted by the Nazi regime. Second, since there was no separation of powers between the executive and judicial branches of government, Hitler had the power "to intervene in any case" through what was called "an extraordinary appeal for nullification of sentence." This inevitably resulted in replacing one sentence with one more severe, usually a death sentence.

Just a few non-Jewish judges demonstrated courage in the face of Nazi persecution and violations of civil liberties. One was Lothar Kressig, a county court judge who issued injunctions against sending hospital patients to extermination camps. When ordered to withdraw his injunctions, Kressig refused. He also attempted to initiate a prosecution of Nazis for their role in the pogrom. Kressig, under pressure, eventually resigned.

In the actual Nuremberg trial, the defendants — prosecutors, judges, and administrators — were charged with involvement in an organized pogrom of cruelty and injustice in violation of the laws of war and humanity. The jurisdiction of the Nuremberg tribunal was based on the Allied Powers' control over Germany, as well as the prerogatives of sovereign states under international law.

Among the defendants, Oswald Rothaug had been appointed to a variety of judicial posts between 1937 and 1945, including presiding judge of the Special Court. He then served as public prosecutor of the Public Prosecution at the People's Court in Berlin. As head of Department I, between May 1943 and April 1945, Rothaug handled cases involving high treason and the undermining of morale. The prosecution at the Nuremberg tribunal focused on the judgments Rothaug issued as presiding judge of the Special Court at Nuremberg, especially in the Katzenberger race defilement case. Katzenberger was charged with violating Article 2 of the Law for the Protection of German Blood, which forbade sexual intercourse between Jews and other German nationals. Katzenberger was accused of having sexual intercourse with Irene Seillor, a nineteen-year-old German photographer. Both Katzenberger and Seillor denied the charge. Katzenberger described the relationship between the two of them as "fatherly." The prosecution produced evidence that Seillor was seen sitting on Katzenberger's lap. Rothaug arranged to have Katzenberger's trial transferred to a special court. In this court, high-ranking Nazi officials—in uniform—took the stand to express their opinions that Katzenberger was guilty. Rothaug said to a medical expert who had been summoned to examine the defendant that, since he had already decided that Katzenberger would be executed by decapitation, the examination was unnecessary. The doctor questioned whether an individual of the defendant's age and agility could commit race defilement. Rothaug allegedly replied that it was sufficient that "the swine said that a German girl had sat upon his lap." Rothaug allowed Katzenberger to testify only for a moment before Rothaug dismissed him from the stand. At the conclusion of the evidentiary phase of the trial, Rothaug met with the prosecution, outlined what he wanted to be included in the closing arguments, and directed the lawyers to ask for the death penalty for Katzenberger, even though the normal punishment for violations of Article 2 was life in prison, and a prison term for defendant Irene Seillor. Rothaug converted the sentence for Katzenberger to death by a creative construction of a law that required death for breaking certain laws "to take advantage of the war effort." Rothaug argued that death was the appropriate punishment for Katzenberger because he exploited the lights-out situation provided by air-raid precautions to develop his alleged romance with Seillor.

The Allied Nuremberg tribunal noted that the fact that only a Jew could be prosecuted for racial pollution was sufficient to establish that the Katzenbeger case was an act in furtherance of the Nazi pogrom to persecute and to exterminate Jews. The tribunal also suggested that Katzenberger was part of a pattern. Rothaug condemned Katzenberger to be executed because he was a Jew and others because they were Poles.

Defendant Curt Rothenberger served as president of the District Court of Appeals in Hamburg between 1935 and 1942. In 1942, he was appointed Under Secretary in the Ministry of Justice under Otto Thierack. While president of the district court, Rothenberger cooperated with the security police in placing informers within the judicial system and gave the police information. Rothenberger participated in conferences that issued a report to the judiciary that warned that extreme caution had to be exercised in weighing the testimony of Jews, that verdicts should not be based upon such evidence, and that after the death of a Jew, his or her property be confiscated.

Rothenberger and other judges visited the Neuengamme and Mauthausen concentration camps in order to investigate charges of poor accommodations, inadequate food, and harsh working conditions. On his return, he claimed that he had failed to find any inmates who had been interred without trial, that the conditions were adequate, and that he had not observed or discovered any abuse. Since this was not the case, his report was seen as a furtherance of the Nazi regime and its "Final Solution."

Defendant Franz Schlegelberger was a legal scholar who steadily rose through the pre-Nazi judicial bureaucracy. In 1931, he was appointed secretary of state in the Reich Ministry of Justice under Minister Franz Guertner. In 1941, Schlegelberger was appointed administrative secretary of state. He resigned when Otto Thierack was named minister of justice on August 20, 1942.

In 1938, Schlegelberger was ordered by Hitler to join the National Socialist Party. He testified that, despite his membership, he remained uninvolved in Nazi affairs and unattached to party doctrines. However, upon Schlegelberger's retirement as acting justice minister, Hitler expressed his appreciation by giving him a gift of 100,000 Reichmarks.

Hitler ordered Schlegelberger to explain the ideological foundations of National Socialist jurisprudence to the public and legal profession. Accordingly, in a 1936 speech, Schlegelberger stated that the creation of justice in harmony with the moral concepts of the new Reich had been made possible by the provision of the criminal code that provided for the punishment of acts that deserved punishment in accordance with the basic concepts of criminal law and the sound instincts of the people.

Schlegelberger also signed the "Night and Fog" decree, which involved the judiciary in the disposition of defendants who had been secretly spirited out of the occupied territories. Less brutal than some of the other judges, Schlegelberger did argue against the deportation from Germany of half-Jews, proposing that they be given the choice of sterilization or deportation. But he also prepared the draft of the "Law against Poles and Jews" that was applied in Germany and in the Incorporated Eastern Territories. On January 31, 1942, he issued a decree providing that the provisions of the Decree against Poles and Jews would be applicable to offenses committed before the decree came into force.

Schlegelberger publicly disapproved of police intervention into the judicial process, and yet he cooperated in the murder of a Jewish defendant at Hitler's request and assured Hitler that he would take any additional action that Hitler believed was required to ensure that sentences were aligned with National Socialist ideology. Schlegelberger cooperated with Hitler in modifying judicial sentences, including ordering the murder of imprisoned defendants.

Herbert Klemm was appointed state secretary by Thierack. One of Klemm's central responsibilities involved the administration of the Night and Fog pogrom. Klemm and Thierack, together, denied clemency in 123 cases.

While Klemm was secretary of state, the practice of lynch justice was initiated against Allied pilots. Thierack received reports of all the killings of Allied pilots, and the Tribunal was unable to find a single instance in which an indictment was filed. Klemm and Thierack both signed off on a Reich Chancellery memo on the matter. Klemm, aware that Allied forces were approaching, also ordered the killing of eight hundred prisoners interned in Sonnenburg prison, many of whom were Jews, Poles and other citizens of occupied territories.

At the Nuremberg trial, the defendants pled that they had adhered to the letter of legal language. They claimed that they possessed little room for either discretion or dissent and only drafted statutes, followed precedents, issued decisions, and crafted arguments that were indistinguishable from those of their colleagues. Rothaug noted that "no proof has been furnished in any single case that ... we ... applied an illegal method." Defendant Wilhelm von Ammon of the Ministry of Justice testified that he would have refused to have followed an order that was contrary to the law. In those instances in which defendants encountered injustices, the defendants claimed to have worked to correct them. However, as noted by Klemm, a state secretary in the Ministry of Justice, "to revoke laws and norms which had existed for years was not in my competency."

Schlegelberger offered a defense that, to varying degrees, also was claimed by other defendants. He said that had he resigned that his successor would have proven to be a harsher and more unbending figure. Schlegelberger explained he was on a "lonely island" in attempting to fairly administer the legal system. In this situation, "sacrifices had to be made to this storm of power in order to protect it [the storm] from triumphing completely." His goal was to maintain the independence of the judiciary "at all costs" as the "most secure guaranty for the law." Schlegelberger complained that the Allied Powers had rewarded his struggle to preserve justice with imprisonment and criminal prosecution.

Defendant Guenther Nebelung, chief justice of the Fourth Senate of the People's Court, noted that he was a German jurist, had followed the laws of his country and his own conscience, and so was indistinguishable from a German soldier. Nebelung challenged the court to convict him if the "law of the victors so demands."

The defendants claimed that any transgressions that they may have committed had been motivated by a desire to preserve judicial independence and integrity.

Schlegelberger testified that he had involved the judiciary in the Night and Fog pogrom in order to avoid consigning defendants to the sole jurisdiction of the police.

He also stated that he had supported the retroactive application of the death penalty for serious cases of conspiracies to commit treason. He feared that without this provision the police would have arbitrarily executed individuals without regard to the seriousness of the case. He did concede that "what I had always tried to achieve by various means had not been achieved; on the contrary, that which I had tried to avoid had come true."

The chief judge for Case No. 3, *U.S. v. Altstoelter* was Judge Carrington T. Marshall until June 19, 1947, and James T. Brand from the Oregon Supreme Court after that date. Other judges were Judge Mallow B. Blau and Judge Justice W. Harding. General Telford Taylor was the chief prosecutor. The trial was held between March 5, 1947, and December 4, 1947. Of the fourteen defendants who were finally tried, ten were found guilty, four were acquitted. The court concluded that the defendants had been aware that they were engaging in criminal conduct and could not credibly claim that they were being subjected to retroactive punishment. The court also rejected the defendants' judicial immunity defense and their claim they were insulated from liability because they had acted in furtherance of governmental authority. The defendants were found to have applied the death penalty in an arbitrary and capricious fashion, to have implemented and administered the "Night and Fog decree." Further, the Ministry of Justice, courts, prosecutors, military and Gestapo caused thousands of civilians in the occupied territories to be arrested, transported to Germany, held incommunicado and denied due process of law, prosecuted in secret without the rights to counsel or to present evidence, imprisoned in cruel and inhumane conditions, and sentenced to death.

The tribunal noted that this new conception of criminal law encroached upon the rights of citizens by subjecting them to the arbitrary opinion of a judge as to what constituted an offense. Individuals no longer could know which acts were approved and which were prohibited. According to the court, this "destroyed the feeling of legal security and created an atmosphere of terrorism."

In its decision, the justice trial tribunal considered what it called Schlegelberger's "hesitant injustices." The tribunal concluded that Schlegelberger "loathed the evil that he did" and that his real love was for the "life of the intellect, the work of the scholar." In the end, the tribunal stated, Schlegelberger had resigned because "the cruelties of the system were too much for him." Despite its obvious sympathy with Schlegelberger's plight, the tribunal found him guilty. It pointed out that the decision of a man of his stature to remain in office lent credibility to the Nazi regime. Moreover, Schlegelberger did sign his name to orders that, in the tribunal's judgment, constituted crimes. One case described in the decision involved the prosecution in 1941 of a Jew (Luftgas) accused of "hoarding eggs." Schlegelberger gave Luftgas a two-and-a-half-year sentence, but then Hitler indicated that he wanted the convicted man executed. Although Schlegelberger may well have protested, he signed his name to the order that led to the execution of Luftgas. Another case cited by the tribunal concerned a remission-of-sentence order signed by Schlegelberger. Schlegelberger explained in his decision that the sentence imposed against a police officer who was convicted of beating a Jewish milking hand would have been bad for the morale of officers.

Although Schlegelberger received a life sentence in Nuremberg, he was released from prison in 1951 on medical parole and received a generous monthly pension until his death.

The tribunal found "no mitigating circumstances" in the case of Oswald Rothaug. In its decision, the tribunal calls Rothaug "a sadistic and evil man." Rothaug, unlike Schlegelberger, had no reservations about enthusiastically supporting the Nazi pattern of human rights abuses. He was sentenced to life in prison, although it was commuted to 20 years.

Klemm was sentenced to life imprisonment. For his orders to kill prisoners at Sonnenburg prison, the tribunal concluded that Klemm must share responsibility "at a high policy level, for the crimes committed in the name of justice which fill the pages of this record."

THE FILM

Judgment at Nuremberg[52] is based not on the most famous Nuremberg trial in which Herman Goering and other Nazi leaders were tried almost immediately after the World War II had ended in 1945[53] but on a later — 1947 — trial held in Nuremberg (Case No. 3, *U.S. v. Josef Altstoelter*) of 16 German judges and prosecutors. The film was adapted by Abby Mann from his 1957 *Playhouse 90* television drama, which aired April 16, 1959, and starred Claude Rains in the role of the lead U.S. judge played in the film by Spencer Tracy. Also in the cast were Melvyn Douglas, Paul Lukas, and Maximilian Schell, who repeated his role as the defense attorney in the film.[54] Mann used the trial transcripts as his source for the teleplay[55] and the teleplay as his source for the movie. (Mann adapted his screenplay for the theater in 2001.[56])

The film was produced and directed by Stanley Kramer, who had, as a producer or director, specialized in socially conscious dramas such *High Noon* (1952), an implicit criticism of McCarthyism dressed up as a western; *The Defiant Ones* (1958), a foray into the issues of race relations dressed up as a prison escape drama; *On the Beach* (1959), which portrayed a world dying after a nuclear explosion, and *Inherit the Wind* (1960), which was discussed earlier. The last film also starred Tracy. In addition to Tracy as Judge Dan Haywood and Schell as defense attorney Hans Rolfe, *Judgment at Nuremberg* had an all-star cast, including Burt Lancaster as defendant Ernst Janning, Richard Widmark as prosecutor Col. Ted Lawson, Montgomery Clift as witness Rudolph Peterson, Marlene Dietrich as Nazi widow Madame Bertholt, William Shatner as Haywood's aide Captain Byers, Werner Klemperer as defendant Emil Hahn, and Judy Garland as witness Irene Hoffman.

The film was nominated for 11 Academy Awards— best picture; actor, Tracy; actor, Schell; supporting actor, Clift; supporting actress, Garland; director, Kramer; writing from material from another medium, Mann; art direction; cinematography; costumes; and film editing. Mann and Schell won. Kramer and Schell received Golden Globe Awards for best director and best actor, respectively, and Schell won the New York Film Critics Awards for best actor.

All of the characters were fictionalized. Some were loosely based on actual personages. The film has no disclaimer, although the writing credit states: "Written by Abby Mann, based on his story"— the word "story" suggesting fictionalization.

The film opens with scenes of Nuremberg, Germany, 1948, with shots of the skeletal remains of the bombed-out, once-mighty city. Judge Dan Haywood — who is loosely based on Judge Brandt, although Haywood is from Maine and not Oregon, presumably to illustrate his deep American, conservative roots— is driven to where he will live during the trial — a palatial home once owned by Nazi General Bertholt.

When the defendants enter their pleas, Ernst Janning, who is partially based on Judge Franz Schlegelberger, refuses to stand until he is gently pulled up by soldiers, indicating he does not recognize the jurisdiction of the court.

In his opening statement, prosecutor Colonel Lawson — very, very loosely based on General Taylor — firmly states that the four defendants — not 16 or even 14 — were on trial not for violation of due process or other constitutional violations but for murder, brutalities, torture, and atrocities committed during the Third Reich. He says that the defendants cannot claim ignorance — they should have known better since, unlike the many young people who were led into Nazism during the rise of Hitler, they were already educated adults when the Nazis came into power.

In his opening statement, Hans Role — who evidently is the defense counsel for all four defendants — states that the purpose of this trial is the reconsecration of the temple of justice and reestablishment of the code of justice. He calls for a clear, honest evaluation of the charges brought by the prosecution and argues that judges do not make the laws, they carry them out. He argues that the love of country led to an attitude of "my country right or wrong." Disobedience to the führer would have been choice between patriotism and treason for the judges. Finally the defense argues that not only are the justices on trial, so are the German people.

Judge Haywood asks his aide for copies of the Weimar Constitution, which Janning helped draft, and Janning's books. He walks around town to think and get a feel for the place. He goes to the auditorium where the Nazis used to have their rallies and seems to hear the echoes of the not-too-distant past when the place was full of cheering German citizens. He turns to the empty podium and hears Hitler's voice.

Colonel Lawson calls Dr. Wiecke — seemingly based on Lothar Kressig and a few other German judges. Wiecke had resigned as a judge in 1935 rather than serve under the Nazi regime. Wiecke describes how the judicial system was corrupted under Hitler, how sterilization was enforced, and how Janning, who had been one of his students, had cooperated with these efforts. In his cross examination of Wiecke, Rolfe disputes that sterilization was a war crime, stating that it was commonly used in dealing with the mentally deficient. Rolfe proudly and even gleefully quotes U.S. Supreme Court Justice Oliver Wendell Holmes in *Buck v. Bell,* in his upholding a sterilization law, that, "Three generations of imbeciles are enough." He then asks Wiecke if he had sworn an oath of loyalty to Hitler in 1934. When Wiecke stammers that it was mandatory, Rolfe badgers him that if he — a respected man of great importance — had resisted, then the Nazis would not have stayed in power. Rolfe is, then, echoing the "man of stature" argument the Nuremberg tribunal raised concerning Schlegelberger, but he does so to impeach a witness not, as the tribunal used the argument, to condemn a defendant's actions.

As a witness on sterilization, Lawson calls Rudolph Petersen, a baker's helper, who testifies that he was sterilized by the Nazis. He says it was because his father and brothers had angered local Nazi officials, but on cross examination Rolfe argues that Petersen was properly sterilized because he was feebleminded. He asks Petersen to perform a test the Nazis gave — to form a sentence with the words "hare," "hunter," and "field" — which Petersen cannot do. When Rolfe tells the court that Petersen is mentally deficient, Petersen shouts that he has been "since that day." Rolfe coldly replies that the tribunal cannot know how he was before, only how he is now.

To bolster his case, Lawson convinces Irene Hoffman — based on Seillor in the Katzenberger case — to testify about the Feldenstein case. Defendant Emil Hahn — loosely based on Judge Rothaug, who had been the judge in the Katzenberger case — was the prosecutor in the Feldenstein case, and Janning was the presiding judge. Hoffman says Hahn had been determined to convict Feldenstein despite evidence that he had merely been a friend of her family. Hahn had told Hoffman that it was no use to deny having relations, that if she protected Feldenstein she would be arrested for perjury. She said she refused to lie and was arrested. She testifies that Emil Hahn mocked Feldenstein, ridiculed him. Feldenstein was found guilty and executed.

In cross-examination, Rolfe again browbeats the witness, but Janning suddenly ends his courtroom silence and stands, demanding that Rolfe stop.

Judge Haywood makes friends with Madame Bertholt, who with her late husband owned the house where he is living. They are obviously attracted to one another. She talks to the judge about the war and that most Germans didn't know what was happening. The scene then focuses on Germans singing in a bar. The message is that the German people are ready to forget.

Prosecutor Lawson takes the stand as a witness — an unusual move that he justifies based on his experience during the liberation of the Nazi concentration camps — and submits documents to prove the judges and prosecutors had sent thousands to their deaths. Actual film footage is shown, with prisoners and dead bodies. Later, talking among themselves, some of the Nazi judges expressed disbelief in the magnitude of the Holocaust. Hahn is especially angered at being made to watch these films since he feels that he and the other defendants were not responsible.

Janning testifies about the Feldenstein case. He says that there was fear in the country, that Hitler told the people to lift their heads, and that once the gypsies, Jews, and others were destroyed all would be well. He claims that he and others let it happen because they loved their country, that they felt that they could go back to the law when the country was in better financial shape and the people were more confident, but what was going to be a passing phase became a way of life. Janning testifies that he was content to sit by during his trial until he realized the same arguments were being used in his defense that had been used in the Feldenstein trial. Janning denies that Germans were unaware of the exterminations. He says that all knew what was going on, maybe not the details, but only because they did not want to know them.

In his concluding argument, Rolfe insists that if the judges are war criminals, so are the U.S. industrialists who sold weapons to Hitler or the Soviet Union that signed a pact with Hitler so that he could avoid Poland.

With the Cold War beginning — the Russians are blockading Berlin — Haywood is urged to pass light sentences on the defendants. And yet, when the tribunal renders judgment, all four are found guilty and all receive life imprisonment. Judge Haywood and Judge Norris, who had lost a son in the war, vote guilty. Judge Ives dissents. In giving the verdict, Judge Haywood holds the defendants responsible:

> The trial has shown that under a national crisis ordinary men, even extraordinary men, can delude themselves into the commission of crimes so vast and heinous that they beggar the imagination.
>
> The principle of criminal law in every civilized society has this in common: any person who sways another to commit murder, any person who provides the lethal weapon for the purpose of the crime, any person who is an accessory to the crime is guilty.
>
> A country is what it stands for. It is what it stands for when it proves most difficult. Before the people of the world let it now be noted that, here in our decision, this is what we stand for: justice, truth, and the value of a single human being.

Rolfe comes to Haywood just as he is leaving for the airport to say that Janning wants to see him in his cell. Janning gives Haywood summaries he had written of his cases. He tells Haywood that he truly did not know that it would all result in mass executions. Haywood replies, "You knew the first time you sentenced an innocent man to death."

The film concludes with the printed legend that none of the 99 defendants sentenced in the various trials were still serving time by the time the movie was made in 1961.

• **Analysis.** While the film did not deal with the trial of well-known figures such as Herman Goering and Rudolph Hess, it appealed to Kramer and Mann especially because it focused on issues of how those who were to dispense justice could so absolutely corrupt justice, whether laws can be established post-facto and individuals held accountable for crimes against laws that did not exist when they were broken, and whether there is an absolute law or a natural law, in which case the laws are not post-facto.

As with any film based on history, events that occurred over two years are telescoped to fit within its running time of 190 minutes. The sixteen original defendants are reduced to four — all judges. While the actual place and circumstances of the "Justice Trial" are used, names of individuals are changed, the four defendants are made composite characters, and other characters undergo various degrees of fictionalization.

Some of the characters become stereotypes. Prosecutor Gen. Telford Taylor becomes Colonel Lawson, who is portrayed by Richard Widmark as a typical Richard Widmark hero — just as when Errol Flynn played General Custer and boxer James J. Corbett as a typical Errol Flynn hero, and when John Wayne played Townshend Harris in the *Barbarian and the Geisha* (1958), David Crockett in *The Alamo* (1960), and a character based on Lieutenant Kelly in *They Were Expendable* (1945), he was playing a typical John Wayne hero. Widmark had depicted the same type of military man throughout the 1950s in such films as *Halls of Montezuma* (1950), *The Frogmen* (1951), and *Hell and High Water* (1954); in *Time Limit* (1957), he had portrayed a military lawyer. As Lawson, Widmark is rough and tough and gets drunk after Rolfe tears the poor Petersen apart on the stand. The film describes how the fictional Lawson had helped to liberate the death camps — giving him a little bit of Gen. George Patton — the memory of which drives him to prosecute Nazis. By giving Lawson this concentration camp connection, Mann and the filmmakers were suggesting that the prosecutor needed some specific motivation. Lawson's real-life counterpart was evidently thought to be not as interesting. Gen. Telford Taylor was a Harvard Law School graduate, on law review, and a classical and jazz clarinetist. He had almost a decade of service as a government lawyer and served in London in army intelligence from 1943 to 1945. He had been second prosecutor to Justice Robert H. Jackson in the first Nuremberg trial and was reportedly more impressive in cross-examining Herman Goering than Jackson had been.

Janning is portrayed very romantically — this tall, silent, brooding figure for the first part of the film — and this jars with what his real-life model was like. After all, Schlegeberger's actual defense was rooted in pragmatism: if he had resigned over the Nazi's conduct, a harsher man would have taken over. While the actual Nuremberg tribunal described Rothaug as an evil, sadistic man, Hahn is played by Werner Klemperer as a party hack. (The same year, Klemperer portrayed Nazi Adolph Eichman, who was captured and tried in Israel, in a low-budget film *Operation Eichman* and four years later played the comic Nazi POW commandant Colonel Klink in the television series *Hogan's Heroes*.) Rothaug was the judge in the Katzenberger case who arranged to have the Jew Katzenberger executed, but the film makes him the prosecutor in a case based on Katzenberger and claims that Janning was the judge — who sat by, again silently, and let it happen. The final effect, then, is not on Rothaug/Hahn's evil designs against a Jew but on Janning's silence.

Janning echoes some of Schlegelberger's arguments in his defense, but the other three defendants are truly less complicit in the Nazi evil than their real-life counterparts appear to have been. Janning even calls them "party hacks." The three judges act the same way as Haywood's servants, saying that they did not know what was going on and, even if they did, what could they do?

Even with its distortion of whom the judge and prosecutor were in the Katzenberger/Feldenstein case, the film presents that aspect of the trial in a fairly straightforward fashion. However, the overall handling of the defense is where the film is most problematic. Rolfe seems to represent all four defendants, while in reality all had separate counsel. Maximilian Schell won the Academy Award as best actor, although today his portrayal seems very much over the top. (Tracy also was nominated and lost to Schell, and his performance today appears to be much more rock-solid and genuine than Schell's.) The film allows Rolfe to humiliate witness Wiecke by getting him to admit that, even though he resigned in 1935, he had sworn an oath of allegiance to Hitler in 1934. Since Hitler came to power in 1933, swearing an oath of allegiance in 1934 — while the Nazi's techniques were becoming better known — and resigning a year later does not seem especially damning. At least it is much less damning than Janning's complicity, which lasted until the war's end. Also in his cross-examination of Wiecke, Rolfe sets up the argument that sterilization of the medically deficient was an accepted medical procedure in the 1930s and 1940s and justifies the sterilization of Petersen by demonstrating that he is mentally deficient. Admittedly, by quoting Holmes in *Buck v. Bell*, the film shows that historically sterilization was performed in such instances. However, Wiecke has some credibility when he says on the stand that the Nazis brought sterilization to a new high. Montgomery Clift as Petersen was also nominated for an Academy Award as best supporting actor, and his falling apart as Rolfe questions him is heartbreaking and draws the audience sympathy. While Rolfe's argument may be historically accurate, the film's presentation of the issue of sterilization illustrates not only how the mentally deficient were treated in the 1930s and 1940s but how the filmmakers viewed them in 1961 in that Rolfe's defense is presented as a reasonable one. Such treatment of the mentally handicapped has long been judged abhorrent and unreasonable.

Rolfe batters both Petersen and Irene Hoffman on the stand in his cross-examination, making him seem also as villainous as Hahn. This is unfortunate since early in the film it appears that he is being set up as the seeker of truth and justice — a touchstone character for the audience. In his last scene, he is nothing more than go-between for Janning and Haywood.

The film has measures of power as well as truth as Haywood articulates his feelings in his announcement of the verdict and answers Janning so powerfully in his concluding one-on-one in Janning's cell. Yet, in the final moments, the film loses its way completely by announcing that none of the defendants were still in prison when the movie was made. That seems especially alarming when the film has shown that the four defendants all received life sentences. In reality, the actual verdicts were much more mixed. Four defendants were acquitted. Although sentenced to life, Schlegelberger was released on medical parole. Some like Rothenberger were only sentenced to seven years. In short, the fact that none of the defendants were still in prison by 1961 is not in itself surprising. Klemm and Rothaug did have their life sentences commuted. Is the film's conclusion meant to suggest — that in spite of the great effort of the tribunal and Haywood's insistence on justice that justice cannot be given? The announcement also is the equivalent of a crawl, telling what happened to the real people that have been fictionalized in a movie, thus confusing fiction and fact.

The film changes the actual date of the "Justice Trial"—from 1947 to 1948 — to move it into the birth of the Cold War era, something in which the world was still immersed in 1961 when the movie was made, and to provide some grounding as to why public and governmental interest was moving away from the war crime trials when the Soviets were "on the move."

The film fictionalizes characters and compresses events, but what it truly fictionalizes— or at least fails to truly come to terms with — is what the real crimes of the defendants were and what the trial was about. This view was shared by historian Arthur Schlesinger, Jr., in a review of the film:

> It is not fair to criticize this film for failing to solve problems
> which will torment moral philosophers for a long time to come.
> Yet even accepting its own assumptions, one is surely justified in

expecting a certain consistency about the impression it is trying to leave in its audience's mind.[57]

• *Litigation.* None known.

Reynolds-Pegler Libel Case (1954)
A Case of Libel (1988)

THE FACTS

Quentin Reynolds was a noted journalist, described as two-fisted and hard living. He covered the rise of Nazism in Germany in the 1930s, and by the start of World War II, he and Edward R. Murrow were the principal U.S. journalists in Europe. He wrote extensively about the war, often from the front lines. He averaged twenty articles a year for *Collier's* magazine and published twenty-five books, including *The Wounded Don't Cry, London Diary, Dress Rehearsal,* and *Courtroom,* a biography of lawyer Samuel S. Leibowitz. Reynolds became such a well-known personality that he played himself in the 1947 movie *Golden Earrings* starring Ray Milland and Marlene Dietrich. Reynolds even wrote a screenplay — *Miracle of the Bells* (1948) starring Frank Sinatra and Fred MacMurray.

Westbrook Pegler began his career as a sports writer, but he soon branched out into other types of journalism, winning the 1940 Pulitzer Prize for exposing labor union racketeers. An arch conservative, he began writing columns known for their withering wit. Over the years, after issuing columns approving of lynch mobs and attacking people mercilessly without cause, he became the epitome of low, nasty journalism. In his 1950 letter to the *Washington Post* music critic Paul Hume, in which he lambasted Hume for criticizing Truman's daughter's singing, President Harry S Truman wrote, "Pegler, a guttersnipe, was a gentleman along side you."

One of Pegler's targets was Reynolds. In one of his columns syndicated in 186 newspapers, Pegler called Reynolds "yellow," an "absentee war correspondent," and someone with "a protuberant belly filled with something other than guts" — Reynolds was 6'5" and weighed 250 pounds. Reynolds sued Pegler and his newspapers for libel, hiring Louis Nizer to represent him. Pegler countersued, claiming Reynolds had libeled him in a book review.

In his autobiography, Nizer describes the preparation for the trial and includes large portions of the trial transcript.[58] Nizer flew to London to interview people who had known Reynolds during the war and obtained an affidavit from Lord Mountbatten, war hero and member of the royal family, attesting to Reynolds' bravery. In his answer to the complaint, Pegler actually embellished his libelous claims and then published portions of these new claims in one of his columns. His attacks continued, and at one point Reynolds' wife went to Pegler and begged him to stop. Pegler agreed to if Reynolds dropped the case. Nizer later scolded Mrs. Reynolds for the "psychological damage" she had caused, but he informed Pegler's attorney that Mrs. Reynolds had had no authority to settle the case.

In his direct testimony, Pegler referred to other articles that he claimed he had relied on in making his statements about Reynolds. On cross-examination, Nizer got Pegler to admit that he had read those articles after he wrote his columns and not before. He caught Pegler in numerous other lies. Concerning Pegler's claim that Reynolds and a woman who was not his wife had been going about nude, Nizer confronted him with the fact that he had added the claim four years after his initial answer to the complaint—suggesting that it had not happened but rather that Pegler had made it up. He got Pegler to admit that it was known that Reynolds was allergic to the sun and that it would then be unlikely that he would have been able to frolic about in the nude on a sunny day. Several times during his testimony, Pegler asked Nizer not to stand too close to him, and Nizer made a great deal of this, causing the judge to caution Pegler that he had no say in where the plaintiff's attorney stood. Nizer then read Pegler columns by Reynolds and asked if Pegler thought that they showed Reynolds to be a communist sympathizer. When Pegler said they did, Nizer read him others that Pegler had written but for which Nizer did not identify the author. Assuming that these were by Reynolds as well, Pegler continued to claim that the author was obviously a "Red" until Nizer let the authorship be known.

Reynolds won $1 in compensatory damages but $175,001 in punitive damages—at the time the largest libel judgment ever. With costs and services added, the amount exceeded $200,000.

The judgment may have weakened Pegler's reputation and marketability but not his opinions. In 1963, at the height of the Civil Rights movement, he claimed that it is "clearly the bounden duty of all intelligent Americans to proclaim and practice bigotry."[59] By then his views had become too extreme even for the Hearst papers, and his column was cancelled in 1962. He continued writing as a freelancer until his death in 1969. Reynolds had died in 1965, his journalistic career too having lessened in its impact, if only because of the coming of television.

The Film

Nizer published his autobiography, *My Life in Court,* in 1961. It stayed on the best seller list for 72 weeks.[60] A section of the book described the Reynolds-Pegler case, and Henry Denker used this part of Nizer's book as the basis for his play, *A Case of Libel.* The play debuted on Broadway at the Longacre Theater on October 10, 1963. Denker took the basic premise of the case and used parts of the trial transcript but then fictionalized the characters. Reynolds and Pegler were both still alive. The Broadway production starred Van Heflin as Robert Sloane — based on Nizer, Larry Gates as Boyd Bendix — based on Pegler, and John Randolph as Dennis Corcoran — based on Reynolds. *A Case of Libel* was well respected by attorneys for the authenticity of its behind-the-scenes interplay against the background of a trial.

The play was filmed for television in 1968 with Heflin repeating his Broadway role, Jose Ferrer taking on the part of Bendix, and Arthur Hill, Corcoran. The play was filmed again in 1983 for the television cable network Showtime.[61] It starred Edward Asner, fresh from his television series roles as Lou Grant in *The Mary Tyler Moore Show* and *Lou Grant,* as Sloane; Daniel J. Travanti, then starring in the series *Hill Street Blues,* as Bendix; and Gordon Pinsent as Corcoran. The 1983 version was released on videotape. Denker, author of the military trial play *Time Limit,* later wrote a trial film — *Twilight of Honor* (1963) — and two trial teleplays — *Judgment: The Court Martial of Lieutenant William Calley* (1975) and *Outrage* (1985). Nizer died in 1994.

In the film, Corcoran sues Bendix for libel based on columns in which Bendix alleges that Reynolds was a coward when he was a war correspondent, that Bendix witnessed Corcoran's "whoring around" with a scantily clad woman, and that Reynolds was a communist sympathizer. Corcoran tells Sloane that he cannot find work because Bendix's columns have harmed his reputation. Unfortunately, Sloane cannot locate any of the people who turned down Corcoran's work who are willing to testify — so afraid are they of Bendix's power. This inhibits their ability to prove actual damages. During trial preparation, Corcoran's wife begs Bendix to stop his attacks. Sloane says this might have been a "fatal mistake," but the trial goes on anyway.

On the stand, Bendix is arrogant and surly to Sloane during cross-examination. He insists on standing while he testifies and objects when Sloane gets too close to him. During Sloane's questioning, he even suggests that Sloane and his colleague are communists.

Sloane's young colleague had seen Bendix writing out phrases — as well as alternative phrases—that in his direct testimony he attributed to other people. The young man is able to read upside down and remembers some of the alternate phrases. The yellow legal pad sheet had been discarded. During his cross-examination of Bendix, Sloane pretends to read from a blank yellow legal pad sheet and asks Bendix if the words Sloane's colleague saw sound familiar. Bendix assumes that Sloane has his discarded paper and becomes frazzled since he thinks Sloane is able to expose his lies. He again demands that Sloane not stand too close to him. Sloane then inquires of Bendix if he feels that Corcoran had always been a communist, and Bendix says the conversion was gradual. Sloane reads a number of passages, all of which Bendix identifies as communist-leaning. Sloane tells Bendix that only the first two were by Corcoran, the rest were by Bendix himself. Furious, Bendix shouts at Sloane that Bendix will destroy him. Sloane snaps at Bendix, "Now, I'm afraid, sir, that you have been standing too close to me. And frankly, I don't like it." For the first time, Bendix sits down. The jury awards substantial punitive damages to Corcoran.

• **Analysis.** The film carries the gist and much of the spirit of the actual case. In adapting Nizer's material for the stage, Denker streamlined it radically, cutting out most of the other witnesses and all of the issues of what Bendix/Pegler read and when he read it. He focuses on the more sensational aspects of Pegler's testimony—nude swimming—and Nizer's trap of getting Bendix to described his own writings as communist-leaning. Some of the dialogue is very close to the actual trial testimony. Pegler did indeed complain that Nizer was standing too close to him.

Bendix, however, has characteristics not only of Pegler but of other famous columnists such as Walter Winchell and becomes a mouthpiece for all forms of ranting, conservative zealotry. Pegler did not stand during his testimony but did rise on several occasions in anger over Nizer's questions and inferences. Denker also fills up the plot with cliché legal tricks. Rather than having Sloane painstakingly show Bendix/Pegler how he had embellished on his earlier deposition statements, as Nizer did, Denker introduces a young associate for Sloane who can read upside down and actually tell Sloane/Nizer that Bendix/Pegler was making things up. The trick with the blank yellow legal pad sheet was seemingly taken from Agatha Christie's *Witness for the Prosecution*, which had been filmed in 1957 starring Charles Laughton as the ingenious barrister Sir Wilfrid Robarts.[62] In that film, Robarts asks Christine Vole, the prosecutor's main witness, if she had written a particular letter and starts to read from a white sheet of paper. When Vole says that the paper cannot be her stationery and describes it, Robarts thanks her for identifying her stationery and then produces the real letter. What he had been pretending to be reading from, he tells the court, had been a bill for Bermuda shorts

All in all, though, the film captures much of the sense and feel of the original trial. It was obviously done with Nizer's approval — since his book is credited as the source.

• **Litigation.** None known. Reynolds criticized the play on a radio program but told the *New York Times* in an interview that he would not sue Nizer.[63]

Big Dan's Tavern Rape Trial (1983)
The Accused (1988)

THE FACTS

On March 6, 1983 a 21-year-old woman entered Big Dan's Tavern in New Bedford, Massachusetts.[64] She was a native of the New Bedford and had just celebrated her older daughter's third birthday. She had told her boyfriend to watch over their three children while she went for cigarettes. However, she stayed at the bar, ordered a drink, and talked with a waitress whom she knew. She enjoyed a few more drinks and then decided to talk to some men over by the pool table. Later that night, three men forced her onto the pool table. They repeatedly raped her while she struggled to get away. No one in the bar helped her; instead, many men continued to stand around the pool table to watch and cheer on the violent act. She finally was able to run screaming from the bar, wearing only a sock and jacket, and flagged down a passing pickup truck for help. She told the driver she had been gang-raped, and he took her to a hospital.

The woman decided to press charges against the men who raped her. The trial was one of the first to receive television coverage. The prosecutor was Ronald A. Pina, who, like the defendants, was of Portuguese descent. The town of New Bedford was the home for first- and second-generation immigrants from Portugal. There were six defendants— three accused of rape, one who had tickled the woman during the rape, and two bystanders who cheered on the rapists. Six men were formally charged with aggravated rape. Among those men were Joseph Vieira, 26; Daniel Silvio, 26; Virgilio Medeiros, 24; Jose Medeiros, 23; and Victor Raposo. The trial date was set for October 11, 1983, by a Bristol County judge. Eventually, Judge William Young granted a defense motion to sever the cases of Vieira and Silvio, resulting in two cases starting on the same day.

The case received extensive press coverage, both print and broadcast, which resulted in community interest and protests, both for and against the victim. The press's continual reference that the defendants were Portuguese fueled resentment and charges of racism in the Portuguese community. Two witnesses later gave interviews in which they claimed the woman had not resisted. In response, the group "Portuguese Americans United" (PAU) charged that media attention has created "a psychological state of siege toward a particular ethnic group." Columnists and women's groups jumped in to defend the woman. One cable television station decided to break tradition and refer to the woman by name.

At trial, the woman testified twice in, what some would describe, a clinical and dispassionate manner. Since there was little question that the men had been in the bar, the defense's strategy was to discredit the woman, both in cross examination and by presenting witnesses that suggested a whole range of arguments, including that the sex was consensual, that the woman was a liar, that she was drunk, that she had previously accused other men of rape, that she had sold her story to a publisher, and that she was a welfare cheat. Virtually all of these charges were, according to Helen Benedict in her book *Virgin or Vamp: How the Press Covers Sex Crimes*, either erroneous or irrelevant — what did her "welfare status" have to do with rape?[65] There was, however, a serious, relevant, and unresolved question about how many men had been in the bar. During the trial, one of the defendants gave an interview in which he said the woman had "asked them for sex."

Three of the defendants were convicted of aggravated rape and sentenced to nine to twelve years and the "tickler" was convicted and received a sentence of six to eight years. The two defendants who had been charged with "joint enterprise" were acquitted. All of the convictions were affirmed by the Massachusetts Supreme Court.

Big Dan's Tavern was closed and converted into a bakery. Judge Young went on to become chief justice of the U.S. District Court for the District of Massachusetts. Ronald A. Pina was voted out of office in 1990 amid some controversy of his handling of his duties. The rape victim moved to Florida, where she was killed in an auto accident, leaving two children. According to reports, she had fled New England after having been in the harsh spotlight of the trial and resorted to drink and cocaine. Her body was found to contain three times the amount of alcohol used to define drunk driving in that state.

Before the rape, *Hustler* magazine ran a feature in January 1983 that showed a woman being gang-raped on a pool table. In response to the Big Dan's Tavern "pool table" rape, which was seemingly modeled on *Hustler's* story, *Hustler* published a postcard of another nude woman on a pool table, this time with the inscription, "Greetings from New Bedford, Mass. The Portuguese Gang-Rape Capital of America."

THE FILM

The Accused is based on the Bedford, Massachusetts, event, although the names are fictionalized and the story tweaked. Jodie Foster, playing Sarah Tobias, the fictional name given to the rape victim, received the Academy Award as best actress. Also in the cast were Kelly McGillis as prosecutor Kathryn Murphy, Bernie Coulson as Kenneth Joyce, Leo Rossi as Cliff "Scorpion" Albrecht, Steve Antin as Bob Joiner, and Carmen Argenziano as Paul Rudolph. The film was directed by Jonathan Kaplan with a screenplay by Tom Topor. In 2000, Topor wrote the teleplay for *Perfect Murder, Perfect Town: Jon Benét and the City of Boulder* about the murder of young Jon Benét Ramsey.

Tobias goes into a local bar one night after getting into an argument with her boyfriend. She has dressed in an alluring manner. She talks to Sally Frazer, a waitress friend, has a few drinks, and smokes some pot at the bar. A little later in the night, a man comes over to her, buys her a drink, and starts to dance with her. Three men then rape her by pinning her against the pinball machine — rather than a pool table. Some customers cheer the rapists on. When Sarah finally gets out of the bar, she runs outside screaming, and someone picks her up and brings her to the hospital.

District Attorney Murphy decides that Tobias' past could be used against her in court. Feeling that she cannot prove rape, especially since many in the bar are likely to testify that Tobias "asked for it," Murphy strikes a plea bargain whereby the rapists plead guilty to "reckless endangerment," for which they will serve no more than nine months in jail. Feeling that Murphy has sold her out, Tobias berates her and then convinces Murphy to charge the men who cheered the attackers on with "criminal solicitation." When Rudolph, Murphy's supervisor, tells her not to pursue the new case, Murphy threatens to quit and to sue the D.A.'s office. He relents.

Murphy finds a fraternity brother of one of the rapists — Joyce — who is ashamed that he did not stop them. He testifies, and the three new defendants are convicted.

• ***Analysis.*** The film is well presented and deals with the important issue of how a rape victim can — on the basis of past behavior — become the accused. It follows the basic outline of the actual rape case and the unusual charging of the men who cheered the defendants on with complicity.

However, the film focuses on this unusual aspect and ignores the actual outcome, which was less unusual in all ways but the more dramatic one. The rapists were convicted. Those who cheered the rapists on were acquitted. In this way alone, the film completely distorts the case.

The film ignores the Portuguese community element of the case. The rapists are more conventional barroom denizens. The case turns on a student discovering a conscience and informing on the others. Again, this was a conventional plot device that had nothing to do with the actual case.

Carol Clover notes that the movie makes the sole source of authority a male spectator — in fact, the rape is only shown during his testimony — who informs on the men in the bar. In some ways, then, the woman's account is shown to be insufficient and requires an objective — and male — affirmation to the believed.[66, 67] The young man serves much the same function as the eyewitness in the Japanese film *Rashômon*[68] and its American remake *The Outrage*,[69] in which, after various versions of the story are told, all benefiting the teller, a third party who has actually seen what happened comes forward to establish "the truth." It is an interesting dramatic technique.

The most obvious fictionalization in the film is the gender of the prosecutor, who has been changed from a man to woman, presumably to indicate more of a bond between the film's two protagonists. The film is, then, able to paint a dual progression of one ambitious young woman becoming more human while a less educated young woman stands up for herself and shows herself to be smart as well as brave. At the same time, however, it can be argued that by making the prosecutor a coprotagonist, the film takes some of the focus off the rape victim's story.

The film portrays Tobias as feeling betrayed by Murphy, although Murphy is not her attorney and in fact has a duty to the state only to prosecute cases that she thinks she can win. Her threat to sue the district attorneys office is undoable since prosecutors have immunity concerning decisions about which cases to prosecute — otherwise, victims and family members would sue them all the time.

By turning the actual prosecution inside out, the film ignores the actual drama of the courtroom trial in which the rapists were punished. Carol Clover writes, *"The Accused* shows the system working — but only barely (only by loophole, actually), and only slowly, and only because a man of goodwill and a very smart, sympathetic, and stubborn female lawyer happened to be in the right place at the right time."[70] This is, then, a well-intentioned fantasy. In reality, the system worked, and it didn't matter. The men were convicted of rape; the woman was condemned. She was named; her past was exposed; she was driven from her community and to drink and, ultimately, self-destruction.

• *Litigation.* None known.

Von Bulow Murder Trial (1985)
Reversal of Fortune (1990)

THE FACTS

Claus von Bulow was born in Copenhagen, Denmark on August 11, 1926.[71] He was the son of a noted playwright, Svend Borberg, and Ionna Bulow Borberg. Claus was well educated at private boarding schools and received his law degree from Cambridge University. He left the practice of law to work for oil billionaire John Paul Getty as his executive assistant. It was at a party at Getty's estate that he met Princess Sunny von Auersperg, born Martha Crawford, an American heiress. She had married an Austrian prince with whom she had two children, Ala and Alexander. Sunny divorced her husband and moved back to the United States. On June 6, 1966, she married von Bulow. They seemed a fairy tale couple — rich, handsome, and cultured. However, shortly after the birth of their daughter, Cosima, the marriage began to disintegrate.

Claus complained publicly about his dissatisfaction with his marriage — his wife was reclusive; he was unemployed and always needed money, but Sunny would not let him work. In 1979, he began an affair with a former soap opera actress Alexandra Isles. Isles, a divorcée and mother of one son, insisted that Claus seek a divorce. But divorce would have left him with a fraction of the wealth he enjoyed with Sunny. In December of 1979 and again in December of 1980, Sunny von Bulow fell into a coma. She recovered from the first one, but the second was irreversible. On both occasions, it was noted that her blood sugar was dangerously low, possibly indicating a high level of insulin in her system. After the second coma, Sunny's children, Ala and Alexander, began an search of their stepfather's room that led to his indictment for attempted murder.

The von Bulow trial drew enormous attention from the public and the media. It was the first time a trial was broadcast on television. Von Bulow was convicted in his first trial and sentenced to 30 years in prison.

Freed on bail, Von Bulow engaged the services of noted Harvard law professor Alan M. Dershowitz to organize his appeal. Dershowitz found some likelihood that Sunny's coma was self-induced, as friends cataloged a lifetime of drug and alcohol abuse interspersed with mammoth food binges, a potentially lethal combination for a known reactive hypoglycemic (someone who suffers from low blood sugar). Even more revealing, Sunny's maid Maria Schrallhammers' memory was seriously flawed. Dershowitz found some notes made at the time by family attorney Richard Kuh, which unveiled grave inconsistencies in the maid's various statements.

Dershowitz filed a new trial motion with the Rhode Island Supreme Court that included arguments he planned to make at trial if the court ordered a new one. The motion drew attention to the new evidence — which would normally only be considered by the trial court if a new trial were ordered — and planted seeds of doubt in the judges' minds. The court reversed the lower court's decision based on the state's failure to disclose Kuh's notes and on unlawful search and seizure — the children did not need a warrant to search the closet, but the police needed one to test the contents of the bag.

The Rhode Island Supreme Court reversed the conviction and ordered a new trial. In neither trial did Claus von Bulow take the witness stand. On June 10, 1985, the jury acquitted Von Bulow on all counts

After his acquittal, Claus no longer felt at home in America and moved back to England in 1987. Von Bulow's acquittal was not the end of his legal woes. His stepchildren sued for $56 million in a civil suit. Later, von Bulow agreed to divorce Sunny and never speak or write about the trials. At this writing, Sunny von Bulow remains in a coma in a private New York hospital.

The Film

The movie *Reversal of Fortune*[72] is based on the book by the same name by Dershowitz. It was directed by Barbet Schroeder, with a screenplay by Nicholas Kazan. (Kazan, interestingly enough, is the son of Elia Kazan, who had directed *Boomerang,* previously discussed.) It starred Jeremy Irons as Claus von Bulow, Glenn Close as Sunny von Bulow, Ron Silver as Alan Dershowitz, and Uta Hagen as Maria. The film was nominated for two Academy Awards — Irons for best actor and Schroeder as best director. Irons won.

The movie is narrated by Sunny von Bulow, who is in a coma. In her remembering, the audience sees the von Bulows, a glittering high-society couple married for 13 years. They dislike each other but remain together — he for her money, she for his companionship. Claus von Bulow is having an affair with Alexandra Isles.

At Christmastime in 1979, Sunny goes into a coma. Claus says that she is sleeping off a hangover and refuses to call a doctor, saying that Sunny detests them. When Sunny has difficulty breathing, he finally calls the doctors, who revive her. A year later, Sunny goes into a coma again and is found unconscious in the bathroom of her Newport home. It is below freezing outside and yet the window is open. Sunny does not recover this time.

Maria tells Sunny's children by her first marriage of her suspicions about von Bulow. With an investigator's help, they break into Claus's closet and find a black bag that contains a syringe with a needle incrusted with insulin, a container of insulin, and Claus's medicines. No one in the family is diabetic. Claus is charged with two counts of assault with intent to commit murder. The prosecution highlights his suspicious behavior and how much he would gain financially with Sunny's death. Claus is convicted and sentenced to 30 years.

Dershowitz agrees to take Claus's appeal so he can support his pro bono work and also because he sees an important constitutional issue at stake involving the family's exerting control over the evidence gathered. Claus tells Dershowitz that Sunny tried to commit suicide and that she took his black bag. Dershowitz finds that there was no inventory kept of the search of Claus's closet or what was in the black bag. He also shows that if the needle had been used to inject Sunny, it would have been wiped clean rather than having a point incrusted with dried insulin. This suggests to Dershowitz that someone has tried to frame Claus.

The Rhode Island Supreme Court reverses von Bulow's conviction and orders a new trial. The jury acquits him on all counts.

• **Analysis.** The film stays very close to the facts, although it provides some unique interpretations. It is colored, for example, by Sunny's narration.

Schroeder and Kazan admittedly tweaked the personal side of Alan Dershowitz in the film for the sake of dramatic effect, making him a brash and loud-talking white knight — but still a white knight. Dershowitz was mainly happy with the way he was portrayed except in one scene where he's shown throwing a portable phone on the ground and smashing it to pieces. Dershowitz even wrote an editorial in the *New York Times* pleading innocent to ever smashing a phone in his entire life. In a June 9, 1999, CNN interview looking back at the O.J. Simpson trial, Dershowitz rather flippantly answered a question about the portrayal of him in the movie:

> I think [it was] was a very accurate portrayal of the legal issues in that case, and its complexity. Of course, no one ever likes the way they are personally portrayed, though I can't complain because

Ron Silver is a lot better looking than I am, though I am a better basketball player.

• *Litigation.* None known about the film. Sunny's children did sue von Bulow for $56 million in a civil case for common law assault, negligence, fraud, and RICO violations. As part of that case, the plaintiffs asked the court to rule that Dershowitz's book amounted to a waiver of attorney-client privilege. The district court ruled that attorney-client privilege had been waived, but the Second Circuit reversed.[73] The plaintiffs agreed to drop the suit in return for von Bulow's renunciation of any claims he might have to his wife's estate.

Conclusions

The 13 films about legal cases discussed here are largely films of merit. Of the 13, six were nominated for best screenplay Oscars—*Young Mr. Lincoln, Boomerang, Court Martial of Billy Mitchell, Inherit the Wind, Judgment at Nuremberg,* and *Man for All Seasons*—and the last two won. *Seasons* also won the Oscar for best film of its year, and *The Andersonville Trial* won the Emmy as best outstanding single program for the year. The 13 films show the range of variances from factual accuracy in films based on facts.

In *The Court Martial of Billy Mitchell, Amistad, The Trials of Oscar Wilde,* and *Reversal of Fortune,* while there are some composite characters and other fictionalizations for dramatic purposes, the names, places, and plots are generally as they were in fact. The films convey the gist and spirit of the actual trials.

A Case of Libel, Compulsion, and *Boomerang* all change the names of the major characters. *A Case of Libel* and *Compulsion,* however, actually quote from the transcripts of the original trials. All three films are true to the historical period of the cases. *A Case of Libel* introduces some unhistorical, cliché courtroom tricks, and *Boomerang* blends in some unhistorical melodrama — blackmailed wife, suicide in the courtroom — and makes the district attorney younger to create more tension as he decides what to do. Reflecting the period in which it was made, *Compulsion* waffles on the sexual orientation of the defendants. All three films, however, are true to the spirit of the actual events.

Young Mr. Lincoln makes the same historical adjustment that *Boomerang* does— making the attorney younger than he was in real life. Perhaps because the historical character in *Boomerang*—Cummings—is less well-known than Lincoln and because *Boomerang* changes the names

of the participants and Lincoln is Lincoln in *Young Mr. Lincoln*, the adjustment seems like a larger lapse in *Lincoln*.

A Man for All Seasons presents the basic story of Thomas More faithfully, but its portrayal of More is an uneasy blend of Brechtian alienation
and saints' plays.

Judgment at Nuremberg, *Inherit the Wind*, *The Andersonville Trial*,
and *The Accused* all fictionalize the characters and events. *The Accused* mis-
represents the verdicts—the actual rapists were convicted and those who
were charged with complicity were acquitted. But more importantly, the
film distorts the facts to promote a particular viewpoint. The *Accused* has
a feminist orientation. It changes the sex of the district attorney arguing
the case to a woman who, with the rape victim, join together to prosecute
those who cheered on the rapists. *Inherit the Wind* turns the actual Scopes
monkey trial into a story of progress versus faith and promotes the myth
of the trial that Drummond humiliated and destroyed Bryan on the stand.
Judgment at Nuremberg changes the date of the actual "justice trial" to
move it closer to the start of the Cold War and seems uncertain of its own
viewpoint. *The Andersonville Trial* invents the motivations of a major character.

It should also be noted that Nizer and Dershowitz were alive when *A
Case of Libel* and *Reversal of Fortune* were filmed and that the movies were
based on their books. Their portrayals in the film emphasize their courage.

IV

What Protection for
Dramatic Fictional Personas?

Oh, my darlin' Clementine.
Do I sound like Gene Autry? Can he sue me, Clementine?
— Bing Crosby, 1941 Decca
recording

The answer to the question that Bing Crosby raised in a parody version of "My Darlin' Clementine"[1]—can an artist sue when another borrows or steals his or her persona—is probably not, but it depends.[2] This is an extension of the issue of fictionalization in film raised in Chapter I. Film and television performers, and even recording artists, with the help of writers and directors, have created personas, sometimes using their own names, that were and are fictionalizations. Charlie, the Little Tramp, was not really Charlie Chaplin. Jack Benny was not really the stingy miser he portrayed in film and television. Yet, who owned the persona? While people may claim that film characters have defamed them or violated their rights of privacy or publicity, what of the rights of the actors who create or at least help create fictional personas identified with them?

Actors can control by contract the use of their image. In roughly half of the United States, there is by statute a right of publicity; in ten of those states, that right can be passed to heirs. There is substantial case law in which movie stars and other celebrities have sued to protect their rights to control use of their likeness, voice, and personality. The comedian and

149

film director Woody Allen, for example, sought an injunction and damages for an advertisement that showed an impersonator of Allen endorsing a product — a misappropriation of Allen's own personality.[3]

The licensing of the images of actors living and dead has become a big business.[4] While most attention has been focused on an individual's right to protect his or her own name, personality, and likeness, there has been some issue or at least question of the protection of a fictional persona with which an individual acquires an identification. Extending the question of whether the events and characters of a motion picture or television show are in and of themselves "fictitious," what happens when the actor and the fiction he or she embodies blend? What happens when an actor becomes so identified with a role that it is the actor and the role and not just the actor's image that is at issue? What happens when there is no contract and the use of the likeness or voice straddles the various applicable laws—copyright, trademark — that none seem to apply.

The actions that are the subject of this chapter go beyond the performer's natural persona and beyond a single performance and instead concern the creation of a fictional persona through a series of performances, usually by playing the same character in several films or television shows— Bela Lugosi as Dracula, Stan Laurel and Oliver Hardy as Laurel and Hardy, Roy Rogers as Roy Rogers King of the Cowboys, and Julius, Arthur, and Leonard Marx as the Marx Brothers.

If there was a specific spark that caused these actions to grow, it was the showing of old movies on television in the 1940s and 1950s.[5] Actors (or their heirs) saw their movies broadcast and sometimes serving as the basis for regular television programming — the Laurel and Hardy Theatre, the Bowery Boys Weekly Movie, the Abbott and Costello Film Festival. Because of their renewed popularity, their likenesses in character — Laurel and Hardy in their bowler hats and narrow ties, for example — were placed on school lunch boxes and other merchandise. Yet for all of this, they received no remuneration because others claimed the right to use their personas. Some of the actors sought protection in the courts.

The dissenting California Supreme Court Justice in *Lugosi v. Universal Studios*, distinguished the various types of claims that had been or might be brought and argued for consistent protection of dramatic fictional personas:

> Because the right [of publicity] prohibits the unauthorised [*sic*] commercial use of an individual's identity, the right clearly applies to the person's name and likeness. However, such protection would appear to be insufficient because many people create public recognition not only in their "natural" appearance but in their portrayal

of particular characters. Charlie Chaplin's Little Tramp, Carroll O'Connor's Archie Bunker, and Flip Wilson's Judge and Geraldine exemplify such creations.... There appears to be no reason why the right of publicity should not extend to one's own likeness while portraying a particular fictional character.[6]

Opinions in the cases under analysis are not clear-cut. Even while denying Bela Lugosi's heirs an inheritable right to promote his likeness in the fictional character of Count Dracula, a justice of the California Supreme Court concurring in the decision conceded that such personas *could* obtain protection:

> An original creation of a fictional figure played exclusively by its creator may well be protectible. [Others besides Lugosi had played the role.] Thus Groucho Marx, with his moustache, cigar, slouch and leer, cannot be exploited by others. Red Skelton's variety of self-devised roles would appear to be protectible, as would creations of Abbott and Costello, Laurel and Hardy and others of that genre.[7]

Because films and television programs are collaborative efforts, an individual performer's rights may often be uncertain. Another thing that has seemingly affected court decisions in these cases is the shifting, ephemeral nature of what is at issue: while the actor's performance is usually *fixed* on film or tape, it is not a single performance that is at issue but a series of performances that create a character that is identified with the actor. These combined performances forming a distinct persona float over the head like an airy mist, like Macbeth's dagger of the mind they seem so real and yet cannot be grasped.

The complexity and fascination of these cases may derive from their crossing over so many areas of law dealt with in previous chapters—copyright, unfair competition, the right of privacy, the right of publicity, and contract. In addition to the variety of causes of action and their simultaneous assertion in many of the suits, the cases have been complicated by a convergence of these various laws. One commentator notes that the "look and feel" copyright infringement test has been used in trademark cases, while the public confusion test for trademark infringement has been utilized in copyright analysis.[8]

In addition, appreciation of these issues has had to evolve over time. It is significant that so many of these cases span years of trials and appeals, remands, and reverses. The Lugosi case covered fourteen years from initial complaint to the decision of the appeals court.

Another early example shows the difficulties of these cases. Victor

DeCosta, a rodeo cowboy, created an Old West character called Paladin, who dressed in black, wore a mustache, and handed out a card that read, "Have Gun Will Travel Wire Paladin." While DeCosta had begun performing his "Paladin" character at rodeos and charitable functions in 1947, in 1957 the Columbia Broadcasting System (CBS) premiered *Have Gun Will Travel*, a weekly television western starring Richard Boone as Paladin, who wore black, had a mustache, and handed out a card that read, "Have Gun Will Travel Wire Paladin." The series ran for six years and was later popular in syndication.[9] It was in the top ten in the Nielsen ratings from 1957 through 1961. Its theme song was a hit single in the early 1960s.[10] Richard Boone, who played Paladin, became a star.[11]

In 1963, as the series was ending its first run, DeCosta applied to register "Have Gun Will Travel Wire Paladin" with its chessman logo with the U.S. trademark office[12] and sued CBS for misappropriation of his idea, common law trademark and/or service mark infringement, and unfair competition. The misappropriation count was severed and tried before a jury. While CBS claimed that the similarity between DeCosta's performances and the CBS television character were the result of "spontaneous creation," the jury awarded DeCosta $150,000 in damages. CBS appealed, and the court held that, while the jury's disbelief in CBS's "spontaneous creation" explanation was certainly understandable, under the existing copyright law DeCosta's copyright had not been registered, the distribution of the calling cards constituted publication without notice, and the work was therefore in the public domain and could be used freely by CBS.[13]

As to whether DeCosta's fictional character could be copyrighted at all, the court appeared to accept CBS's contention that DeCosta's "creation being a personal characterization was not reduced and could not be reduced to an [identifiable, durable, material] form" and added,

> [We] think it sensible to say that the constitutional clause extends to any concrete, describable manifestation of intellectual creation, and to the extent that a creation may be ineffable we think it ineligible for protection against copying simpliciter under either state or federal law.[14]

Seven years later, on the trademark issue, a magistrate found for DeCosta,[15] and once again the First Circuit reversed,[16] finding no deliberate "deceiving" by CBS and insufficient similarity between marks. Ultimately, the patent and trademark office granted DeCosta's trademark application.[17] Meanwhile, CBS had assigned syndication rights to the series to Viacom, and DeCosta sued Viacom in 1991 for trademark infringement and unfair competition. Nearly thirty years after DeCosta's initial complaint, the First Circuit held that the judgment against DeCosta in the prior case collaterally had estopped his relitigation of the issue of likelihood of confusion.[18]

DeCosta argued that there had been significant changes in the trademark law between his first trial in 1967 and the 1992 decision. In addition, the 1976 copyright law had weakened the registration requirement on which the 1967 court had relied. But the First Circuit summed up DeCosta's 29-year saga succinctly, noting the difficulty of fixing the infringement within established standards:

> Mr. DeCosta's original legal problem lay in his inability to bring his case within a particular set of protective rules. Copyright law, for example, might in principle have offered protection for his "Have Gun — Will Travel" calling card, but he had brought the card into the public domain by distributing it widely, without giving the kind of specific "copyright" notice that federal copyright law requires.... Mr. DeCosta's present legal problem is that he sued CBS and lost."[19]

The "inability to bring [a] case within a particular set of protective rules" has been a characteristic of actions concerning fictional dramatic personas. As the following discussions will show, the cases evidence a searching by plaintiffs through various laws—copyright, trademark, unfair competition, right of privacy, right of publicity, forsaking one when it has failed for others and pursuing another — attempting to find a proper fit.

Another aspect of the initial DeCosta case that is significant, especially given the seeming inability to find a "fit" for fictional personas, is the First Circuit's assertion that performers' rights were governed by *Sears, Roebuck & Co. v. Stiffel*[20] and *Compco Corp. v. Day-Brite Lighting, Inc.*,[21] in which the court affirmed a "strong federal policy favoring free competition in ideas which do not merit or qualify for patent protection."[22]

Relevant law to the issue include copyright, trademark and unfair competition, right of privacy/publicity, and contract law.

Copyright

PERFORMER'S COPYRIGHT
(AND THE IDEA OF PERFORMERS' RIGHTS)

The copyright for the works themselves in which actors and other performers appear have inevitably been registered by the studios or companies that have produced the films, broadcasts, or recordings. The copyright law invests initial ownership of a copyright in the author or authors or a work.[23] The problem is, of course, that a performance is but a part of a dramatic work. Performers in these roles are typically regarded as employees doing work for hire,[24] and the copyright is consequently owned by the employer. In the first 75 years of the twentieth century, U.S. performers' rights claims in the manner of their performance were made through common law copyright. However, the 1976 copyright law revision eliminated common law copyrights.[25] Discussions of performers' rights in these earlier cases, however, provide important background for later decisions.

In 1937, a radio station played recordings of Fred Waring's orchestra that were marked "not licensed for radio broadcast." The Pennsylvania court held that a performing artist can have a property right in his performance in the nature of a common law copyright:

> [I]t must be clear that such actors, for example, as David Garrick, Mrs. Siddons, Rachel Booth, Coquelin, Sarah Bernhardt, and Sir Henry Irving, or such vocal and instrumental artists as Jenny Lind, Melba, Caruso, Paderewski, Kreisler, and Toscanini, by their interpretations, definitely added something to the work of authors and composers which not only gained for themselves enduring fame, but enabled them to enjoy the financial rewards from the public, in recognition of their unique genius.... The law has never considered it necessary, for the establishment of property rights in intellectual or artistic productions, that the entire ultimate product should be the work of a single creator. Such rights may be acquired by one who perfects the original work or substantially adds to it in some manner.[26]

The 1909 copyright law, which was in effect at the time, did not provide any copyright protection for sound recordings. As a result, since the work was not registered, Waring, as "creator" of the work was the only possible litigant under common law. The *Waring* decision, however, has been viewed as an anomaly, limited to its circumstances and jurisdiction. In a similar case three years later involving the orchestra leader Paul Whiteman, Judge Learned Hand found that the performer had no property right.[27]

A persistent fear expressed in many decisions has been that any protection afforded a performer's interpretation of the role would adversely affect the ability of other actors to perform the same role. "Could John Barrymore have claimed a common law property right in his memorable interpretation of Shakespeare's *Hamlet*?" asked a 1952 commentator.[28] The concurring opinion in the *Lugosi* decision concluded that "neither Lugosi during his lifetime nor his estate thereafter owned the exclusive right to exploit Count Dracula any more than Gregory Peck possesses or his heirs could possess common law exclusivity to General MacArthur, George C. Scott to General Patton, James Whitmore to Will Rogers and Harry Truman, or Charlton Heston to Moses."[29]

Copyright is a property right. Even when performers in later cases avoided assertions of copyright protection, since such protection had not been given others in similar circumstances, some still argued that they had a property right in their persona. Yet the existence of copyright law often defeated such arguments. The actress Shirley Booth asserted a property right in her persona when an actress in a commercial imitated Booth's voice as the television character "Hazel," even though the holder of the copyright for "Hazel" had given the creators of the commercial permission to use the character. The court gave three reasons why performers should not have such a right:

1. "Policing" would be difficult for a court of equity.

2. There would be undue restraint on the potential market of the copyright proprietor.

3. Such a right would be the equivalent of vesting a monopoly in the performer and preventing others from using his or her gestures—this would impede rather than promote the useful arts as required by the copyright provision of the U.S. Constitution.[30]

In suing Goodyear Tire and Rubber Company for a commercial that utilized the song she had made famous, "These Boots Are Made for Walking," and, she claimed, her singing style,[31] Nancy Sinatra specifically did not allege copyright infringement for the simple reason that she did not own the copyright. Instead, she claimed that the song had become identified with her and that the song and the arrangement used by Goodyear had acquired a "secondary meaning"; by using the song in this manner, Sinatra alleged, Goodyear was purposefully deceiving the public.[32] Sinatra's claim was similar in concept to later claims in *Lugosi*, *Price*, and *Groucho Marx* in that she claimed a right in the overall "persona" projected in her performance, even though she lacked copyright or trademark protection. The difference was that hers was a claim based on voice and arrangement and not film and visual likeness.

The court held that there was no unfair competition because Goodyear and Sinatra were not in competition with one another in the production of products. Because Goodyear had obtained permission to use the song from the copyright holders, the court found that Sinatra's claims clashed with the federal objectives: "The plaintiff had not obtained the same rights which would have protected the secondary meaning she asserts."[33] Jane M. Gaines suggests that the court's decision was an attempt "to forestall the possibility of multiple claims; had Sinatra's style become attached to the composition, it would make the use of the song by others prohibitively expensive."[34]

For performer's rights, copyright law evidently provides no protection for the performer who does not hold a copyright in the work in which he or she performs and in fact favors the performers' employer or the assignee of the copyright.

COPYRIGHT IN FICTIONAL CHARACTERS

Because fictional personas are created by performers in dramatic presentations, protection could be sought for these persona through a copyright for the fictional characters. Fictional characters themselves are not among the eight categories of works that can obtain copyright protection.[35] It has long been established that fictional characters *can* be afforded protection within the copyright of the overall work.[36] But this has led at least one commentator to describe fictional characters as "second-class citizens in the realm of intellectual property law [in that they] are protected only within the context of the work in which they appear."[37]

The *extent* to which fictional characters in a copyrighted work can be given protection against unauthorized copying has been variously decided, with decisions differing from jurisdiction to jurisdiction. As noted earlier, the *DeCosta* court in addressing the issue simply (and unhelpfully) acknowledged that "a concrete, describable manifestation of intellectual creation" was protected by the Constitution and one that was "ineffable" was not.[38]

Much of the discussion of the protectibility of fictional characters has been developed in infringement cases, where authors claimed that characters in their works were copied by others. The author of the play *Abie's Irish Rose* sued the creators of the film *The Cohens and the Kellys*, claiming that a similarities of characters and events constituted infringement. Judge Hand in *Nichols v. Universal Pictures* highlighted the difficulties in determining infringement in these cases by noting that if the right were limited literally to the text, the plagiarist would escape by immaterial variations.[39] Yet, by allowing that something other than a line-by-line borrowing could constitute infringement, Hand acknowledged that a "line had to be drawn in the dirt" to determine how much similarity was necessary for infringement, a line that he was certain some would find arbitrary.[40]

In determining that the "similarity" of *The Cohens and the Kellys* to *Abie's Irish Rose* was too generalized, that the characters in *Abie's* were stock and conventional, *Nichols* established an "abstractions" test to determine "substantial similarity" of not only the "ideas" but the "expression" of fictional works:

> Upon any work, and especially upon a play, a great number of patterns of increasing generality will fit equally well, as more and more of the incident is left out ... but there is a point in this series of abstractions where they are no longer protected, since otherwise the playwright could prevent the use of his "ideas," to which, apart from their expression, his property never existed.[41]

In short, Judge Hand concluded, "It follows that the less developed the characters, the less they can be copyrighted; that is the penalty an author must pay for making them too indistinctly."[42]

Nearly forty years later, the court in *Sid and Marty Kroft* established a two-part test to determine substantial similarity:

1. an "extrinsic" test to determine a substantial similarity of ideas, which would include an analysis of similarities and expert testimony, and

2. an "intrinsic" test to determine whether there is a substantial similarity of expression.

The plaintiffs claimed that commercials for McDonald's, the hamburger chain, had used characters that the plaintiffs argued were substantially similar to the ones in their television show *H.R. Pufnstuf*. The court concluded that McDonald's had captured the "total concept and feel" of *H.R. Pufnstuf*, that the commercials were "intrinsically" similar to the Kroft's children's program.[43]

By way of illustration of the various considerations involved and in the evolution of the analysis, a brief look at cases concerning the comic book character of Superman is in order. In 1940, DC Comics, the owners of the copyright in the Superman comics, sued the publishers of comics about "Wonderman," who wore similar clothing and performed stupendous feats like Superman.[44] The defendant claimed that both Superman and Wonderman were based on prototypes from classical mythology and that, therefore, there had been no infringement. The court, using the *Nichols'* "abstractions" test, found that the creators of Superman had developed specific characteristics for Superman that transcended the mythic prototype and which were also found in Wonderman.

In 1982, DC Comics and Warner Brothers, Inc., producers of *Superman, The Movie* (1978), sued American Broadcasting Companies (ABC) and the producer of the television show *The Greatest American Hero* for copyright infringement, unfair competition, and trademark dilution.[45] The plaintiffs claimed that the TV hero, Ralph Hinkley, who wore a cape and who flew through the air like Superman, was "substantially similar" to Superman. Summary judgment was granted to the defendants. On appeal, the Second Circuit affirmed,[46] basing its decision on a lack of similarity in the "total concept and feel" of the two works. While acknowledging specific similarities between the television series and the "Superman" works, the court labeled these as parody.[47] The court examined the "totality" of Ralph's Hinkley's traits: he was not from another planet as was Superman; he was a bumbler, a reluctant hero, and not a bold super-man. The case was resolved on copyright grounds alone; the unfair competition claim did not receive an independent analysis.

A logical question to follow is whether a fictional character has any protection separate from the work in which he or she appears. This has relevance in that performers who claim an identification with a fictional persona they have played are asserting that the personas have lives apart from the works themselves. In *Warner Brothers Pictures v. Columbia Broadcasting Systems*, the Ninth Circuit held that the right to the characters is reserved to the author, even after he or she assigns rights in the first work in which the characters appear, unless the character in question is a mere "chessman."[48] This case has been variously used to argue both that fictional characters are not copyrightable (since the right to the characters did not automatically "go along" with the assignment in the copyright instrument)[49] and that they are copyrightable (that is, characters may acquire protection if they are well delineated and constitute the "whole story"). Later, the same Ninth Circuit hedged on the feasibility of the *Warner Brothers* test[50]; it suggested that the test might be more applicable to comic book characters than literary characters since the distinct delineation that would evidence unique elements of expression required in *Warner Brothers* would be more ascertainable in graphic than literary creations.[51] The Second Circuit has suggested that the issues in *Warner Brothers* are still to be resolved.[52] In a case concerning the 1981 remake of *Tarzan of the Apes*, the Second Circuit expressed "no opinion on whether the character of Tarzan is covered by copyright."[53] Lacking a specific copyright registration for fictional characters, the issue is not neatly decided.

The argument, then, of performers who create or become identified with a persona would be that they had created a fictional character and that unauthorized use of that persona would constitute infringement. In accordance with *Nichols* and *DC Comics*, the persona would have to be sufficiently delineated for a "substantial" similarity argument to survive.

The performers would argue that the rights of the holders of the copyrights for the films or plays were limited to those works or that any "assignment" of the right was limited to the particular films or plays.

Copyright issues have not figured prominently in litigation concerning dramatic fictional personas. The Marx Brothers characters are obviously fictional creations, and yet when ruling on the claim of unauthorized use of their personas the court did not address the copyright issues and, according to some commentators, went out of its way not to address them.[54] The fact that the copyrights for the film or broadcast have been registered in names other than the performers' and the fact that the films were usually scripted by others may have caused litigants to seek alternative causes of actions. A possible exception would be when the performer is also the sole creator of the persona, as in the case of Charlie Chaplin's "Little Tramp," since Chaplin wrote the scripts and the film scores, directed the movies, and exclusively played the Little Tramp. Chaplin's "control" of this persona was so established, in contrast to Laurel and Hardy whose personas appeared in films copyrighted, directed, and coscripted by others, that his "Little Tramp" persona was dutifully licensed by IBM for a series of broadcast and print ads for IBM copiers starting in 1981[55] and revived in 1991.[56]

An interesting question, however, in arguing for a copyright by Charlie Chaplin in the Little Tramp character or in any fictional character that has evolved over time is determining exactly what the "fixed" persona is and when it is "fixed." Chaplin played "The Little Tramp" with his bowler hat, little mustache, twirling cane, and funny walk from 1916 until 1936. The character evolved in the early silent film days from a sometimes violent and selfish individual, in keeping with the filmic style of Chaplin's first director Mack Sennett, to a gentle and sentimental figure who resorted to violence only to protect the unprotected.[57] This was especially true in his final appearances in two sound films—*City Lights* (1931)[58] and *Modern Times* (1936)[59]. The character softened and changed as its creator and technology and the times changed. (It has also been noted that even the cartoon character Mickey Mouse evolved from a rambunctious, sadistic creature to a well-behaved, likable role-model.[60]) The 1976 copyright law revision provided that copyright exists from the date of creation and has a general duration of life of the author plus 50 years,[61] with works "made-for-hire" having a copyright duration of 75 years.[62] If a "persona" is by definition something that is established over time, how could it be determined at what point copyright protection would begin and how long it would last? Could someone theoretically appropriate Chaplin's "Little Tramp" persona by limiting any reference to or copying of the character to the version that existed in the early films before the "persona" was well established?

A similar contention could be made about the character of Ralph Kramden, the loud-mouthed bus driver with the heart of gold, as played exclusively on television by Jackie Gleason. The character was originated on the DuMont Cavalcade of Star for the DuMont network in 1951 and performed live on *The Jackie Gleason Show* on CBS until 1955. In 1956, thirty-nine shows were filmed under the title *The Honeymooners*. The character was sporadically revived on Gleason's variety shows throughout the late 1950s and 1960s, some of which were videotaped. From 1966 to 1970, *The Jackie Gleason Show* produced periodic musical comedy shows in which Ralph Kramden and the other *Honeymooner* cast members sang.[63] Recently discovered kinescopes of the early live performances shows a cruder and angrier Ralph Kramden.[64] The 1956 filmed shows are the most frequently seen. The 1960s embodiment of the character was very sentimental and was also musical. Which of these embodiments would obtain copyright protection? All of them? The most popular? And at what point would it be fixed?

Trademark and Unfair Competition

Federal and common law trademark laws protect against the unauthorized use of the same mark by a second comer where confusion, mistake, or deception by the consumer is likely.[65] The test for protectibility has as a separate analysis of whether or not a mark has acquired a secondary meaning that will cause consumers to connect a second mark with the first.[66]

> [Secondary meaning] contemplates that a word or phrase originally, and in that sense primarily, incapable of exclusive appropriation with reference to an article on the market ... might nevertheless have been used so long and so exclusively by one producer with reference to his article that, in that trade and to that branch of the purchasing public, the word or phrase had come to mean that the article was his product; in other words, had come to be, to them, his trademark.[67]

Trademark protection for a fictional character has been afforded where the character identifies a single source of a work containing the character,[68] an example being "Amos and Andy" from the radio and television program that aired from the 1930s to the mid–1950s.[69]

Unfair competition, at common law and as codified on the federal level in the Lanham Act,[70] is an extension of trademark violation in that any false and misleading designations that may cause confusion or mistake are prohibited. The test for violation of the relevant provision in the Lanham Act is:

1. Defendant has made false and misleading statements.

2. There is an actual deception or at least a tendency to deceive a substantial portion of the intended audience.

3. The deception is material in that it influences purchasing decisions.

4. The advertised goods traveled in interstate commerce.

5. There is a likelihood of injury to the plaintiff in terms of declining sales or loss of goodwill.[71]

The Lanham Act has been held to apply to situations that would not qualify as trademark infringement but that involve unfair competitive practices resulting in actual or potential deception.[72] As such, it has often been utilized in persona-related cases on the argument that the public has been deceived as to the performer's involvement in the enterprise and/or that the performer's own ability to market his or her persona has been affected. The preliminary draft of the Restatement of Unfair Competition includes a section on misappropriation of the commercial value of personal identity.[73]

In 1986, Ginger Rogers, the film actress and famed dancing partner of Fred Astaire, sued the producers of the Federico Fellini film *Ginger and Fred*, claiming false light invasion of privacy, misappropriation and infringement of her public personality, and violation of Section 43(a) of the Lanham Act in that the title of the film allegedly created a false impression that she had endorsed the film. The court held that film's title was not deliberately misleading in that it was justified by the film's story about two performers who were called "Ginger and Fred" because they imitated Fred Astaire and Ginger Rogers. In ruling against Rogers, the court stated that the violation must be "explicit," that the Lanham Act does not bar the minimally relevant use of a celebrity's name in the title of an artistic work where the title does not explicitly denote authorship, sponsorship, or endorsement or explicitly mislead by the content.[74]

The actor Bert Lahr, best known as the "Cowardly Lion" in *The Wizard of Oz* successfully sued for unfair competition for the imitation of his voice in a commercial.[75] Lahr's voice, with prizefighter's intonation and its manneristic tics and honks, was very distinctive. A later court noted that *Lahr* "was decided on the basis of the singular uniqueness of the quality of voice that made his situation not just different in degree but different in kind."[76] As noted previously, Nancy Sinatra had failed in her unfair competition action where her voice and style were imitated; the difference with *Lahr* was that *Sinatra* involved a clash with copyright law and *Lahr* did not.[77]

Right of Privacy/Right of Publicity

Many of the early suits regarding fictional persona were at least partially invasions of privacy actions or held by the courts to be rooted in privacy law. The concept of a right of privacy was first suggested in the 1890s in response to abusive gossip columns[78] and evolved to include an individual's right to restrain the unauthorized use of his or her name or likeness for product endorsements or other advertising uses.[79] The characteristics of the individual that are protected will vary from state to state. Not all states recognize a right of privacy. Two states that do — California and New York — also host the stage and film capitals of the United States. New York's right of privacy law reads as follows:

> [Any] person whose name, portrait or picture is used within this state for advertising purposes or for the purposes of trade without the written consent first obtained ... may ... restrain the use thereof; and may also sue and recover damages for any injuries sustained by reason of such use.[80]

At this time, it is unclear whether or not the right of privacy under the New York Law descends to heirs.

California's right of privacy law reads,

> Any person who knowingly uses another's name, voice, signature, photograph, or likeness, in any manner, on or in products, merchandise, or goods, or for purposes of advertising or selling ... without such person's prior consent ... shall be liable for any damages sustained by such person.[81]

Whether the right of privacy — the right to be left alone — is inheritable or vested in the individual also varies from jurisdiction. Films and television in the 1940s and 1950s saw litigation by the heirs of individuals who were the subject of films or television programs — the gangster Al Capone in TV's *The Untouchables*[82]; Jesse James, in the *Playhouse 90* April 17, 1958, television presentation "Bitter Heritage"[83]; and the composer

Robert Schumann in the 1947 film MGM *Song of Love*.[84] In the first two cases, the right in an individual's personality was found to reside in and die with the individual in the particular states, and since the heirs themselves were not portrayed in the broadcast or show they could not prevail. In the *Schumann* case, it was held that the 91 years distance between when Schumann, who owned this right of privacy, died and the date of the film was too great to allow recovery.

In 1969, the satirical television program *That Was the Week That Was* awarded a recently deceased 99-year-old woman with a large family the "First Annual Booby Prize in the Birth Control Sweepstakes." The court held that there was no right of action in relatives in Ohio for invasion of privacy of a deceased.[85] In litigation concerning the tax consequences of Glenn Miller's widow's agreement with MGM Studios for use of her husband's name and likeness in the 1954 MGM film *The Glenn Miller Story*, the court held that for tax purposes, a property right in the band leader's name and likeness were not inheritable.[86]

The 1950s saw the development of a recognizable right of publicity that was distinct from the right of privacy: "The right of publicity is the right of a person to own, protect, and commercially exploit his own name, likeness, and persona."[87] While the right of privacy is concerned with the feelings, hurt, and damages done as a result of the invasion of privacy, the right of publicity addresses the loss of compensation by the plaintiffs through the unjust enrichment of the defendants.[88] Where the right of privacy is seen to reside in the individual, the right of publicity has been regarded as a "property" right.[89] Right of publicity suits by *heirs* of performers or other public figures against dramatic works that portray these individuals have often been unsuccessful, turning on the issue of descendibility[90] or on the degree of fictionalization.[91]

Nonpersona decisions concerning the rights of privacy and publicity and the confusion between the two rights were influential in the persona cases *Price*, *Lugosi*, and *Marx Brothers*.

The significance of this "new" right of publicity argument for fictional persona cases can be seen in *Midler v. Ford Motor Co.*[92] Like Nancy Sinatra, Bette Midler sued a manufacturer for imitating her voice in a commercial — in her case the imitator sang a song Midler had popularized, "Do You Want to Dance." The court bluntly stated that if Midler had claimed a secondary meaning or unfair competition, as Sinatra had, she would have lost, like Sinatra.[93] Since California Civil Code §3344 was limited to protection of "likeness," the court extended the protection to situations involving misappropriation of voice, stating, "The singer manifests herself in the song; to impersonate her voice is to pirate her identity."[94] This tort was reaffirmed in California in *Waits v. Frito-Lay*.[95] The *Midler* decision has been the subject of much discussion, most of its centering on the earlier fears of the *Sinatra* court.[96] Gaines claims that,

> Midler signaled a new development in intellectual property law, one that had been evolving since the fifties but that was not recognized in common law until the early seventies: the introduction of the right of publicity paradigm.... [I]ntellectual property law moved to reinsert the legal subject and its rights squarely into the work. Nancy Sinatra argued only that she had produced a secondary meaning in her product, that is, her style of singing. Bette Midler's complaint was that her very identity-property had been stolen.[97]

Contract Law

Of course, the litigation in the area of a performer's right to a persona has been greatly dependent on the specific contractual agreements. Whatever theory is used, what will control is what has been agreed to. The movie cowboy Roy Rogers claimed that the exhibition of his movies on television was an unauthorized use of his name, picture, and voice, but the court held for the studio since the language of the contractual agreements gave the studio the right to exhibit the films without limitation and perpetually.[98] Another singing cowboy, Gene Autry, sued the same studio for editing seven minutes from each of his films when they were shown on television in order to allow commercials. Upon review of the contract, the court held that the studio had acquired all rights, including the right to edit.[99] The specific contract wording was central to the courts' decisions in *Price* and *Lugosi*. Interestingly enough, Bing Crosby's concerns about being sued by Gene Autry, expressed at the start of this chapter in his 1941 recording, proved to have some validity 13 years later — but only regarding contracts, not imitation.

Fictional Dramatic Persona Cases

LUGOSI V. UNIVERSAL STUDIOS

Bela Lugosi,[100] a Hungarian-born actor, played the character of Count Dracula on the stage in 1927 and then in the 1931 Universal film *Dracula*.[101] He reprised the role of Count Dracula in 1948 for Universal in the parody

Abbott and Costello Meet Frankenstein. During the 1930s and early 1940s, he appeared in a wide variety of roles in numerous horror films for Universal as well as other studios, and even played the Frankenstein Monster.[102] However, he was best known for playing Count Dracula, intoning "Good e-vening," and wearing a long black cape. Lugosi also played vampire characters in *Return of the Vampire* for RKO Studios in 1943 and the 1952 British film *Mother Riley Meets the Vampire.* His career, however, was hampered by his typecasting, drug addiction, and, according to his fellow horror star Boris Karloff, his failure to master the English language.[103] Lugosi died bankrupt in 1956, leaving, according to one of his biographers, his "reputation" as his only legacy.[104] Ironically, in his last film, *Plan 9 from Outer Space,*[105] arguably the worst film ever made,[106] the fatally ill Lugosi was a silent figure, an image, a likeness. He died during filming, and his role was taken by a double who covered the lower half of his face in a Dracula cape to create the likeness of the late Lugosi.[107]

In 1960, Universal Studios entered into merchandising agreements for Lugosi's image as Dracula. The image being marketed was clearly Lugosi in his Dracula cape. The merchandise included child phonograph records, plastic toy pencil sharpeners, greeting cards, molded plastic figures, T-shirts, Halloween costumes and masks, toys, comic books, self-erasing slates, candy dispensers, belt buckles, wallets, luggage, and toy horoscope viewers with flip cards.[108] The Lugosi/Dracula image was not the only one licensed. It was part of a package that included other characters from Universal Pictures horror films, including the Frankenstein Monster, the Wolf Man, the Mummy, the Creature from the Black Lagoon, the Phantom of the Opera, Mr. Hyde, the Mutant, the Mole Man, and the Hunchback of Notre Dame.[109] Except for Count Dracula, all of these characterizations rely heavily on makeup, so the features of the actors who played the roles are disguised; as a result, Lugosi was the only actor who was recognizable in the merchandise. There is no indication that any of the actors who played these roles, including Boris Karloff, who created the role of Frankenstein's Monster on film, initiated actions against Universal.

Lugosi's son and last wife sued Universal in 1963 but withdrew the suit pursuant to the reopening of the probate of Lugosi's estate. They filed suit again in 1966, claiming that they had inherited Lugosi's exclusive right to exploit the commercial value of his likeness.[110]

The character of Count Dracula was in the public domain, since Bram Stoker, the novel's author, had not registered its copyright in the United States. Universal had acquired the rights to the 1927 play based on the novel by Hamilton Deane and John Balderston. Since neither Lugosi nor Universal claimed a copyright in the Dracula character, copyright was not an issue in the case. Universal argued that Lugosi had given Universal the right to use his likeness in his 1931 contract for the first Dracula film. However, in analyzing the contract, the court held that that right was limited to promotion of the 1931 film; it also noted that Universal had asked Lugosi to give them permission to use a wax dummy of his face for the corpse of Count Dracula in the sequel *Dracula's Daughter* (1936) in which he did not appear[111] and reasoned that Universal would not have done that had it acquired perpetual rights to his likeness in 1931.[112] While Universal had copyrighted its photoplay and, even though the character was in the public domain, it might have acquired a copyright for the unique characteristics its treatment gave to the Dracula character, the court stated,

> But the very essence of the Count Dracula character in the photoplay *Dracula,* produced by the defendant consists of the characteristics, makeup, and mannerisms of Bela Lugosi in the role. Only the dress was not created by the actor. In licensing the use of the Count Dracula's characteristics, makeup, and mannerisms, of necessity Bela Lugosi's appearance and likeness in the role are the thing being licensed. The horror character, Count Dracula, is, as taken from the films, *Dracula* and *Dracula's Daughter,* cannot be divorced from Bela Lugosi's appearance in the role.[113]

The court held that Lugosi's right to his likeness was an inheritable property right.[114]

In its language, even though the first *Lugosi* court did not cite *Waring,*[115] the court seemed to echo the thinking that a performer had indeed brought a uniqueness to a role. The decision, of course, went beyond the reasoning of *Waring*, dealing as it did not just with performance but with likeness and publicity value.

In January 1974, after two years of "haggling," the Los Angeles Supreme Court awarded $53,023 to Lugosi's son and wife.[116] Universal appealed, and in 1979 the California Supreme Court reversed,[117] finding that the right of privacy was not inheritable in the state of California after all, citing *James, Schumann*, and *Maritote*. While the trial court had also cited these precedents, it had argued that these were rights of privacy cases and Lugosi's rights at issue were those of publicity:

> In the James, Werner, and Kelly cases, the injury asserted was that of an injury to feelings or the depicting of or exposing to public view uncomplimentary phases of private life. In none of these cases was there any assertion of a pecuniary loss due to appropriation of a celebrity's publicity value in his name, likeness, appearance, or personality. Although Prosser has classified the *right of publicity*

as constituting a right of privacy, it must be recognized that an invasion of such a right causes a pecuniary loss, as contrasted with the typical loss in a right of privacy invasion as an injury to a person's feelings and emotion.[118]

The response of the appeals court to this reasoning was to re-cite *Prosser* and hold that the rights to publicity and privacy are inseparably intertwined; as a result, the right of publicity must be exercised in the person's lifetime and is not inheritable:

> The so-called right of publicity means in essence that the reaction of the public to name and likeness, which may be fortuitous or which may be managed or planned, endows the name and likeness of the person with commercially exploitable opportunities. The protection of name and likeness from unwarranted intrusion or exploitation is the heart of the law of privacy.[119]

The appeals court did hypothesize that if Lugosi had established a business during his lifetime licensing his likeness, then that business could have been inherited, like any other business.

> Assuming arguendo that Lugosi, in his lifetime, based on publicity he received and/or because of the nature of his talent in exploiting his name and likeness in association with the Dracula character had established a business under the name of Lugosi Horror Pictures and sold licenses to have "Lugosi as Dracula" imprinted on shirts, and in doing so built a large public acceptance and/or good will for such a business, product or service, there can be little doubt that Lugosi would have created during his lifetime a business or a property wholly apart from the rights he had granted Universal to exploit his name and likeness in the characterization of the lead role of Count Dracula in the picture *Dracula*.[120]

But as a rule, the court countered, the right, if not utilized by the actor in his lifetime, is not assignable.

> Thus, under present law, upon Lugosi's death anyone, related or unrelated to Lugosi, with the imagination, the enterprise, the energy and the cash, could, in [his or her] own name or in a fictitious name, or a trade name coupled with Lugosi's, have impressed a name so selected with a secondary meaning and realized a profit or loss by so doing depending on the value of the idea, its acceptance by the public and the management of the enterprise undertaken. After Lugosi's death, his name was in the public domain. Anyone, including [plaintiffs], or either of them, or Universal, could use it for a legitimate commercial purpose.[121]

The court's contention that Lugosi had not exploited his likeness in his lifetime struck some at least one commentator as leaving too many questions unanswered.[122] It seemed to associate the exploitation with full-fledged merchandising, which Universal "got to" first. Since Lugosi did not create the court's imagined business during his lifetime, the court held that his right of publicity died with him. Later, the *Groucho Marx* court, in attempting to determining the intention of the appellate court in *Lugosi,* relied on an earlier passage in the *Lugosi* decision stating that Lugosi had not used his likeness as Dracula "in connection with any business product or service so as to impress a secondary meaning on such business."[123] The later court reasoned:

> [This] is the language of trademark law, under which the strength or public recognition of a mark as identifying the source of a particular product is significant in determining whether the proprietor may prevent the use of the mark on similar products.... Perhaps Lugosi was relegating the heirs solely to their rights under trademark law.[124]

Even if the *Lugosi* appellate court was recognizing a distinct descendible right of publicity, the *Groucho Marx* court held that the right is limited to the particular "commercial situations"—products or services—that the celebrity promoted with his name and likeness during his lifetime.

Another commentator has used the two *Lugosi* decisions to illustrate the inconsistency of courts' approaches to intellectual property issues by noting that there are three different views of what was at issue — the trial court and the majority in the court of appeals viewed the case a property right issue; the concurring opinion in the appeals court focused on Lugosi's persona as a work product of the employer; while the dissent presented a detailed copyright analysis.[125]

The court also made much of the fact that other actors had played Count Dracula — Christopher Lee, Jack Palance, John Carradine, Lon Chaney, Jr.— in addition to Lugosi, thereby diluting Lugosi's "right." A strong and lengthy dissent repeated much of the arguments and conclusions of the trial court, distinguished between the rights of privacy and publicity, and cited for support a similar case that had been decided between the first trial and the appeal — *Price v. Hal Roach Studios.*[126] *Price* had, ironically, relied heavily on the lower court's opinion in *Lugosi.*

PRICE V. HAL ROACH STUDIOS

Stanley Laurel and Oliver Hardy were a comedy team, appearing in nearly 90 films together from 1926 to 1950, primarily for Hal Roach

Studios, although they worked for MGM in a few films in the 1930s and under contract from 1941 to 1945.[127] Hardy died in 1957. In 1961, Laurel, Hardy's widow (Price), and the Laurel and Hardy Productions[128] sold the rights to the likenesses of Laurel and Hardy to Larry Harmon, who created a pilot for an animated television series.[129] Laurel died in 1964. But Hal Roach Studios also licensed the likenesses of Laurel and Hardy.

The two widows sued Hal Roach Studios for misappropriation of their rights.[130] There was no dispute that the studio owned the right to the individual films. As had been the case in *Lugosi,* the studio claimed that the contracts with Laurel and Hardy had given it the right to their likenesses, but the court found that right limited to promoting individual films.[131] Just as the *Lugosi* opinion had noted Universal's act of requesting Lugosi's permission to use his image in *Dracula's Daughter* as evidence that it had not acquired the rights to Lugosi's Dracula persona, the *Price* court cited Hal Roach's failure to claim any entitlement to Laurel and Hardy's name and likenesses when they severed their contract with the studio in 1939 and entered into one with MGM as proof that Roach's right to their likenesses was never contemplated.

The *Price* court distinguished between the rights of privacy and publicity, claiming that the defendants were confusing them.[132] Citing *Lugosi* as precedent, the court added that this case was easier than Lugosi's since Laurel and Hardy were playing themselves.

> The present case is easier to decide than *Lugosi* since we deal here with actors portraying themselves and developing their own characters rather than fictional characters which have been given a particular interpretation by an actor. This distinction removes the case from the kind of criticism lodged against recognition of such a right in *Supreme Records v. Decca Records*, 90 F. Supp. 904 (S.D.Cal. 1950). There it was noted that if the court were to protect performers from imitations, "[it] would have to hold that ... for instance ... that Sir Laurence Olivier could prohibit anyone else from adopting some of the innovations which he brought to his performance of Hamlet" [90 F. Supp. at 909].[133]

The court found for the plaintiffs, holding that the right to Laurel and Hardy's likenesses was inheritable according to the laws of New York state.[134]

The court sidestepped the issue of fictional personas by claiming that Laurel and Hardy were playing themselves. It is true that Laurel and Hardy usually — although not always — were called by their own names in their films, but their characters were fictional creations. Early silent films were the result of intense collaboration between actors, directors, and gag men.

Of course, their sound films were scripted. In real life, Laurel and Hardy did not throw pies at one another or twiddle their ties. A fairly dramatic distinction between the public and private Laurel and Hardy occurred in 1954 when the television program *This Is Your Life*, which surprised famous people and brought them in contact with old friends and family, surprised Laurel and Hardy. Laurel refused to go on the program, leaving host Ralph Edwards to stall on camera until Laurel was persuaded by his wife and friends to continue. When asked later, Laurel said, "I don't like to be unprepared…. It was very difficult for me because I wasn't in character and I didn't know what was coming."[135]

The court found an easy answer by claiming that Laurel and Hardy were playing themselves since it thereby could avoid the question of whether John Barrymore or Laurence Olivier could prevent others from playing Hamlet. The court could then restrict its decision to the right of publicity, which is covered by the privacy laws of New York. It also noted, however, that Laurel and Hardy were the sole performers of these characters. This was not the case with Dracula, which was played by performers other than Lugosi. The court may well have been influenced by the fact that the original license agreement with Harmon was signed by Laurel himself and that Laurel had established a production company, which had started in his lifetime to promote his likeness, which Lugosi had not. Even though *Price* preceded the appellate court's *Lugosi* decision, it anticipated its arguments—especially the systematic promotion of the persona during the individual's lifetime — and won protection for an actor's personas, while hedging on the protection of fictional personas.

Ironically, the animated series was abandoned during the lengthy litigation.[136] However, with the benefit of the *Price* ruling, the widows of Laurel and Hardy were able to prevent the production of a television series portraying their husbands.[137]

GROUCHO MARX PRODUCTIONS
V. DAY AND NIGHT COMPANY

Julius, Leonard, and Adolph Marx performed as Groucho, Chico, and Harpo and were collectively known as the Marx Brothers. They acted on the stage in the 1920s—*I'll Say She Is* and *Animal Crackers*—and in fourteen films as a team from 1929 to 1949.[138] The Marx Brothers on stage and film had very distinctive personalities—Groucho wore glasses and a straight black mustache and loped around the stage and sets with his back hunched, a cigar in his mouth, and a leer on his face. Chico used a burlesque Italian accent and dressed like an organ grinder; he was also an idiosyncratic pianist. Harpo did not speak on stage but instead used pantomime. He had frizzy blond hair, pop eyes, and blew staccato wolf whistles while chasing women; he was also an accomplished harpist.

Chico died in 1961, Harpo in 1964, and Groucho in 1977. Harpo's daughter and Groucho Marx Productions, which received the rights to Groucho's likeness from Groucho himself in 1976 and to Chico's from his daughter in 1979, sued Day and Night Company for the play *A Day in Hollywood/A Night in the Ukraine.*[139] In part two of the play, actors impersonated the Marx Brothers performing in a burlesque dramatization of Anton Chekov's "The Bear." The suit was for misappropriation of property rights, for interference with contractual relations, and for infringement of common law copyright. Although one commentator claims that the decision is really a traditional copyright infringement analysis, the focus of the court's decision was the right of publicity.[140]

The Marx Brothers were fictional creations. In real life, the brothers had other names and personalities. Their fictional personalities were the result not only of their own contributions but of such noted writers as George S. Kaufman and S.J. Perleman who worked on the scripts for their Broadway shows and movies. Yet, the issue of fictional creations and copyright for the characters was not examined by either the trial or the appellate court.[141] Another commentator concluded that the court's approach was dictated by its implicit contention that fictional characters cannot be copyrighted apart from a work.[142]

Instead, the action was based on the right of publicity in New York (since the injury had occurred in a Broadway play). The defendant cited the second *Lugosi* opinion holding that the right to promote one's name and likeness does not survive death. Relying mostly on *Price,* the court found that the right of publicity existed in New York and was inheritable if exercised in the person's lifetime, that the Marx Brothers had exercised it, and that the Marx Brothers right of publicity was infringed.

The court of appeals reversed,[143] very simply holding that the appropriate law was not New York's, the site of the injury, but California's. All three Marx Brothers were domiciled in California at the time of their deaths. Plaintiff Susan Marx was a California resident asserting Harpo Marx's right of publicity as a trustee of a residuary trust under his will which was probated in California. The contract assigning Chico's right of publicity to Groucho Marx Production provided that it was governed by the laws of California. Citing the appellate court's *Lugosi* decision for the proposition that in California the right to exploit one's likeness is not inheritable, the court of appeals reversed.[144]

The appellate court took the time and space to justify its decision in light of the hypothesis of the appellate court in *Lugosi* that if Lugosi had created a business exploiting his persona as Dracula, the right to protect his image might be protectible and inheritable. Groucho Marx had exploited his image in his films and in commercials[145] and created such a business by assigning the rights to his image and personality to Groucho Marx Productions before his death. However, the court held that any descendible right of publicity in the state of California is limited to products or services that the owner had promoted during his or her lifetime. Since what was at issue in *Groucho Marx* was not the promotion of a product but the impersonation of the Marx Brothers in an original play, the plaintiffs could not prevail under California law. It would appear, then, that if the case had involved the promotion of products using the Marx Brothers' personas, their heirs and assignees would have won on proof that the brothers had promoted the products in their lifetimes.

LEGISLATIVE CHANGE

When the Lugosi suit began, Bela Lugosi, Jr., was in law school. He went on to become a lawyer. In one of the many ironies of these events, Lugosi built up a practice representing the heirs of such movie personalities as the Three Stooges, Boris Karloff, and Lon Chaney — his father having performed with the last two — and negotiating licensing agreements concerning the images and likenesses of their parents.[146]

Also, after the 1979 *Lugosi* decision, Lugosi Jr. and others lobbied for a change in the state law. The result was California Civil Code Section 990, which was enacted in 1988. It provides in section (a) that

> [a]ny Person who uses a deceased personality's name, voice, signature, photograph, or likeness in any manner, on or in products, merchandise, or goods, or for the purposes of advertising or selling, or soliciting purchases of, or products, merchandise, goods or services, without prior consent ... shall be liable for any damages sustained by the person or persons injured as a result thereof.

Section (h) defines "deceased personality" as "any natural person whose name, voice, signature, photograph, or likeness [that] has commercial value at the time of his or her death, whether or not during the lifetime of that natural person the person used his or her name, voice, signature, photograph, or likeness on or in products, merchandise, or goods, for the purposes of advertising or selling, or solicitation of purchase of, products, merchandise goods or services." The "decreased personality" is defined in the section as any natural person who has died within 50 years prior to January 1, 1985. Section (c) requires consent from the person or persons to whom the right of consent has been transferred; section (e) states that the rights set for in section (a) will terminate without transference. Section (n) provides exceptions for use in plays, books, magazines, newspaper, musical composition, film or radio, not including commercial announcements or advertisements.[147]

The legislation was obviously influences by the *Lugosi* case and others. It removes the requirement that the right be exercised during the individual's lifetime. It allows transference and inheritability. It, however, specifies that the "personality" have "commercial value" at the time or the person or persons' death and does not define "personality," leaving a question as to whether Lugosi as Dracula or Julius Marx as Groucho are specifically covered. Whether there will be test cases of the statute or whether the specific circumstances of the 1950s and 1960s will never recur thanks to licensing agreements and other contracts remains to be seen.

ROBOTS AND COMPUTERS

Unknown elements at this writing are the effect of one decision and one new technology.

In *White v. Samsung*,[148] the Ninth Circuit found triable issues of fact regarding whether the likeness of game show hostess Vanna White was misappropriated in Samsung's print advertisement depicting a futuristic robot game-show hostess.

White claimed that the advertisement violated her rights under the California civil code, the common law right of publicity, and the Lanham Act. The advertisement, which hypothesized "outrageous future outcomes" for the future such as a feminine robot dressed in a wig, gown, and jewelry standing in a *Wheel of Fortune*–like game show set with the caption, "Longest-running game show, 2012 A.D."

The U.S. District Court for the Central District of California granted summary judgment in favor of Samsung on each claim. The Ninth Circuit reversed, holding that White's common law right of publicity was not limited to appropriation of her "name or likeness" and included any method of invoking an individual's identity. After remand, the jury awarded damages of $403,000 in response to White's claim of $6 million in compensatory damages.

The decision has been widely criticized as threatening to harm the First Amendment and chill speech, making the right of publicity a tort to merely evoke a celebrity's image in the public mind.[149]

New technology includes the ability to digitally create images of actors and other celebrities long deceased. There is the potential to use these images in movies and television, and Californian Civil Code 990 provides an exemption for the use of name, voice, signature, photograph, or likenesses in plays, books, film, radio, television, magazines, newspapers, and musical compositions in anything but an advertisement. While the archival footage itself is presumably copyrighted, the reanimation by computer, which translates data into images, results in new images.

The practice has been used to create a "Virtual Ed Sullivan Show" on the UPN Network in June 1998, with the image of the late Ed Sullivan, who had hosted a variety show on CBS from 1948 to 1971, generated by computer and his voice supplied by the impressionist John Byner.[150]

Paramount Pictures Corp. v. Wendt[151] was going to deal with the issue or robots and — by inference — the whole problem of rights to fictional personas— once and for all.

George Wendt and John Ratzenberger — actors who portrayed barflies named Norm and Cliff on the popular television series *Cheers* during the show's 11-year run —filed the suit in 1993. They brought the suit against Paramount Pictures Corporation, the owner of the Norm and Cliff characters, for granting Host International, Inc., a license to open a series of airport bars with two life-size animatronic figures that resembled the Norm and Cliff characters. Unappeased by the fact that Host changed the names of the robots to Hank and Bob, Wendt and Ratzenberger alleged that the Host license violated their California statutory and common law right of publicity, as well as federal unfair competition law. Paramount intervened, claiming that, under section 301(a) of the U.S. Copyright Act, it had the right to create derivative works based on the series, and that this right preempted the plaintiffs' state right of publicity claims.

Agreeing with Paramount's argument, the U.S. District Court for the Central District of California granted summary judgment in favor of the defendants. The U.S. Court of Appeals for the Ninth Circuit reversed and remanded, stating that there was no preemption "'so long as the [claims] contain additional elements, such as invasion of personal rights ... that are different in kind from copyright infringement.'"

On remand, the district court again granted the defendants summary judgment, finding no similarity between the robots and the actors. The Ninth Circuit again reversed and remanded, relying on its decision in *White v. Samsung Electronics*. The Ninth Circuit concluded that the case contained material facts that might cause a reasonable jury to find that the robots are similar enough to the plaintiffs to violate California Civil Code section 3344.

In a dissenting opinion, Ninth Circuit judge Kozinski noted that, unlike *White*, *Wendt* pits actor against copyright holder. Judge Kozinski asked, "Can Warner Brothers exploit Rhett Butler without also reminding people of Clark Gable? Can Paramount cast Shelley Long in the *Brady Bunch* movie without creating a triable issue of fact as to whether it is treading on Florence Henderson's right of publicity? How about Dracula and Bela Lugosi? Ripley and Sigourney Weaver? Kramer and Michael Richards?"[152]

Wendt and Ratzenberger did not claim rights to Norm and Cliff but, relying on California Civil Code section 3344, claimed rights to their own likenesses. Which right takes precedence: the actors' right of publicity, or the studio's copyrights to the Norm and Cliff characters? The Ninth Circuit majority in *Wendt* flirted with the conflict, addressing the performer's side: "While it is true that appellants' fame arose in large part through their participation in 'Cheers,' an actor or actress does not lose the right to control the commercial exploitation of his or her likeness by portraying a fictional character."[153]

Judge Kozinski's dissent, which was echoed in Paramount's *certiorari* petition, expresses frustration over the majority's refusal to address the ultimate copyright/right of publicity dilemma: "We pass up yet another opportunity to root out this weed. Instead, we feed it Miracle-Gro."[154]

There was hope that the U.S. Supreme Court would step in and review the *Wendt* case. The Court passed, and, with the case headed back to California, Paramount and the *Wendt* plaintiffs came to an out-of-court agreement in July 2001, leaving the issue unresolved.

Conclusion

In answer to the question, "what protection is afforded a dramatic fictional persona," analysis of case law shows a dearth of findings, analysis, or even discussions involving copyright or trademark protection for these personas and weak evidence for any protection under the right of publicity. Under New York law, the right to exploit the personas of Laurel and Hardy and the Marx Brothers were found to be protected during their lives and afterwards if the right had been exercised during their lifetimes. In both cases, the exercise of the right was basically taken for granted, especially in *Price*, since the court asserted that Laurel and Hardy had been playing themselves. However, this assertion in *Price* and the avoidance of discussion about fictional characters by the *Groucho Marx* trial court illustrates that the decisions in these cases provides no specific authority for protecting dramatic fictional personas.

The appellate court in the *Lugosi* court *did* specifically discuss fictional personas. Even though the *Lugosi* decision went against the Lugosi family, that decision and the appellate court decision in *Groucho Marx* allow that in California the rights to the personas of Lugosi and the Marx Brothers would have been protected after their deaths if the violations were in regard to products Lugosi and the Marx Brothers had promoted in their lifetimes. As the appellate *Groucho Marx* decision illustrates, such an interpretation provides limited protection.

In its discussions of dramatic fictional personas, the appellate *Lugosi* court clearly had difficulty in establishing protection for these personas. It is also telling that the statement in the appellate *Lugosi* decision that "Groucho Marx just being Groucho Marx ... cannot be exploited by others"[155] was refuted by the appellate *Groucho Marx* court.[156]

The history of relevant and related cases shows a searching for a cause of action that fits the subject matter of fictional personas. As the court observed in the final *DeCosta* case, his problems could be attributed at least in part to the inability to find such a fit.[157] The right of publicity has provided the closest approach to a good fit. As the dissent in the appellate court's *Lugosi* decision argued, if the right of publicity protects an individual's "natural" appearance, there is "no reason why the right of publicity should not extend to one's own likeness while portraying a particular fictional character."[158] However, the results will vary from state to state, with Groucho Marx Productions winning under New York law and losing under California's. At the moment, the right of publicity seems the only path available with which courts have shown any sympathy for actors who created a persona without the ability to protect it upfront.

The cleanest form for protection of fictional personas would require extensive legislative revision. This sometimes desperate searching for appropriate causes of action has often occurred because the copyright law does not afford protection for fictional characters. One commentator specifically referenced the *Groucho Marx* case while arguing for the ability to copyright fictional characters:

> [*Groucho Marx*] reveals the need for an effective remedy under the copyright law. By first recognizing that the Marx Brothers were protected, the court could have applied a standard two-part infringement analysis.[159]

As another commentator notes, such a proposal for protecting fictional characters is not new, but counterarguments from the U.S. copyright office have stressed that case law already affords appropriate protection. Since, as previously noted, case law concerns infringement, this commentator states that the copyright office's contention confuses copyrightability and infringement.[160]

One commentator, noting that the *Groucho Marx* courts avoided discussion of copyright protection for the Marx Brothers as fictional characters, suggested establishing in actors' contracts who owns the copyrights to personas.[161] It may seem impractical for producers to turn over rights in *all* actors' contracts for performances for which filming has not even begun, especially since it will be years before it is clear whether a persona has been established by the actor. As illustration of this point, the 1979 dissent in *Lugosi* suggested that Charlie Chaplin's Little Tramp, Carroll O'Connor's Archie Bunker, and Flip Wilson's Geraldine should be given protection.[162] In the subsequent years, while awarding such status to Chaplin's Little Tramp still seems appropriate, Wilson's Geraldine has faded from public memory, and recognition of Archie Bunker is not what it was. Fame is indeed fleeting and selective.

If copyright protection were made available for fictional characters, there would be a special need to establish up front who owned the copyright — the actor or the producer. The creation of such a category would give at least well-known actors the opportunity to secure joint registration for themselves, based on their performance in the role. Another option would be to include a contract provision to allow the actor the ability to share in the rights to the persona if sequels were indeed produced. It is imaginable that lesser-known actors with little bargaining power would be unable to secure these contract provisions or that producers, forced to share rights in a character in a series of films with the actor who first played the role, would try to hire another actor for subsequent films rather than give up such rights. However, at the very least, the availability of protection would be established.

The issue remains as solid and as intangible as Macbeth's dagger or Hamlet's ghost. The courts have demonstrated a reluctance to deal with the issue of protection for fictional representations that cannot be easily trademarked or copyrighted, that cannot be analyzed within previously established causes of action. Subsequent manifestations of the combination of circumstances that occurred in the Lugosi, Laurel and Hardy, and Marx Brothers cases, the combination of fictional personas developed over time plus the usurpation of these personas, may well be necessary to establish in greater detail the existence of such rights.

Afterword

While each chapter has a conclusion, there is an overall conclusion to this book: the legal considerations concerning fictionalization of actual people and events in films and television still don't fit.

In the course of this book, we have seen courts struggle with the alternative universes created in which films claim to be both based on actual events and also fictionalizations totally or in part. We have seen people who claim they have been falsely portrayed in films grapple with the question of identification and the spouses and children of these people confronting the legal fact that they have no standing to sue for libel — only the dead would have standing, and the dead cannot sue for libel. Having confronted this fact, these family members have — as shown in detail in the suit regarding the film *The Perfect Storm* — searched for other causes of action under which they could seek legal satisfaction — invasion of privacy, violation of the right of publicity, and commercial misappropriation — so far with little success. We have seen filmmakers try to present films that are entertaining, exercise their First Amendment right of freedom of expression, and deal with complaints from those portrayed or their families. (I'll always remember director Ridley Scott, when asked about the fictionalizations in *Black Hawk Down*, fixing me with an exasperated stare and saying, "Look.") We have even seen actors whose personalities have merged with the film personas struggle with the fact that the law is evolving. Individuals like Mr. DeCosta, who felt he had created the character of Paladin in the TV series *Have Gun Will Travel*, were basically told they were caught between recognizable causes of action.

We have also seen the ironies that come with perspective. If the case of *Youssoupoff v. MGM* were tried today in the light of *Sullivan v. New York Times*, the plaintiff probably would have lost — as the Youssoupoffs did when they sued MGM 30 years after the MGM case. Robert B. Kelly won a defamation suit against MGM for its portrayal of him in *They Were Expendable,* and 30 years afterwards his commanding officer said that Kelly had sued because MGM depicted him for exactly the type of person he was. Of the legal films analyzed, arguably the most compelling — *The Andersonville Trial*— takes the most liberties, not with events but with the motivation of the characters.

While plaintiffs sue for depictions of themselves of family members in films and television shows, filmmakers like Oliver Stone, supported by some film scholars, claim they are *deliberately rewriting* history and "playing with our minds."

Things still don't fit. There is an evolution at hand. Things are changing; the issues are being discussed. As the prosecutor says at the end of *The Andersonville Trial,* "We try, we try."

Chapter Notes

Introduction

1. *From Noon to Three,* MGM/UA 1976. Directed and written by Frank Gilroy. Starring Charles Bronson, Jill Ireland, and Douglas V. Fowley.

2. *Butch Cassidy and the Sundance* Kid, 20th Century–Fox, 1969. Directed by George Roy Hill. Starring Paul Newman, Robert Redford, and Katherine Ross.

3. William Goldman, *Butch Cassidy and the Sundance Kid* (1969), 160. The excised scene is included in this, the published screenplay. The silent film being projected in this scene is used instead in the opening credits of the released film.

4. *The Return of Frank James,* 20th Century–Fox, 1940. Directed by Fritz Lang. Starring Henry Fonda, Gene Tierney, Jackie Cooper, Henry Hull, and John Carradine.

5. *Jesse James,* 20th Century–Fox, 1939. Directed by Henry King. Starring Tyrone Power, Henry Fonda, Nancy Kelly, and Randolph Scott.

6. See William Settle, *Facts and Fiction Concerning the Careers of the Notorious James Brothers of Missouri* (1977), and Ted P. Yeatman, *Frank and Jesse James: The Story Behind the Legend* (2000). There was also a 1957 film that pointedly advertised itself as *The True Story of Jesse James,* 20th Century–Fox, directed by Nicholas Ray and starring Robert Wagner and Jeffrey Hunter.

7. See Richard Patterson, *Butch Cassidy: A Biography* (1998).

8. *JFK,* Warner Bros., 1991. Directed by Oliver Stone. Starring Kevin Costner, Tommie Lee Jones, and Kevin Bacon.

9. See Art Simon, *Dangerous Knowledge: The JFK Assassination in Art and Film* (1996), 210–211.

10. *The Conqueror Worm,* AIP, 1968. Directed by Michael Reeves. Starring Vincent Price, Rupert Davies, and Ian Ogilvy.

11. *Glory,* TriStar, 1989. Directed by Edward Zwick. Starring Matthew Broderick, Denzel Washington, Morgan Freeman, and Cary Elwes.

12. Mackubin Thomas Owens, "History and the Movies: The Lessons of 'The Patriot' and 'Glory,'" *USA Today,* August 1, 2000.

13. *The Man Who Shot Liberty Valance,* Warner Bros., 1962. Directed by John Ford. Starring John Wayne, James Stewart, Vera Miles, Lee Marvin, and Edmond O'Brien.

14. Robert A. Rosenstone, *Visions of the Past: The Challenge of Film to Our Idea of History* (1995), 12.

15. *Mississippi Burning,* Orion, 1988. Directed by Alan Parker. Starring Gene Hackman, Willem Dafoe, and Frances McDormand.

16. *Walker,* MCA, 1987. Directed by Alex Cox. Starring Ed Harris and Richard Masur.

17. Sumiko Higashi, "*Walker* and *Mississippi Burning*: Postmodernism Versus Illusionist Narrative," in *Revisioning History: Film and the Construction of a New Past,* ed. Robert A. Rosenstone (1995), 198.

18. *Nixon,* Hollywood Pictures, 1995.

Directed by Oliver Stone. Starring Anthony Hopkins, Joan Allen, and James Woods.

19. Mark C. Carnes, "Past Imperfect: History According to the Movies" (interview with film director Oliver Stone), *Cineaste* 22, no. 4 (Fall 1966): 33. Reprinted from *Past Imperfect: History According to the Movies*, eds. Ted Mico, John Miller-Monzon, and David Rubel (1996).

20. "A Conversation between Eric Foner and John Sayles" in *Past Imperfect: History According to the Movies*, eds. Ted Mico, John Miller-Monzon, and David Rubel (1996), 16.

21. Higashi, 198.

22. Quoted in Janet Maslin, "A Movie's Power Over Attitudes and Action," *New York Times*, February 22, 2004, 5.

23. See William A. Rusher, "How Reliable Is History?" Daily Ardmoreite (Ardmore, OK), October 29, 1997.

24. *Hoodlum*, United Artists, 1997. Directed by Bill Duke. Starring Lawrence Fishburne, Tim Roth, Vanessa L. Williams, and Andy Garcia.

25. *Patton*, 20th Century–Fox, 1970. Directed by Franklin J. Schaffner. Starring George C. Scott, Karl Malden, and Edward Binns.

26. *History in the Movies*, The History Channel, broadcast November 2001.

27. Goldman, iii.

28. *The Perfect Storm*. Warner Bros., 2000. Directed by Wolfgang Petersen. Starring George Clooney, Diane Lane, Mary Elizabeth Mastrantonio, Mark Wahlberg, and John C. Reilly.

29. *Tyne v. Time-Warner*, case No. 02-13281, Movant's Initial Brief on Question Certified by the 11th Circuit, July 2003.

30. Laurence Darmiento, "Hollywood's Liability Tab Skyrocketing," *Los Angeles Business Journal*, July 2, 2001.

31. Max Frankel, "One Peep vs. Docudrama," *New York Times Magazine*, March 16, 1997, 26.

32. Jack Valenti, "'False History' on a Screen Near You," *Washington Post*, March 23, 2004, A23.

Chapter I

1. *Contact*. Warner Bros., 1997. Directed by Robert Zemeckis. Starring Jody Foster, Tom Skerritt, and James Woods.

2. White House Release, July 15, 1997.

3. Steve Steakey, producer, on "Crossfire," broadcast on CNN Cable, July 15, 1997. The closing credits for the film list a number of real-life television personalities as playing "himself" or "herself," but there is no credit for the person who plays the president.

4. *Hennessy*, American International, 1975. Directed by Don Sharp. Starring Rod Steiger, Lee Remick, Patrick Stewart, and Richard Johnson.

5. *Hoodlum*, United Artists, 1997. Directed by Bill Duke. Starring Lawrence Fishburne, Tim Roth, Vanessa L. Williams, and Andy Garcia.

6. R. H. Kurtz, "Georgia Anne Unamused by Sitcom Nonsense," *Washington Post*, January 28, 1993, C1:4.

7. *Entertainment Tonight*, February 1, 1993.

8. Kurtz, C2:4.

9. *Tyne v. Time Warner Entertainment*, No. 6:00 CV-1115-ORL-22-C, M.D. Fla., filed August 24, 2000.

10. "CBS Pulls Reagan Miniseries," AP Report, November 5, 2002. See also Lisa de Moraes, "The Reagans: Too Hot for CBS to Handle?" *Washington Post*, November 4, 2003, C01.

11. Tom Shales, "'The Reagans': Not Quite a Hatchet Job," *Washington Post*, November 30, 2003, D1. Shales concluded, "There's enough nastiness and character assassination in the film — even without the line about AIDS — to make CBS look wise in pulling it off the network and foolish in having scheduled it in the first place. It's a matter of bad timing as well as bad manners; former president Reagan is not only still alive but seriously and terminally ill, making a drama riddled with slurs unseemly and hugely inappropriate."

12. Herodotus, *Histories*, 6:21.

13. Quoted in E.K. Chambers, *The Elizabethan Stage*, vol. 4. (1923), 332.

14. William H. Hudson, *Treatise of the Court of Star Chamber*. London, 1791–92, Vol. 2 of *Collectionsea Juridicia*, Francis Hargrave. ed.

15. For a complete look at this incident, see Margaret Dowling, "Sir Edward Hayward's Troubles over His Life of Henry IV," *The Library* ser. 4, no. 11 (1930–31), 213–16. Dowling reproduces Coke's notes from the examinations, now in the Public Record Office.

16. Bodleian Library, Tanner MS. 76. f. 49r, a seventeenth-century manuscript.

17. J. Dover Wilson, ed. *The Tragedy of Richard the Second*. New Cambridge edition, 1984, xvi–xxxvi.

18. Dowling, 216–17.

19. F.J. Levy, "Hayward, Daniel, and the Beginnings of Politic History in England," Huntington Library Quarterly 18 (1987), 50.

20. A.R. Braunmuller, "King John and Historiography," 55 *ELH* [English Literary History] (1988), 322.

21. Quoted in Stanley Weintraub, *General Washington's Christmas Farewell: A Mount*

Vernon Homecoming (2003), 161. The 1824 painting, "General Washington Resigning his Commission," is in the Capitol Rotunda in Washington, D.C. Weintraub notes that, in other paintings depicting this period, General Washington did not risk the safety of the boat by standing as he is shown to have done in Emanuel Leutze's 1851 depiction of Washington crossing the Delaware, and it was General Charles O'Hara who surrendered his sword to Washington at Yorktown rather than General Cornwallis as shown in another Trumbull painting. Admiral Nelson did not die on the deck of his ship surrounded by his officers and crew as depicted in Benjamin West's 1806 painting "Death of Nelson" but rather in a small cabin below.

22. See, among other Cody books, Bobby Bridger, *Buffalo Bill and Sitting Bull: Inventing the Wild West* (2003). Robert Altman's 1976 film *Buffalo Bill and the Indians* (United Artists) uses Cody's life to explore the subject of mythmaking.

23. *Binns v. Vitagraph,* 210 N.Y. 51; 56.

24. Youssoupoff's 1916 fortune has been valued at $500,000,000 by T. Berkman, *The Lady and the Law: The Remarkable Life of Fanny Holtzman* (1976), 138, and $350,000,000 by *New York Times,* October, 16, 1965, 1:5 (testimony at 1965 lawsuit by Youssoupoff against CBS television).

25. For more information on this period, see E. Radzinsky, *The Last Czar: The Life and Death of Nicholas II* (1992); Leon Trotsky, *The History of the Russian Revolution* (1932); as well as Youssoupoff's own account: F.F. Iusupov [Youssoupoff], *Rasputin* (1927).

26. Youssoupoff testified in his action against MGM that he had filed suit against the German filmmakers of this 1930 film but had dropped it when his Berlin attorneys settled without getting the defamatory segments excised. Rather than compromise his honor, Youssoupoff said, he refused the money and abandoned the action. D. Napley, *Rasputin in Hollywood* (1990), 134.

27. Veidt had costarred in the 1919 classic *The Cabinet of Dr. Caligari* and later moved to the United States, where he played mostly villains in such films as *Casablanca* (Warner Bros., 1942).

28. Oddly, given the litigation that ultimately affected *Rasputin and the Empress*, Ethel Barrymore contemplated suing Kaufman and Ferber for defamation for the play's depiction of the characters based on her and her brother John (Lionel was not portrayed) and contacted the attorney Max Steuer. She was told that the only Barrymore who might have a claim was John, whose counterpart in the play was care-less, egocentric, and slightly deranged. Ferber even admitted that they had based the character of Tony Cavendish on John Barrymore, or at least some of him, saying, "He was, of course, too improbable to copy from life." True to his persona, John Barrymore refused to speak to Steuer and the matter was dropped. See M. Peters, *The House of Barrymore* (1990), 300; J. Kobler, *Damned in Paradise: The Life of John Barrymore* (1977), 227.

29. Gene Fowler, *Goodnight, Sweet Prince* (1943, rpt. 1947), 307.

30. John Kobler, *Damned in Paradise* (1977), 271.

31. J. Kotsitibas-Davis, *The Barrymores* (1981), 130.

32. Berkman, 153.

33. B. Thomas, *Thalberg: Life and Legend* (1969; rpt. 1970), 210.

34. M. de Acosta, *Here Lies the Heart* (1960), 245. ("I don't need you to tell me a lot of nonsense about what is libelous or what is not. I want this sequence in and that's all there is to it," de Acosta quotes Thalberg as saying.)

35. Hyman later produced *San Francisco* (1936, about the 1906 earthquake), *The Good Earth* (1937), *Conquest* (1937, about Napoleon) and *The Great Waltz* (biography of Johann Strauss, Jr.).

36. Kotsilibas-Davis, 141.

37. *Rasputin and the Empress*, MGM, 1932. The film became available on videotape in April 1993.

38. Napley, 44–5.

39. Iusopov.

40. Napley reports that the case was dismissed by the French court because it dealt with political issues in a foreign jurisdiction. Napley, 44.

41. de Acosta, 246.

42. J. Robert Rubin, MGM New York vice president and general counsel, told Fannie Holtzman, "Anyway, the damn thing stinks. Audiences won't go near it." Berkman, 142.

43. As listed in *The American Movies: The History, the Films, the Awards* (1969), 377.

44. As listed in *The American Movies*, 381.

45. R. Behlmer, ed., *Memo from David O. Selznick* (1972), 65.

46. Napley, 66–7.

47. Berkman, 143.

48. L. H. Elderidge, *Law of Defamation* (1978), §10 at 50; R. A. Smolla, *Law of Defamation* (1993), §4.07 [b].

49. Berkman, 143.

50. Berkman, 147.

51. Berkman, 151.

52. Berkman, 142.

53. An almost complete transcript of the trial is presented in narrative form in Napley.

The book, however, is a narrative, with almost no legal analysis or discussion. Press accounts and the recollections of participants provide additional details, however.

54. Beckman, 151.

55. *New York Times*, February 28, 1934, 4:3.

56. What was not apparently cited during the trial was that there had been contemporary rumors that Rasputin had lusted after Princess Irina and that these were suspected to have been started by the assassins themselves to give them more justification for their act. See Radzinsky, 163. ("Vera Leonidovna: "The legend about the holy man lusting after Irina was created later by the assassins themselves.") It is possible, then, that from the filmmakers' interviews and research that these rumors were "in the air" and somehow ended up in the finished film. In Youssoupoff's 1965 invasion of privacy suit against CBS television for its telecast of a dramatization of the murder of Rasputin, one of his allegations was that the broadcast falsely suggested that he had used his wife as bait to lure Rasputin to his home. Princess Irina admitted on the stand that Rasputin had most probably come to their home in the hope of being with her but denied that her husband had planned it. *New York Times*, 26 October 1965, 36:5.

57. *New York Times*, March 1, 1934, 1:2; March 2, 1934, 9:1.

58. Berkman, 157.

59. Napley, 147.

60. William Shakespeare, *The Rape of Lucrece*, 692. In *The Riverside Shakespeare* (1974).

61. *New York Times*, March 6, 1934, 9:1.

62. *Youssoupoff v. Metro-Goldwyn-Mayer Pictures*, 50 Times L.R. 581 (1934); rpt. 92 A.L.R. 864.

63. 50 Times L.R. 581; rpt. 99 A.L.R. at 874.

64. 50 Times L.R. 581; rpt. 99 A.L.R. at 875.

65. 152 N.Y.S. 829 (1915).

66. 152 N.Y.S. at 831.

67. 270 N.Y.S. 544 (1934).

68. 50 Times L.R. 681; rpt. 99 A.L.R. at 869.

69. 50 Times L.R. 581; rpt. 99 A.L.R. at 870.

70. *Time*, March 12, 1934, 23.

71. 50 Times L.R. 581; rpt. 99 A.L.R. at 868.

72. 50 Times L.R. 581; rpt. 99 A.L.R. at 868: "Part of the defence in the action seems really to be: 'It is quite true that the defendants said that this is a story of fact, but it is really all fiction. We ought to have used, if we described it properly, the formula which is now put at the beginning of most novels: 'All circumstances in this novel are imaginary, and none of the characters in it are real.' Of course, that would not have fitted in with a representation that it was really a representation of the rela-tions of the Royal Family with Rasputin and the people who killed Rasputin."

73. *New York Times*, 11 August 1934, 14:2.

74. *New York Times*, 22 September, 1934, 17:4.

75. Note, 31 *Mich. L. Rev.* 1013–4 (1934).

76. For brief histories of the Hays Office and the Legion of Decency, see "Censorship," *The Oxford Companion to Film* (1976), 119–20. See also J. Vizard, *See No Evil: Life Inside a Hollywood Censor* (1970) and P. Facey, *The Legion of Decency: A Sociological Analysis of the Emergence and Development of a Social Pressure Group* (1974).

77. Max Steiner, film music composer, quoted in T. Thomas, *Music for the Movies* (1973), 113.

78. 50 Times L.R. 581; rpt. 99 A.L.R. at 877.

79. 50 Times L.R. 581; rpt. 99 A.L.R. at 977.

80. *New York Times*, February 28, 1934, 4:3 ("'The episodes in dispute were made after I left Hollywood,' [Ethel Barrymore] said. 'As a matter of fact, I have never seen the film right through. My sympathies are with the Youssoupoffs, whom I have known personally for some years.'").

81. Behlmer, 65. A film version of *The Man of Property*, the first volume in *The Forsyte Saga*, was made in 1949 at MGM under the title *That Forsyte Woman;* it was released in Great Britain as *The Forsyte Saga*. Errol Flynn, a friend and protégé of John Barrymore who would portray him in the 1958 film *Too Much, Too Soon*, played Soames Forsyte, the role presumably designated for John Barrymore. The other leads were Greer Garson and Walter Pidgeon.

82. *New York Times*, November 9, 1965, 1:3; 34:3 (producer and two authors of teleplay were unaware when the program was broadcast that Prince Felix Youssoupoff, portrayed in the program, was still alive).

83. *Youssoupoff v. C.B.S.* 244 N.Y.S. 2d. 201, 19 A.D.. 2d 865 (1963).

84. 224 N.Y.S. 2d at 203.

85. 244 N.Y.S. 2d. at 203.

86. *New York Times*, November 9, 1965, 1:3; 34:3.

87. 244 N.Y.S. 2d at 706.

88. 244 N.Y.S. 2d at 706.

89. 244 N.Y.S. 2d at 708.

90. 244 N.Y.S. 2d 1 (1963).

91. *N.Y. Times,* October 16, 1965, 1:5.

92. *N.Y. Times*, November 9, 1965, 1:3; 34:3. The story notes that when the verdict was handed down, jewels from the necklace Czar Nicholas had given Princess Irina as a wedding gift were being sold across town at Bruckner & Morton; the Youssoupoffs had sold the necklace for cash thirty years before.

93. The Princess Irina died in March 1970 at the age of seventy.

94. Radzinsky, 141 (again quoting Vera Leonidovna: "Handsome Felix had what are called 'grammatical errors,' that is, he was bisexual, plain and simple.") In the film, Prince Chegodieff is dashing and kind. In an early scene, he stops the guards from opening fire on peasants, only to have one of the peasants spit at him. When the officer in charge tells him, "Do you see what you get for being kind to them?" Chegodieff wipes the spittle away and says, "Well, at least it isn't blood."

95. See J. D. Eames, *The MGM Story* (1982).

96. *They Died with Their Boots On*, Warner Bros., 1941. Directed by Raoul Walsh. Starring Errol Flynn, Olivia de Havilland, and Arthur Kennedy.

97. *Little Big Man*, National General, 1970. Directed by Arthur Penn. Starring Dustin Hoffman, Faye Dunaway, Chief Dan George, and Richard Mulligan.

98. Oliver Stone, "Who Is Rewriting History," *New York Times*, December 20, 1991, A35.

99. Max Frankel, "One Peep vs. Docudrama," *New York Times Magazine*, March 16, 1997, 26.

100. *The Great Ziegfeld*, MGM, 1936. Directed by Robert Z. Leonard. Starring William Powell, Myrna Loy, and Anna Held.

101. *Yankee Doodle Dandy*, Warner Bros., 1942. Directed by Michael Curtiz. Starring James Cagney, Joan Leslie, and Walter Huston.

102. McGilligan, Patrick, ed., *Yankee Doodle Dandy* (1981), 16, 18.

103. See Comment, "Defamation by Fiction," 42 *Md. L. Rev.* 387–427 (1983).

104. "*Smith, Jones v. Hulton*: Three Conflicting Judicial Views As to Question of Defamation (p.2)," 60 *U. Pa. L. Rev.* 461, 476 (1917). Subsequent case law has shown, for both fiction and films, that announcement that a work is fiction is not an absolute bar to libel. But the thought had currency at the time of *Rasputin* and affected the formation of the disclaimer.

105. For a contemporary view of the use of disclaimers in modern novels, see Peter Mack, "Thou Art Not He Nor She: Authors' Disclaimers and Attitudes to Fiction," *Times Literary Supplement*, December 15, 1995, 12.

106. *The Life of Emile Zola*, Warner Bros., 1937. Directed by William Dieterle. Starring Paul Muni, Gale Sondegaard, and Donald Crisp.

107. *The Charge of the Light Brigade*, Warner Bros., 1936. Directed by Michael Curtiz. Starring Errol Flynn, Olivia de Havilland, and David Niven.

108. There was a 1968 film entitled *The Charge of the Light Brigade* that attempted to tell the "true" story of the blunder that was the charge at Balaklava. It was distributed by MGM, directed by Tony Richardson, and starred Trevor Howard, Vanessa Redgrave, John Gielgud, and David Hemmings. In promoting the film on TV talk shows, Howard, who had starred in *The Roots of Heaven* with Flynn in 1958, compared the 1969 and 1936 films by saying, "Well, with Errol, he always won."

109. *Louisiana Purchase.* Music and Lyrics by Irvin Berlin. Book by Morris Ryskind. Produced by B.G. de Sylva. 1940. Manuscript in the Library of Congress. The musical was made into a 1941 Paramount film starring Bob Hope. As was the custom, most of the songs from the show were jettisoned, with the interesting exception of an abbreviated version of the disclaimer song, which forms the first five minutes of the film, although the initial singer is the attorney and not his secretary. The film was released on videotape in May 1993.

110. *The Wings of Eagles*, MGM, 1957. Directed by John Ford. Starring John Wayne, Maureen O'Hara, Dan Dailey, and Ward Bond.

111. John Ford quoted in Peter Bogdanovich, *John Ford* (1968), 96.

112. *Somebody Up There Likes Me*, MGM, 1956. Directed by Robert Wise. Starring Paul Newman, Pier Angeli, and Everett Sloane.

113. Quoted in Mason Wiley and Damien Bona, *Inside Oscar: The Unofficial History of the Academy Awards* (1984), 266.

114. Samuel Taylor Coleridge wrote in 1817 in Chapter IV of his autobiography *Biographia Literaria*, "In this idea originated the plan of the 'Lyrical Ballads'; in which it was agreed, that my endeavours should be directed to persons and characters supernatural, or at least romantic; yet so as to transfer from our inward nature a human interest and a semblance of truth sufficient to procure for these shadows of imagination that willing suspension of disbelief for the moment, which constitutes poetic faith."

115. *Hollywood Canteen*, Warner Bros, 1943. Directed by Delmer Daves. Starring Joan Leslie, Dane Clark, and Robert Hutton.

116. *Adaptation*, Columbia, 2002. Directed by Spike Jonze. Starring Nicolas Cage, Meryl Streep, and Chris Cooper.

117. Quoted in Karen Butler, "The Screenplay Thief," *Book Magazine*, January/February 2003.

118. Andy Seiler, "An Amused Orlean Plays

Along with Preposterous 'Adaptation,'" *USA Today,* January 3, 2003, 13D.

119. *Green Grow the Rushes,* British Lion, 1951. Directed by Derek Twist. Starring Richard Burton and Robert Livesey.

120. *The Great Dictator,* United Artists, 1940. Directed and written by Charles Chaplin. Starring Charlie Chaplin, Paulette Goddard, Billy Gilbert, Henry Daniel, and Jack Oakie.

121. R. Weinstein, "The Legal Effect of Disclaimers of Liability on Motion Pictures Based on Fact," 9 *Glendale L. Rev.* 74, 77 (1990).

122. R. A. Smolla, "Law of Defamation," §4.09 [7][b], fn.174 (1993).

123. *Kelly v. Loewe's Inc.,* 76 Supp. 473, 485 (1948).

124. Note, 31 *Mich. L. Rev.* 1013–4 (1934).

125. *Davis v. RKO Radio Pictures,* 16 F. Supp. 195 (S.D.N.Y., 1936).

126. *Bunker Bean,* RKO, 1936. Directed by William Hamilton and Edward Kelly. Starring Owen Davis, Jr., and Louise Latimer; Lucille Ball appears in a small role.

127. 16 F. Supp. at 196.

128. *Levey v. Warner Bros. Pictures,* 57 F. Supp. 40 (1944).

129. 57 F. Supp. at 41.

130. The court's indifference to a plaintiff's feelings is apparent in other unsuccessful suits. The songwriter and comedian Harry Fox sued 20th Century– Fox for portraying him as "a lowly songwriter" in its 1945 film *The Dolly Sisters,* and lost, as did boxer and war hero Barney Ross when he sued the makers of the film biography *Monkey on My Back* (1957). The latter film depicted Ross' descent into drug addiction, and Ross claimed the movie portrayed his life as one of "filth, bilge, and cheap sensation." Ross had been an advisor on the film.

131. 55 F. Supp. 639 (1944).

132. *Primrose Path,* RKO, 1940. Directed by Gregory La Cava. Starring Ginger Rogers, Marjorie Rambeau, and Joel McCrea.

133. *Fighting Father Dunne.* RKO, 1948. Directed by Ted Tetzlaff. Starring Pat O'Brien and Darryl Hickman.

134. 191 F. 2d 901 (8th Cir., 1951).

135. 174 Cal. App. 3d 384; 219 Cal. Rptr. 891 (1985).

136. *Zoot Suit,* Universal, 1981. Directed by Luis Valdez. Starring Edward James Olmos, Tyne Daly, Charles Aidman, and John Anderson. The movie is a filmed version of a stage production that was theatrically released.

137. 191 F. 2d at 904; 174 Cal App. 3d at 391.

138. 174 Cal. App. 3d at 391 (the reference is to the television series *Mork and Mindy,* in which "Mork" is a character from outer space).

139. *Anatomy of a Murder,* Columbia, 1959. Directed by Otto Preminger. Starring James Stewart, Ben Gazarra, Lee Remick, and Joseph L. Welch.

140. 300 F. 2d 372 (1962).

141. *Bindrim v. Mitchell,* 92 Cal. App. 3d 61; 155 Cal. Rptr. 29 (1979), distinguished *Wheeler:* "In the case at the bar, the only differences between plaintiff and the Herford character in [the novel] *Touching* were physical appearances and that Herford was a psychiatrist rather than a psychologist. Otherwise, the character Simon Herford was very similar to the actual plaintiff. We cannot say, as did the court in *Wheeler,* that no one who knew plaintiff Bindrim could reasonably identify him with the fictional character." 92 Cal. App. 3d at 75.

142. 200 F. 2d at 376.

143. 200 F. 2d at 376.

144. S. Warren and L. Brandes, "The Right of Publicity," 4 *Harv. L. Rev.* 196 (1890).

145. The right of publicity is the right of a person "to own, protect, and commercially exploit his own name, likeness, and persona." *Lerman v. Chuckleberry,* 521 F. Supp., 232 (S.D.N.Y., 1981). The right of publicity has been distinguished from the right of privacy, although they do interrelate, in that the right of publicity may not involve the hurt of personal feeling but focuses instead on the loss of compensation. *Harlen Laboratories v. Topps Chewing Gum,* 202 F. 2d 866, 868 (2d Cir. 1953).

146. *Time,* November 8, 1982, 71.

147. *Taylor v. NBC,* No. BC 110922 (Cal. Super. Ct., September 29, 1994).

148. *John Goldfarb, Please Come Home,* 20th Century–Fox, 1965. Directed by J. Lee Thompson. Starring Shirley MacLaine, Peter Ustinov, and Richard Crenna.

149. *University of Notre Dame Du Lac v. Twentieth Century–Fox,* 256 N.Y.S. 2d 301 (1965).

150. "Plaintiff expressly states that the action is in no sense a libel action and that any libel involved is immaterial and beside the point." 256 N.Y.S. 2d at 301.

151. 256 N.Y.S. 2d at 307.

152. 256 N.Y.S. at 304.

153. *Agatha,* Warner Bros., 1979. Directed by Michael Apted. Starring Vanessa Redgrave and Dustin Hoffman.

154. 464 F. Supp. at 432.

155. 464 F. Supp. at 433.

156. *The Ghost of Flight 401,* NBC-TV, 1978. Directed by Steven Hilliard Stern. Starring Ernest Borgnine, Gary Lockwood, Tina Chen, and Kim Basinger.

157. *Loft v. Fuller,* 408 So. 2d 619, 624 (1982).

158. *They Were Expendable,* MGM, 1945. Directed by John Ford. Starring Robert Montgomery, John Wayne, Donna Reed, and Ward Bond.

159. *MacArthur,* Universal, 1977. Directed by Joseph Sargent. Starring Gregory Peck, Ed Flanders, and Dan O'Herlihy.

160. *Kelly v. Lowe's Inc.,* 76 F. Supp. 485 (1948).

161. Bulkeley recalled, "Bob Kelly turned around and sued 'em because they portrayed him as he actually is, a very rambunctious Irishman, very difficult to get along with.... He's a good man, good sailor, but he's a stubborn bastard. He's one of those guys who shoots his mouth off when he should be listening, so that's when he gets into trouble." Quoted in Joseph McBride, *Searching for John Ford* (2001), 407.

162. 76 F. Supp. at 486. The screenwriter was, however, not a layman but Commander Frank Wead, USN, whose life was later filmed by the same director, John Ford, as the movie *The Wings of Eagles* (MGM, 1957).

163. 76 F. Supp. at 485.

164. 76 F. Supp. at 489.

165. *New York Times,* December 4, 1948, 1.

166. Quoted in Joseph McBride, *Searching for John Ford* (2001), 409.

167. *Orlando Sentinel,* March 1, 1993, p. A8; *Houston Chronicle,* Feb. 28, 1993, p. 24.

168. Cook, K. Douglas, "Addendum to *They Were Expendable,*" September 4, 2003, Internet response to essay "*They Were Expendable*: A Critique of John Ford's 1945 War Film" by David M. Cross. http://history.sandiego.edu/gen/filmnotes/They_Were_Expendable2.html. Cross is identified as Chief, Public Affairs and Congressional Liaison, U.S. Army, Fort Jackson, S.C., and was asked by the Walchers to organize their boxes of documents for possible publication.

169. T. Brooks and E. Marsh, *The Complete Directory to Prime Time Network TV Shows, 1946–Present* (1979), 652–4.

170. Interestingly enough, the 1992 TV series *The Untouchables* claimed to be based on the Ness-Fraley book and the 1959–63 original TV series. There is a disclaimer that "some" of the characters are fictitious. While the original series was true to life in that Ness and Al Capone were never shown meeting, the new series had them meet, and frequently. Both Ness and Capone are, of course, dead.

171. *Maritote v. Desilu Productions, Inc.,* 230 F. Supp. 721 (N.D. 1964), aff'd 345 F. 2d 418 (7th Cir. 1965) (finding no action under Illinois law for misappropriation of name, likeness, and personality by descendants of the person in question), cert. denied 382 U.S. 883, 86 S. Ct. 176 (1965).

172. 345 F. 2d at 421.

173. 345 F. 2d at 421.

174. 345 F. 2d at 421.

175. *American Broadcasting–Paramount Theatre, Inc. v. Simpson,* 106 Ga. App. 230, 126 S.E. 2d 873 (1962).

176. 106 Ga. App. at 241.

177. 106 Ga. App. at 242–3.

178. 106 Ga. App. at 242.

179. Settlement, Satisfaction, and Dismissal Order, Fulton Superior Court [Fulton County, Georgia], Case Number A-86281, February 1, 1963.

180. While litigation of claims that characters in movies and television are based on actual people usually state that the portrayal was unwanted and defamatory, there have been cases where plaintiffs actually wanted to prove identification with movie characters. The family of the late Geoffrey F. Bowers sued the creators of the 1993 movie *Philadelphia* for breach of contract. Bowers had sued the law firm of Baker & McKenzie, alleging that he had been fired because he had AIDS. Bowers had died in 1987 after testifying and before the case was decided in his favor. The family claimed that the makers of *Philadelphia* had promised them $1 million and 5 percent of the net proceeds from the movie for the use of Bowers' story. TriStar Pictures argued in response that the movie was fictional and also that any material based on Bowers' lawsuit were taken from public sources. The movie carried the traditional disclaimer. *Cavagnuolo v. Rudin,* 94 Civ. 0585 (S.D.N.Y.); see also "'Philadelphia' Story," *Washington Post,* March 13, 1996. The suit was ultimately settled. TriStar admitted that the film was "inspired in part" by Bowers' story. The terms of the settlement were not disclosed.

181. Broadcast on February 2, 1962, on CBS. Written by Rod Serling, based on an idea by Frederic Louis Fox. Starring Larry Blyden as Rance McGrew and Arch Johnson as Jesse James.

182. 376 U.S. 254 (1964).

183. 365 U.S. at 271.

184. *Curtis Publishing Co. v. Butts,* 388 U.S. 130 (1967).

185. 418 U.S. 323 (1974).

186. 418 U.S. at 347.

187. D. Smirlock, "Clear and Convincing Libel: Fiction and the Law of Defamation," 92 *Yale L. J.* 520 (1983).

188. 92 Cal. App. 3d 61 (1979).

189. 645 F. 2d 1227 (1981).

190. *Judge Horton and the Scottsboro Boys,* NBC-TV, 1978. Starring Arthur Hill.

191. 645 F. 2d at 1235.

192. *Missing*, Universal, 1986. Directed by Constantin Costa-Gavras. Starring Jack Lemmon, Sissy Spacek, Richard Venture, Charles Cioffi.

193. *Davis v. Costa-Gavras*, 654 F. Supp. 653 (1987).

194. 654 F. Supp. at 654, 656.

195. 654 F. Supp. at 658.

196. *George Wallace*, broadcast on TNT-cable TV, 1997. Directed by John Frankenheimer. Starring Gary Sinise, Mare Winningham, and Joe Don Baker.

197. Rick Bragg, "A Movie on His Life Enrages George Wallace," *New York Times,* February 25, 1997, 9.

198. *Journey for Margaret*, MGM, 1943. Directed by W. S. Van Dyke II. Starring Robert Young, Laraine Day, Nigel Bruce, and Margaret O'Brien.

199. *Fort Apache*, RKO, 1948. Directed by John Ford. Screenplay by Frank Nugent. Starring Henry Fonda, John Wayne, Shirley Temple, and Ward Bond.

200. *Three Faces of Eve*, 20th Century–Fox, 1957. Written and directed by Nunnally Johnson. Starring Joanne Woodward, Lee J. Cobb, and David Wayne.

201. The book *Three Faces of Eve* by Drs. Corbett H. Thigpen and Harvey M. Cleckley was published in 1957. The film's director and screenwriter Nunnally Johnson was concerned about the need to "convince somebody that this wasn't simply fiction," and it was for this reason that he secured the services of Alistair Cooke, a respected journalist and host of the CBS TV series *Omnibus*. Unfortunately — and ironically, given Cooke's introduction — Chris Coster Sizemore, the "real life" Eve, in writing her own memoirs—*I'm Eve, My Story,* 1977, and *A Mind of My Own,* 1985 — denounced the book and film, claiming that much of the story had been made up. She also stated that, rather than being "cured" as the book and movie claim, she had had recurrences of her illness and had gone to Dr. Thigpen —fictionalized as "Dr. Luther" in the film — who, sadly, did not help her. She inferred that Thigpen did not want to detract from his reputation as the man who had "cured" Eve.

202. *Hammett*, Warner Bros./Zoetrope, 1982. Directed by Wim Wenders. Starring Frederic Forrest, Peter Boyle, and Marilu Henner.

203. *Raiders of the Los Ark*, Paramount, 1981. Directed by Steven Spielberg. Starring Harrison Ford and Karen Allen. *Indiana Jones and the Temple of Doom*, Paramount, 1984. Directed by Steven Spielberg. Starring Harrison Ford and Kate Capshaw. *Indiana Jones and the Last Crusade*, Paramount, 1989. Directed by Steven Spielberg. Starring Harrison Ford and Sean Connery.

204. *JFK*, Warner Bros., 1991. Directed by Oliver Stone. Starring Kevin Costner, Tommy Lee Jones, and Kevin Bacon.

205. The theory that President Kennedy was killed as a result of a conspiracy in which Vice President Johnson was complicit was dramatized in 1968 in a play entitled *Macbird* — a takeoff of Shakespeare's *Macbeth*— by Barbara Garson. The play's popularity was fueled by antiwar sentiment against then–President Johnson. In November 2003, the cable TV History Channel aired a documentary that expressed the same theory. After criticism was received from the LBJ Foundation and noted supporters of President Johnson, the History Channel reviewed the program and agreed "that indeed we did not make it apparent that the material presented in this program is a theory." The channel said it would add a new introduction for future airings (Howard Kurtz, "LBJ Aides Push History Channel for Probe of Show," *Washington Post,* February 5, 2004, C2) and aired a rebuttal by historians.

206. *JFK* ends with the written statement that in 1979, Helms, who had been director of covert operations in 1963, testified that Clay Shaw had been employed by the CIA. Helms *had* given such testimony in a libel case, but the employment that he referred to was between 1948 and 1952 — not in 1963 when the president was assassinated — and Shaw was basically one of thousands of "business" contacts who were debriefed by the CIA during that period.

207. *Executive Action*, National General, 1973. Directed by David Miller. Starring Burt Lancaster, Robert Ryan, Will Geer, and John Anderson.

208. For a comparison of the two films against the background of the Kennedy Assassination, see Simon, *Dangerous Knowledge: The JFK Assassination in Art and Film.*

209. *Quiz Show*, Buena Vista, 1994. Directed by Robert Redford. Starring Ralph Fiennes, John Turturro, Rob Morrow, and Paul Scofield.

210. Millicent Bell, "Top of the Frauds," *Times Literary Supplement,* February 25, 1995, 19.

211. *Nixon*, Hollywood Pictures, 1995. Directed by Oliver Stone. Starring Anthony Hopkins, Joan Allen, and James Woods.

212. The prologue also appears in the published version of the screenplay. *Nixon: An Oliver Stone Film,* Eric Hamburg, ed. (1995), includes the screenplay by Christopher Wilkinson, Oliver Stone, and Stephen J. Rivele.

213. Janet Maslin, "Stone's Embrace of a Despised President," *New York Times*, December 20, 1995, C11.

214. It is true that Shakespeare did not write plays about his contemporaries. Whether he had a political agenda to push is open to discussion. There are theories that Shakespeare was a closet Catholic and that he was a follower of the Earl of Essex. As noted in this book's section on the interrogation of John Hayward during the Essex affair, Shakespeare's *Richard II* was performed just before Essex and his followers staged their rebellion against Queen Elizabeth.

215. Stephen E. Ambrose, "The Nixon Inside Stone's Head: The 'Beast' Is the Director's Own Warped View of History," *Washington Post*, January 1, 1996.

216. Amy E. Schwartz, "Get the Crawl," *Washington Post*, October 8, 1994, A19.

217. *Titanic*, 20th Century–Fox, 1953. Directed by Jean Negulesco. Starring Clifton Webb, Barbara Stanwyck, Richard Basehart, and Robert Wagner.

218. *A Night to Remember*, Rank, 1958. Directed by Roy Ward Baker. Starring Kenneth More, Honor Blackman, and David McCallum.

219. *Titanic*, 20th Century–Fox, 1997. Directed and written by James Cameron. Starring Leonardo DiCaprio, Kate Winslet, and Billy Zane.

220. See John Aquino, *Film in the Language Arts Class*, National Education Association, 1978.

221. *Saving Private Ryan*, Paramount, 1998. Directed by Steven Spielberg. Starring Tom Hanks, Edward Burns, and Matt Damon.

222. Chris Hastings, "D-Day Hero Fury at Knighthood for Spielberg," *Daily Telegraph*, December 31, 2000.

223. *Objective Burma!* Warner Bros., 1945. Directed by Raoul Walsh. Starring Errol Flynn, George Tobias, and Henry Hull.

224. Tony Thomas, *The Films of Errol Flynn* (1969), 140.

225. *Hoodlum*.

226. *The Desperate Hours*, Paramount, 1955. Directed by William Wyler. Starring Humphrey Bogart, Frederic March, and Arthur Kennedy.

227. *Time Inc. v. Hill*, 385 U.S. 374, 389–390 (1966).

228. *The Extraordinary Seaman*, MGM, 1969. Directed by John Frankenheimer. Starring David Niven, Alan Alda, and Faye Dunaway.

229. *Zelig*, Orion, 1983. Written and directed by Woody Allen. Starring Woody Allen, Mia Farrow, and John Buckwalter.

230. *Forrest Gump*, Paramount, 1994. Directed by Robert Zemeckis. Starring Tom Hanks, Robin Wright Penn, Sally Field, and Gary Sinise.

231. Both *Contact* and *Forrest Gump* were directed by Robert Zemeckis.

232. Jonathan Mandell, "In Depicting History, Just How Far Can the Facts Be Bent?" *New York Times*, March 3, 2002, 2, 7.

233. See Front & Center Online, the Online Version of Roundabout Theatre Company's subscriber magazine, www. roundabouittheatre.org/fc/winter02/daz zle1.htm.

234. Mandell, 2,7.

235. Mandell, 7.

236. Mandell, 7.

Chapter II

1. 408 So. 2d 619 (Fla. 4th DCA 1981).

2. 221 N.E. 2d 543 (N.Y. 1966), vacated 387 U.S. 239, adhered to on remand and reargument, 233 N.E. 2d 840 (N.Y. 1967).

3. 103 N.E. 1108 (N.Y. 1913).

4. *New York Times Co. v. Sullivan*, 376 U.S. 254 (1964).

5. *Time Inc. v. Hill*, 385 U.S. 374 (1966).

6. 994 F. Supp. 525 (S.D.N.Y. 1998).

7. *Kelly v. Loewe's Inc.*, 76 F. Supp. 485 (1948).

8. The *Loft* case mainly involved allegations against the book, which was *nonfiction*, and consequently there were "no allegations of false or slanderous statements" in the plaintiff's complaint. 408 So. 2d 619 at 625. The plaintiffs in *The Perfect Storm* did make allegations that the depictions of deceased family members in the movie are false.

9. *Runaway Bride*, Paramount, 1999. Directed by Gary Marshall. Starring Julia Roberts, Richard Gere, Joan Cusack, and Hector Elizondo.

10. *Cast Away*, 20th Century–Fox, 2000. Directed by Robert Zemeckis. Starring Tom Hanks and Helen Hunt.

11. See www.courses:washington.edu/cmu wo1/Jan16MovieBiz.htm.

12. See www.edu/roc/adv/research/papers/ Turcotte. This is a 1995 research paper from the University of Texas that predates *The Perfect Storm* but describes product placement in the movie industry in detail.

13. *A Beautiful Mind*, Universal, 2000. Directed by Ron Howard. Starring Russell Crowe, Ed Harris, Christopher Plummer, and Jennifer Connelly.

14. *Black Hawk Down*, Columbia, 2001. Directed by Ridley Scott. Starring Josh Harnett, Ewan McGregor, and Tom Sizemore.

15. A video transcript of the press conference is on www.c-span.org.

16. *Il Miracolo,* Italy, 1948. Directed by Robert Rossellini. Starring Anna Magnani and Federico Fellini.

17. *Tyne v. Time Warner,* 11th Cir., No. 02-13281, 7/9/03.

18. *Tyne v. Time-Warner,* Fla. S.C. Case No. 02-13281, Movant's Initial Brief on Question Certified by the 11th Circuit, 7/xx/03.

19. *Tyne v. Time Warner,* Fla. S.C. Case No. 02-13281, Defendant's Answer, 8/19/03.

20. *Tyne v. Time Warner,* Fla. S.C. Case No. 02-13281, Plaintiffs' Reply, 8/19/03.

21. *Tyne v. Time Warner,* Fla. S.C. Case No. 02-13281, Amicus Curiae Brief, 8/5/03.

22. *Tyne v. Time Warner,* Fla. S.C. Case No. 02-13281, Amicus Curiae Brief, 8/25/03.

Chapter III

1. The facts in this section are based on Peter Ackroyd, *The Life of Thomas More* (1980); William Roper, *Lives of Saint Thomas More [by] William Roper & Nicholas Harpsfield,* E. E. Reynolds, ed. (1963); "St. Thomas More," *The Catholic Encyclopedia; Great World Trials,* Edward W. Knappman, ed. (1997), 29–32; Cindy Wooden, "Pope Proclaims England's St. Thomas More Patron of Politicians," The *Catholic Standard,* November 2, 2000, 32; and Richard Marius, *Thomas More* (Knopf, 1984).

2. *A Man for All Seasons,* Columbia, 1966. Directed by Fred Zinnemann. Starring Paul Scofield, Wendy Hiller, Robert Shaw, and Orson Welles.

3. Robert Bolt, *A Man for All Seasons* (1962).

4. *Becket* was filmed two years before *A Man for All Seasons;* this 1964 film starred Peter O'Toole and, Scofield's theater rival at the time, Richard Burton. Both O'Toole and Burton—both better known in films than Scofield—were briefly considered for the role of More before the filmmakers settled on Scofield.

5. Warner Bros., 1939. The film repeats the historical alterations of the play. The strange title of the film is due to a legal concern. Bette Davis was assigned to play Elizabeth; Errol Flynn, Essex. After his success in *The Adventures of Robin Hood* (1938), Flynn was arguably the greater star, and his agents demanded that the title of the play—*Elizabeth the Queen*—be changed to reflect Flynn's role. The first suggestion was *The Knight and the Lady,* but Davis thought that made it sound like a romantic comedy. *Elizabeth and Essex* was suggested, but Lytton Strachley had written an historical book

using that title and there were concerns that his publisher might seek legal action—although for what is unclear since a title cannot receive copyright protection and the phrase is probably too generic for trademark protection. But, to avoid litigation, the title was changed to *The Private Lives of Elizabeth and Essex.*

6. See Graham Bartran and Anthony Waine, *Brecht in Perspective* (1982); John Fuegi, *Bertolt Brecht: Chaos, According to Plan* (1987); and John Willett, ed., *Brecht on Theatre* (1964).

7. Richard Marius, "A Man for All Seasons," in *Past Imperfect: History According to the Movies,* eds. Ted Mico, John Miller-Monzon, and David Rubel (1996), 70–73.

8. See teachwiththemovies.com.

9. Laurence Olivier, *On Acting* (1986), 124.

10. *Amistad,* Universal, 1997. Directed by Steven Spielberg. Starring Morgan Freeman, Anthony Hopkins, Nigel Hawthorne, and Matthew McConaughey.

11. See review of *Amistad* (film by Stephen Spielberg) by Sally Hadden, Florida State University, www.h-net.org.~shear/thread/h_law_film_review_had den_on_amistad.htm.

12. Warren Goldstein, "Bad History Is Bad for a Culture," *Chronicle of Higher Education,* April 10, 1998; reprinted http://chronicle.com/colloquy/98/reelism/background.htm.

13. *Chase-Riboud v. Dreamworks,* U.S. District Court of the Central District of California, Western Division. Case No. CV-97-7619 ABC (JGx) (1997).

14. For the defendant's own recollection of the trial, transcribed in 1896, three years before his death and 38 years after the trial, see "Duff Armstrong's Own Story," rpt. in W. Barton, *The Life of Abraham Lincoln* (1925). See also J.R. Frank, *Lincoln as a Lawyer* (1961).

15. *Young Mr. Lincoln,* 20th Century–Fox, 1939. Directed by John Ford. Starring Henry Fonda, Ward Bond, Alice Brady, and Marjorie Weaver.

16. Paul Bergman and Michael Asimow, *Reel Justice: The Courtroom Goes to the Movies* (1996), 150–1.

17. Norman Rosenberg, "Young Mr. Lincoln: The Lawyer as Super-Hero," *Legal Studies Forum,* 15, no. 3 (1991), 225.

18. Rosenberg, 225.

19. Marsha Kinder, "The Image of Patriarchal Power in 'Young Mr. Lincoln' (1939) and 'Ivan the Terrible,' Part 1 (1945), *Film Q.* 39 (1987), pp. 29–30.

20. Rosenberg, 225–6.

21. Some of the historical information in this section is derived from James Madison Page, *The True Story of Andersonville* (1908); Gary Waltrip, "Andersonville: The Trial and

Execution of Henry Wirz," *The Confederate Sentry,* reprinted on www.rebelgray.com/andersonville2.htm.

22. N.P. Chipman, *The Trial of Andersonville: Trial of Captain Henry Wirz, the Prison Keeper* (1911), 366.

23. N.P. Chipman, "Relations of the District of Columbia to the General Government. Is Washington City the Capital of the United States, or the Capital of the District of Columbia? The Duty of the Nation toward Its Capital." Speech of Hon. Norton P. Chipman, of the District of Columbia, in the House of Representatives, February 28, 1874.

24. Chipman, *The Trial of Andersonville,* 22.

25. Chipman, *The Trial of Andersonville,* 18.

26. Chipman, *The Trial of Andersonville,* 364.

27. Chipman, *The Trial of Andersonville,* 366.

28. Chipman, *The Trial of Andersonville,* 11.

29. See Robert S. Davis, "An Historical Note on 'The Devil's Advocate': O.S. Baker and the Henry Wirz/Andersonville Military Tribunal," *Journal of Southern Legal History* 10 (2002), 25–57.

30. *The Andersonville Trial,* Public Television, 1970. Directed by George C. Scott. Starring William Shatner, Richard Basehart, Cameron Mitchell, and Jack Cassidy.

31. *The Trial of the Catonsville Nine,* Melville/Cinema5, 1972. Directed by Gordon Davidson. Starring Ed Flanders, Richard Jordan, Donald Moffat, William Schallert, and Peter Strauss.

32. For a detailed account of the first trial of Oscar Wilde see H. Montgomery Hyde, *Oscar Wilde: A Life* (1975), which uses then-available versions of the trial transcripts, which Hyde also published; and *Great World Trials,* Edward W. Knappman, ed. (1997), 155–160. *The Real Trial of Oscar Wilde: The First Uncensored Transcript of the Trial of Oscar Wilde vs. John Douglas* (Marquess of Queensberry, 1895) (2003), collates other transcripts of the trial. A possibly more accessible version of the trials is the play *Gross Indecency: The Three Trials of Oscar Wilde* by Moises Kaufman (1998), which employed Hyde's transcripts, contemporary newspaper accounts, and memories and diaries of the participants.

33. *The Trials of Oscar Wilde,* United Artists, 1960. Directed by Kenneth Hughes. Starring Peter Finch, James Mason, and Nigel Patrick.

34. *Oscar Wilde,* Vantage, 1960. Directed by Gregory Ratoff. Starring Robert Morley, John Neville, and Ralph Richardson.

35. For a film critic's comparison of both 1960 Wilde films, see Stanley Kauffman, "The Trials of Oscar Wilde," in Stanley Kauffman, *A World in Film: Criticism and Comment* (1967), 194–196.

36. This section is based on Clarence Darrow (foreword by Irving Younger), *Clarence Darrow's Sentencing Speech in State of Illinois v. Leopold and Loeb,* Classics of the Courtroom Series (1988); Clarence Darrow and Robert E. Crowe, *Attorney Clarence Darrow's Plea for Mercy and Prosecutor Robert E. Crowe's Demand for the Death Penalty in the Loeb Leopold Case; the Crime of a Century* (1923); and Clarence Darrow, *The Story of My Life* (1932).

37. *Compulsion,* 20th Century–Fox, 1959. Directed by Richard Fleischer. Starring Bradford Dillman, Dean Stockwell, and Orson Welles.

38. *Leopold v. Levin,* 45 111 2d 434 (S.C. Ill. 1970).

39. This section is based on Homer Cummings, *The State of Connecticut vs. Harold Israel,* Government Printing Office, Washington (1937); and "Cummings Backs Indirect Evident," *New York Times,* February 26, 1935, 11.

40. See James E. Hamby and James W. Thorpe, "The History of Firearm and Toolmark Identification," *Association of Firearm and Tool Mark Examiners Journal* (Summer 1999).

41. *Boomerang,* 20th Century–Fox, 1947. Directed by Elia Kazan. Starring Dana Andrews, Arthur Kennedy, Jane Wyatt, and Ed Begley.

42. This section is based on Darrow, *The Story of My Life*; Carol Iannone, "The Truth About *Inherit the Wind,*" *First Light* (February 1997), 28–33; David N. Menton, "*Inherit the Wind*: A Hollywood History of the 1925 Scopes Monkey Trial," Missouri Association for Creation, rpt. www.gennet.org/SCOPES/HTM.; Lawrence M. Bernarbo and Celeste Michele Condit, "Two Stories of the Scopes Trial," in Robert Hariman, ed., *Popular Trials: Rhetoric, Mass Media, and the Law* (1990).

43. *Inherit the Wind,* United Artists/Lomitas, 1960. Directed by Stanley Kramer. Starring Spencer Tracy, Frederick March, and Gene Kelly.

44. Jerome Lawrence and Robert E. Lee, *Inherit the Wind* (1955).

45. Stanley Kramer, *It's a Mad, Mad, Mad, Mad World: A Life in Hollywood,* 172 (1997).

46. "A New Image of Bryan," *Life* (undated article, c. 1960).

47. The play was filmed twice more for television: in 1988 on NBC with Jason Robards as Drummond, Kirk Douglas as Brady, and

Darren McGavin as Hornbeck, and in 1999 for Showtime cable with Jack Lemmon as Drummond, George C. Scott as Brady, and Beau Bridges as Hornbeck. Both Lemmon and Robards received Emmys for best actor. Spencer Tracy as Brady had been nominated for a Best Actor Oscar, but lost.

48. See Isaac Don Levine, *Mitchell: Pioneer of Air Power* (1943); Emile Gauvreau and Lester Cohen, *Billy Mitchell: Founder of Our Air Force and Prophet Without Honor* (1942); and Cathy Packer, *Freedom of Expression in the American Military* (1989). Burke Davis had access to the trial transcript in his *The Billy Mitchell Affair* (1967). In his Ph.D. dissertation, "Trial of Faith: The Dissent and Court Martial of Billy Mitchell" (Rutgers, 1991), Michael L. Grumelli argued that Mitchell was convicted because of errors made by his attorneys and because of his own arrogance.

49. See sources noted above (n. 48).

50. *The Court Martial of Billy Mitchell*, Warner Bros., 1955. Directed by Otto Preminger. Starring Gary Cooper, Charles Bickford, Ralph Bellamy, Elizabeth Montgomery, and Rod Steiger. Cooper and Steiger repeated their courtroom exchange as Mitchell and Gullion on CBS-TV's *Ed Sullivan show* on December 25, 1955. Omnibus, the CBS-TV series introduced by Alistair Cook, ended its 1955–56 season with a 90-minute version of the trial starring James Daly (who had been Col. Herbert White in the Preminger film) as Mitchell and Jack Lord as Gullion.

51. The historical data is this section were derived from Matthew Lippman, "The White Rose: Judges and Justice in the Third Reich," 15 *Connecticut Journal of International Law* 95, Winter/Spring 2000; "Famous Trials" by Doug Linder, http://www.law.umkc.edu/faculty/projects/ftrials/ftrials.htm.

52. *Judgment at Nuremberg*, United Artists/Roxlom, 1961. Directed by Stanley Kramer. Starring Spencer Tracy, Maximilian Schell, Burt Lancaster, Richard Widmark, Montgomery Clift, and Judy Garland.

53. An interesting contrast is a television film of the first Nuremberg trial—*Nuremberg*—that was produced in 2000 for the cable TNT network. It starred Alec Baldwin (who also acted as executive producer) as Supreme Court Justice Robert H. Jackson, who served as chief prosecutor. Also appearing were Brian Cox as Herman Göring, Christopher Plummer as British prosecutor Sir David Maxwell-Fyfe, Jill Hennessy as Jackson's secretary Elsie Douglas, Len Cariou as Judge Francis Biddle, and Max Von Sydow as Samuel Rosenman. The film was directed by Yves Simoneau with a screenplay by David W. Rintel from a

nonfiction novel by Joseph Persico. The movie was nominated for a Golden Globe award for Best Motion Picture Made for Television, as were Baldwin and Cox for Best Actor.

54. In addition to its inspiring the movie, the television version is best remembered for being censored. One of the sponsors was the American Gas Association, which insisted that all references to gas ovens having been used in the camps be deleted from the script. When the producer refused, the word was "bleeped" when the actors said it.

55. Mann claimed that Gen. Telford Taylor, chief prosecutor at the "Justice Trial," suggested that he might want to dramatize the trial, although Taylor added that Mann might think it "too intellectual." On reading the trial transcript, Mann decided that "once the objectivity of justice goes, everything goes." See Karen Lipson, "Judgement Call," *Newsday*, March 4, 2001 (on Mann's Broadway version of his teleplay and screenplay).

56. The Broadway version premiered on March 26, 2001, at the Longacre Theater, produced by the National Actors Theater. Maximilian Schell, who had played defense attorney Hans Rolfe in both the television and movie versions, portrayed Ernst Janning, and George Grizzard played Judge Dan Haywood.

57. Arthur Schlesinger, Jr., Review of *Judgment at Nuremberg* in *Show* magazine, quoted in Donald Descher, *The Films of Spencer Tracy* (1968), 244.

58. See Louis Nizer, *My Life in Court* (1961).

59. Quoted in Diane McWhorter, "Dangerous Minds," *Slate*, March 4, 2004 — a reaction to William F. Buckley's appreciation of Pegler in the March 1, 2004, *New Yorker*.

60. "Louis Nizer, Lawyer to Famous, Dies at 92," *New York Times*, November 11, 1994.

61. *A Case of Libel*, Showtime, 1983. Directed by Eric Till. Starring Daniel J. Travanti, Edward Asner, and Gordon Pisenti.

62. *Witness for the Prosecution*, United Artists, 1957. Directed by Billy Wilder. Starring Charles Laughton, Tyrone Power, Marlene Dietrich, and Elsa Lancaster.

63. Interview with Quentin Reynolds in *The New York Times*, October 17, 1963, 41.

64. Facts in this section are drawn from Fox Butterfield, "Trial of Six Starts Today in Pool Table Rape in Massachusetts," *New York Times*, February 6, 1984, 14; Joyce Wadler, "Woman Leaves Seclusion to Tell Court of Assault, Cheering in Dan's Bar," *Washington Post*, February 25, 1984, A3; and Ruth Marcus, "Four Receive Prison Terms in Barroom Rape," *Washington Post*, March 26, 1984, A3. For a detailed analysis of the case and press coverage, see Helen Benedict, *Virgin or Vamp:*

How the Press Covers Sex Crimes (1992), 89–146.

65. Benedict, 89–146.

66. *The Accused,* UIP/Paramount, 1988. Directed by Jonathan Kaplan. Starring Jodie Foster and Kelly McGillis.

67. Carol Clover, *Men, Women, and Chain Saws: Gender in the Modern Horror Film* (1992), pp. 149–150.

68. *Rashômon,* Daiei Motion Picture Co. Ltd., Japan, 1950. Directed by Akira Kurosawa. Starring Toshirô Mifune.

69. *The Outrage,* MGM, 1964. Directed by Martin Ritt. Starring Paul Newman, Laurence Harvey, Claire Bloom, William Shatner, and Edward G. Robinson.

70. Clover, 150.

71. Facts in this section are drawn from Allen M. Dershowitz, *Reversal of Fortune* (1992), and *State v. Bulow*, 475 a. 2d 995 (R.I. 1984).

72. *Reversal of Fortune,* Warner Bros., 1992. Directed by Barbet Schroeder. Starring Jeremy Irons, Glenn Close, and Ron Silver.

73. *In re von Bulow*, F2d 94 (2d Cir. 1987).

Chapter IV

1. "Clementine," Decca Recording, 1941, Bing Crosby accompanied by the Mary Maids and the John Trotter Orchestra. This recording reached #20 on the music charts.

2. Jane M. Gaines, *Contested Culture: The Image, the Voice, and the Law* (1991), deals with some of the same cases, although not from the perspective of fictional personae. Its focus, however, is not just films but iconography in general, including art and photography. It examines the phenomenon of images as property. The book is described as a synthesis of a number of disciplines, methods, and theories, including film history, film theory, critical legal studies, popular cultural studies, feminism, and Marxist Cultural theory.

3. *Allen v. National Video, Inc.,* 610 F. Supp. 612 (S.D.N.Y. 1985).

4. "Why Marilyn and Bogie Still Need a Lawyer," *New York Times*, March 3, 1994, B18.

5. H. Silverberg, "Televising Old Films— Some New Legal Questions About Performers' and Proprietors' Rights," 38 *Va. L. Rev.* 615 (1952).

6. *Lugosi v. Universal Pictures*, 25 Cal. 3d, 813, 844 (1979).

7. 25 Cal. at 826–7.

8. M. Helfand, "When Mickey Mouse Is as Strong as Superman: The Convergence of Intellectual Property Laws to Protect Fictional Literary and Pictorial Characters," 44 *Stanford L. Rev.* 623 (1992).

9. T. Brooks and E. Marsh, *The Complete Directory to Prime Time Network TV Shows 1946–Present* (1979), 252.

10. 25 Cal. at 804–5.

11. A radio version of the show was broadcast from 1958 to 1960 and starred John Dehner as Paladin.

12. The delay in DeCosta's submitting a trademark application, at least from 1957, when the series premiered, to 1963 was never satisfactorily explained; the delay could conceivably have influenced the decisions against DeCosta.

13. *Columbia Broadcasting Sys. v. DeCosta*, 377 F. 2d 315 (1st Cir. 1967).

14. 377 F. 2d at 320.

15. *DeCosta v. Columbia Broadcasting Sys.,* Civil Action No. 2310 (D.R.I Apr. 15, 1974).

16. *DeCosta v. Columbia Broadcasting Sys.*, 520 F. 2d 499 (1st Cir. 1975).

17. *Columbia Broadcasting Sys. v. DeCosta*, 192 U.S.P.Q. 453 (P.T.O. Trademark Trial and Appeal Bd. 1976).

18. *DeCosta v. Viacom International*, 981 F. 2d 602 (1992).

19. 981 F. 2d at 605.

20. 376 U.S. 225, 84 S. Ct. 784 (1964).

21. 376 U.S. 234, 84 S.Ct. 779 (1964).

22. Comments on Sears and Compco in *Lear Inc. v. Adkins*, 395 U.S. 653, 655, 89 S.Ct. 1902, 1940 (1969).

23. 17 U.S.C. §201 (1976).

24. 17 U.S.C. §201 (1976).

25. 17 U.S.C. §301 (1976).

26. *Waring v. WDAS Broadcasting*, 127 Pa. 433, 437, 194 Atl. 631, 633 (1937).

27. *RCA Mfg. Co. v. Whiteman*, 114 F. 2d 86 (2d Cir.), cert. denied, 111 U.S. 712 (1940), reversing 28 F. Supp. 787 (S.D.N.Y. 1939).

28. Silverberg, 623.

29. 25 Cal. 3d 813 at 825. The works alluded to in the statement are the films *MacArthur* (1977) and *Patton* (1977); stage productions of *Will Rogers* and *Give 'Em Hell, Harry*, which were filmed and commercially released; and the film *The Ten Commandments* (1956).

30. *Booth v. Colgate Palmolive*, 362 F. Supp. 343, 347 (1973).

31. *Sinatra v. Goodyear Tire and Rubber Co.,* 435 F. 2d 711 (9th Cir. 1970).

32. 435 F. 2d at 713.

33. 435 F. 2d at 717.

34. Gaines, p. 138.

35. 17 U.S.C. at §102 (1976).

36. *Empire City Amusement Co. v. Wilton*, 1134 F.132 (C.C.D. Mass. 1903).

37. F. Owens, "Sam Spade, Tarzan, and Copyright Law," *Science Fiction and Fantasy*

Writers of America Bulletin 26, no. 2 (Summer 1992), 14.

38. 377 F. 2d at 320.

39. *Nichols v. Universal Pictures,* 45 F. 2d 119, 121 (1930).

40. 45 F. 2d at 123.

41. 45 F. 2d at 121.

42. 45 F. 2d at 121.

43. *Sid and Marty Kroft Television Productions v. McDonald Corp.,* 562 F. 2d 1157 (9th Cir. 1977).

44. *Detective Comics v. Bruns Publications,* 111 F. 2d 432 (2d Cir. 1940).

45. *Warner Bros. Inc. v. American Broadcasting Companies,* 530 F. Supp 1187 (S.D.N.Y. 1982).

46. *Warner Bros. Inc. v. American Broadcasting Companies,* 720 F. 2d 231 (1983).

47. 720 F. 2d at 242.

48. 216 F. 2d 945 (9th Cir. 1954), cert. denied, 348 U.S. 971, 75 S. Ct. 532 (1955).

49. *Hospital for Sick Children v. Milady Fare,* 516 F. Supp. 67, 72 (E.D. Va. 1980).

50. *Walt Disney Productions v. Air Pirates,* 345 F. Supp. 108 (1972), aff'd in part and revers'd in part 581 F. 2d 751, 755 (9th Cir. 1978).

51. 581 F. 2d at 755.

52. *Burroughs v. Metro-Goldwyn-Mayer, Inc.,* 683 F. 2d, 610, 631, n.3 (1982).

53. 683 F. 2d at 631.

54. M. Apfelbaum, "Copyright and the Right of Publicity: One Pea in Two Pods?" 71 *Georgetown L. Rev.* 1567, 1584, fn. 140–141. See discussion in Section III, infra.

55. See S. Halpern, "The Right of Publicity: Commercial Exploitation of the Associative Value of Personality," 29 *And. L. Rev.* 344 (1986), concerning IBM's obligations to Chaplin's estate.

56. "IBM's Little Tramp Returns to Ads," *Advertising Age,* September 2, 1991, 1:4.

57. J. Franklin, *Classics of the Silent Screen* (1959), 144–6.

58. *City Lights,* United Artists, 1931. Directed and written by Charlie Chaplin. Starring Charlie Chaplin and Virginia Cherrill.

59. *Modern Times,* United Artists, 1936. Directed and written by Charlie Chaplin. Starring Charlie Chaplin and Paulette Goddard.

60. S. Gould, "A Biographical Homage to Mickey Mouse," in *The Panda's Thumb* (1980), 9.

61. 17 U.S.C. at 302(a).

62. 17 U.S.C. at 302(c).

63. Brooks and Marsh, 270.

64. T. Shales, "The Honeymooners: How Sweet It Was," *Washington Post,* 2 May 1983, TV Times 5.

65. J. Thomas McCarthy, Trademarks and Unfair Competition §2:1 at 44; (2d ed. 1988 & Supp. 1988).

66. Id. at §3:1 at 104; §15:2 at 659.

67. *G. & C. Marriam Co. v. Saalfield,* 198 F. 369, 373 (6th Cir. 1912).

68. *DC Comics Inc. v. Filmation Associates,* 486 F. Supp. 1273 (S.D.N.Y. 1980).

69. *Silverman v. CBS Inc.,* 632 F. Supp. 1344, 1356 (S.D.N.Y. 1966).

70. Lanham Act, 15 U.S.C. §1125(a), Section 45(a).

71. *American Home Prods. Corp. v. Johnson & Johnson,* 577 F. 2d 160, 165–6 (2d Cir. 1978).

72. *Allen v. National Video, Inc.* 610 F. Supp. at 614.

73. Restatement (Third) of Unfair Competition §§46–49 (Preliminary Draft No. 6, 1992), §46, Misappropriation of the Commercial Value of Personal Identity: The Right of Publicity.

74. *Ginger Rogers v. Alberto Grimaldi,* 695 F. Supp. 112, 124 (1988), aff'd 875 F.2d 994 (1989).

75. *Lahr v. Odell Chemical Co.,* 300 F. 2d 256 (1st Cir. 1962).

76. *Sinatra v. Goodyear Tire and Rubber Co.,* supra at 716.

77. Id. at 716.

78. S. Warren and L. Brandes, "The Right of Publicity," 4 *Harv. L. Rev.* 196 (1890). The New York Right of Privacy Act was enacted in 1903.

79. J. Prosser, "Privacy," 48 *Calif. L. Rev.* 383, 408 (1960).

80. N.Y. Civil Rights Law §51 (McKinney Supp. 1981).

81. California Civil Code §3344 (Deering 1993)

82. *Maritote v. Desilu Productions, Inc.,* 345 F. 2d 418 (7th Cir. 1965). See Chapter I for discussion of other litigation involving "The Untouchables."

83. *James v. Screen Gems, Inc.,* 174 Cal. App. 2d 650, 344 P. 2d 799 (1959).

84. *Schumann v. Loewe's Inc.,* 135 N.Y.S. 2d 361 (Sup. Ct. 1954), final amended complaint dismissed, 144 N.Y.S. 2d 27 (Sup. Ct. 1955). The 1946 MGM motion picture starred Katharine Hepburn as Clara Schumann, Paul Heinreid as Robert Schumann, and Robert Walker as Johannes Brahms.

85. *Young v. That Was the Week That Was,* 423 F. 2d 265 (6th Cir. 1970).

86. *Miller v. Comm. of Int. Rev.,* 299 F. 2d 706 (2d Cir. 1962).

87. *Lerman v. Chuckleberry,* 521 F. Supp., 232 (S.D.N.Y., 1981); *Douglass v. Hustler Magazine,* 769 F. 2d 1128, 1138 (7th Cir. 1985) (Posner, J.) ("the right to prevent others from using one's name or picture for commercial purposes without consent"), cert. denied, 47 U.S. 1094 (1985); J. T. McCarthy, "The Right of Publicity and Privacy" at vii (1992) ("the inherent

right of every human being to control the commercial use of his or her identity"); M.B. Nimmer, "The Right of Publicity," 19 Law & Contemp. Probs. 203, 216 (1954) ("the right of each person to control and profit from the publicity values which he has created or purchased").

88. *Harlen Laboratories v. Topps Chewing Gum*, 202 F. 2d 866, 866 (2d Cir. 1953), cert denied, 346 U.S. 813 (1953).

89. See, e.g., *Cepeda v. Swift & Co.*, 415 F. 2d 1205, 1206 (8th Cir. 1969); *Ettore v. Philco Television Broadcasting Corp.* 229 F. 2d 481, 487 (5th Cir.), cert. denied, 351 U.S. 926 (1956); *Motschenbacher v. R.J. Reynolds Tobacco Co.*, 498 F. 2d 821, 826 n.14 (9th Cir. 1974).

90. *Guglielmi v. Spelling-Goldberg Productions*, 25 Cal. 3d 860 (1979) (an action by an alleged nephew of the actor Rudolph Valentino against producers of a TV movie biography of Valentino, dismissed, citing the appellate court in Lugosi, infra).

91. *Hicks v. Casablanca, Inc.*, 464 F. Supp. 432 (1979). The film *Agatha* was a fictionalized account of Agatha Christie's disappearance in 1926. The action was by her heirs for violation of her right of publicity. The court held that the right of publicity does not attach when the fictionalization of the life of a public figure is obviously fiction and will not be mistaken for anything else. See Chapter I for more discussion of this film.

92. 849 F. 2d 460 (9th Cir. 1988), cert. denied, 112 S. Ct. 1513, 1514 (1992).

93. 849 F. 2d at 462.

94. 849 F. 2d at 463.

95. 23 U.S.P.Q. 2d (BNA) 1721 (1992).

96. M.M. Davis, Note, "Voicing Concern: An Overview of the Current Law Protecting Singers' Voices," 40 *Syracuse L. Rev.* 1255 (1989); E. Windholz, Comment, "Whose Voice Is It Anyway?" 8 *Cardozo Arts & Ent. L. J.* 201 (1989).

97. Gaines, 142.

98. *Republic Pictures Corp. v. Roy Rogers*, 213 F. 2d 662 (1955), aff'd 222 F.2d 950 (1954), cert. denied 348 U.S. 858, 75 S.Ct. 83 (1954).

99. *Autry v. Republic Studios*, 213 F. 2d 667, 101 U.S.P.Q. (BNA) 478 (1954).

100. His real name was Béla Lugosi Blasko. He was born in 1888.

101. *Dracula*, Universal Studios, 1931. Directed by Tod Browning. Starring Bela Lugosi, Helen Chandler, and Dwight Frye. Although he played the role on the stage, Lugosi was not the first choice for the role. But Lon Chaney, frequent star of Browning's silent horror films, died in 1930 before *Dracula* went into production.

102. *Frankenstein Meets the Wolfman*. Uni-versal, 1943. Directed by Roy William Neill. Starring Lon Chaney, Jr., and Bela Lugosi.

103. D. Gilford, *Karloff: The Man, The Monster, The Movies* (1973), 58. Gilford quotes Karloff as saying, "Poor Bela had two troubles. I think he remained slightly old fashioned in his acting. He didn't grow with the times, and I think one must. He didn't really learn the language in which he earned his bread and butter, and that made it difficult for him."

104. A. Lenning, *The Count: The Life and Films of Bela Lugosi* (1974), 317.

105. *Plan 9 from Outer Space*, Reynolds, 1958. Directed by Edward D. Wood, Jr. Starring Gregory Walcott and Mona McKinnon. With Bela Lugosi.

106. E. Snead, "Oddball Director Ed Wood Gains Fame, If Not Respect," *USA Today*, July 20, 1993, 8D:1.

107. R. Bojarski, *The Films of Bela Lugosi* (1980), 231.

108. Petition for Hearing, at 11 n.4. *Lugosi v. Universal Pictures*, Civil No. L.A. 30824 (Cal Sup. Ct., filed July 19, 1977).

109. See *Lugosi v. Universal Pictures*, 25 Cal. 3d at 830.

110. *Lugosi v. Universal Pictures*, 172 U.S.P.Q. 1972) at 541–542.

111. The sequel story begins seconds after the original *Dracula* ended. Lugosi did not appear in the sequel primarily because Dracula was killed at the end of the first film by a stake driven through his heart. Some of the other players from *Dracula* appeared in the sequel. Rather than hire Lugosi to play the corpse of Dracula, Universal simply created a Lugosi mask and asked for his permission to use it. The sequel was directed by Lambert Hillyer and starred Gloria Holden as Dracula's daughter. Interestingly enough, the death of Dracula in the original story did not stop Christopher Lee, who played the role in a British version in 1957, from reprising the role in a half dozen sequels. The producers reasoned that Dracula, one of the undead, could be resurrected, having conquered death before.

112. 172 U.S.P.Q. at 550.

113. 172 U.S.P.Q. at 550.

114. 172 U.S.P.Q. at 551.

115. *Waring v. WDAS Broadcasting*, supra.

116. *L.A. Times*, January 16, 1974, 1. See also Lennig, 317.

117. *Lugosi v. Universal Pictures*, 25 Cal. 3d 813 (1979).

118. 172 U.S.P.Q. at 548.

119. 25 Cal. 3d at 824.

120. 25 Cal. 3d at 820.

121. 25 Cal. 3d at 825.

122. J. B. Eisenberg, "Lugosi v. Universal Pictures: Descent of the Right of Publicity," 29

Hastings L. J. (1978) 751, 770: "No answers were provided as to the possibility of exercise in other ways, for example engaging in or ratifying a minor or token business enterprise. The use of the term 'exercise' without accompanying definition or explanation contributes more uncertainty to an area of the law already fraught with confusion."

123. 25 Cal. 3d at 818.

124. *Groucho Marx Productions v. Day and Night. Co.,* 689 F. 2d at 322.

125. Comment, "An Assessment of the Copyright Model in Right of Publicity Cases," 70 *Cal. L. Rev.* 786 (1982).

126. *Price v. Hal Roach Studios,* 400 F. Supp. 836 (S.D. New York 1975).

127. See W. Everson, *The Films of Laurel and Hardy,* 1967. See also J. McCabe, *Mr. Laurel and Mr. Hardy* (1966), 164– 170.

128. The company had been created in 1939 to employ Laurel and Hardy to produce motion pictures. *Price v. Hal Roach Studios,* 400 F. Supp. at 838, n.2.

129. F. Guiles, *Stan: The Life of Stan Laurel* (1980; rpt. 1991), 225.

130. *Price v. Hal Roach Studios,* F. Supp. 836 (S.D. New York 1975).

131. 400 F. Supp. at 840.

132. 400 F. Supp. at 844.

133. 400 F. Supp. at 844.

134. 400 F. Supp. at 847.

135. B. Verb, "Laurel Without Hardy," *Films in Review* (March 1959), 153, 156.

136. Guiles, 225.

137. *Price v. Worldtelvision Enterprises, Inc.,* 455 F. Supp. 252 (S.D.N.Y. 1979), aff'd without opinion, F. 2d 214 (2d Cir. 1979). The First Amendment issues were not discussed.

138. P. Zimmermann and P. Goldblatt. *The Marx Brothers at the Movies* (1968).

139. *Groucho Marx Productions, Inc. v. Day and Night Co.,* 523 F. Supp. 484 (1981).

140. Apfelbaum, 1584.

141. Apfelbaum, 1584, n.141–142.

142. D. Feldman, "Finding a Home for Fictional Characters: A Proposal for Change in Copyright Protection," 78 *Calif. L. Rev.* 687 (1990).

143. *Groucho Marx Productions v. Day and Night Co.,* 689 F. 2d 317 (1982).

144. 689 F. 2d at 320.

145. The plaintiffs noted that during their lifetimes the Marx Brothers had performed in commercials for products ranging from cars to liquor. 689 F. 2d at 373 n.7.

146. Joel Engel, "Now It's the Heirs of the Stooges Who Are Bopping Each Other," *New York Times,* November 6, 1994, C13; C15.

147. This California law was modified in 1999 by the "Astaire Celebrity Image Protection Act," so called because it was initiated by Robyn Astaire, the widow of Fred Astaire. The act strengthened Section 990 and the ability of heirs to prevent unauthorized commercial use of a celebrity's identity, likeness, voice, or signature. The act added 20 years to the protection — bringing it to 70 years — and required judicial review of the purpose for each unauthorized use.

148. *White v. Samsung,* 971 F. 2d 1395 (9th Cir, 1992), cert. denied, 113 S.Ct. 2443 (1993).

149. See Russell J. Frackman and Tammy C. Bloomfield, "The Right of Publicity: Going to the Dogs," *L.A. Daily Journal,* September 1996.

150. "Raising the Dead for Guest Appearances," *New York Times,* May 14, 1998, B1.

151. *Wendt v. Host International Inc.,* No. CV-93-00142-R (C.D. Cal. 1993); rev'd and remanded 50 F. 3d 18 (9th Cir. 1995; 125 F. 3d 806 (9th Cir. 1997); U.S. No. 991567, cert. denied, 10/2/00.

152. *Wendt,* 197 F. 3d at 1826.

153. 125 F. 3d at 811.

154. *Wendt,* 197 F. 3d at 1289

155. 25 Cal. 3d at 825.

156. 689 F. 2d at 322.

157. 981 F. 2d at 605.

158. 25 Cal. 3d at 844.

159. Feldman at 690.

160. L. Kurtz, "The Independent Legal Lives of Fictional Characters," *Wis. L. Rev.* 429, 450 (1986).

161. Apfelbaum, 1584.

162. 25 Cal. 3d at 844.

Bibliography

Ambrose, Stephen E. "The Nixon Inside Stone's Head: The 'Beast' Is the Director's Own Warped View of History." *Washington Post*, January 1, 1996.

Apfelbaum, M. "Copyright and the Right of Publicity: One Pea in Two Pods?" 71 *Georgetown L. Rev.* 1567 (1983).

Bell, Millicent. "Top of the Frauds." *Times Literary Supplement*, February 25, 1995, p. 19.

Benedict, Helen. *Virgin or Vamp: How the Press Covers Sex Crimes.* New York: Oxford University Press, 1993.

Bergman, Paul, and Michael Asimow. *Reel Justice: The Courtroom Goes to the Movies.* Kansas City: Andrews McMeel, 1996.

Berkman, T. *The Lady and the Law: The Remarkable Life of Fanny Holtzman.* Boston: Little, Brown, 1976.

Black, David A. *Law in Film: Resonance and Representation.* Urbana and Chicago: University of Illinois Press, 1999.

Bogdanovich, Peter. *John Ford.* University of California Press, 1968.

Butler, Karen. "The Screenplay Thief." *Book Magazine*, January/February 2003.

Carnes, Mark C. "Past Imperfect: History According to the Movies" (an Interview with film director Oliver Stone," *Cineaste* 22, no. 4 (Fall 1966): 33. Reprinted from *Past Imperfect: History According to the Movies,* ed. Ted Mico, John Miller-Monzon, and David Rubel. New York: Holt, 1995.

Clover, Carol. *Men, Women, and Chain Saws: Gender in the Modern Horror Film.* Princeton, N.J.: Princeton University Press, 1992.

Cummings, Homer. *The State of Connecticut vs. Harold Israel.* Washington, D.C.: Government Printing Office, 1937.

Darmiento, Laurence. "Hollywood's Liability Tab Skyrocketing." *Los Angeles Business Journal,* July 2, 2001.

Davis, M.M. "Note: Voicing Concern. An Overview of the Current Law Protecting Singers' Voices." 40 *Syracuse L. Rev.* 1255 (1989).

de Acosta, M. *Here Lies the Heart.* New York: Reynal, 1960.

de Moraes, Lisa. "The Reagans: Too Hot for CBS to Handle?" *Washington Post*, November 4, 2003, p. C01.

Descher, Donald. *The Films of Spencer Tracy.* New York: Lyle Stuart, 1968.

Dowling, Margaret. "Sir Edward Hayward's Troubles over His Life of Henry IV." *The Library* ser. 4, no. 11 (1930-1): 213-16.

Eisenberg, J.B. "*Lugosi v. Universal Pictures*: Descent of the Right of Publicity." 29 *Hastings L. J.* 751 (1978).

Feldman, D. "Finding a Home for Fictional Characters: A Proposal for Change in Copyright Protection." 78 *Calif. L. Rev.* 687 (1990).

Foner, Eric. "A Conversation between Eric Foner and John Sayles." In *Past Imperfect: History According to the Movies*, ed. Ted Mico, John Miller-Monzon, and David Rubel. New York: Holt, 1995.

Frackman, Russell J., and Tammy C. Bloomfield. "The Right of Publicity: Going to the Dogs." *L.A. Daily Journal*, September 1996.

Frankel, Max. "One Peep vs. Docudrama." *New York Times Magazine,* March 16, 1997, p. 26.

Gaines, Jane M. *Contested Culture: The Image, the Voice, and the Law.* Chapel Hill: University of North Carolina Press, 1991.

Goldman, William. *Butch Cassidy and the Sundance Kid.* New York: Bantam, 1969.

Goldstein, Warren. "Bad History Is Bad for a Culture." *Chronicle of Higher Education,* April 10, 1998.

Halpern, S. "The Right of Publicity: Commercial Exploitation of the Associative Value of Personality." 29 *And. L. Rev.* 344 (1986).

Helfand, M. "When Mickey Mouse Is as Strong as Superman: The Convergence of Intellectual Property Laws to Protect Fictional Literary and Pictorial Characters." 44 *Stanford L. Rev.* 623 (1992).

Higashi, Sumiko. "Walker and Mississippi Burning: Postmodernism Versus Illustionist Narrative." In *Revisioning History: Film and the Construction of a New Past*, Robert A. Rosenstone. Princeton, N.J.: Princeton, 1995.

Kinder, Marsha. "The Image of Patriarchal Power in *Young Mr. Lincoln* (1939) and *Ivan the Terrible*, Part 1 (1945)." *Film Quarterly* **39** (1987): 29-30.

Kobler, J. *Damned in Paradise: The Life of John Barrymore.* New York: Atheneum, 1977.

Kotsitibas-Davis, J. *The Barrymores.* New York: Crown, 1981.

Kurtz, L. "The Independent Legal Lives of Fictional Characters." 1986 *Wis. L. Rev.* 429, 450 (1986).

Kurtz, R. H. "Georgia Anne Unamused by Sitcom Nonsense." *Washington Post*, January 28, 1993, p. C1, col. 4.

Levy, F.J. "Hayward, Daniel, and the Beginnings of Politic History in England." *Huntington Library Quarterly* **50** (1987): 18.

Mack, Peter. "Thou Art Not He Nor She: Authors' Disclaimers and Attitudes to Fiction." *Times Literary Supplement,* December 15, 1995, p. 12.

Mandell, Jonathan. "In Depicting History, Just How Far Can the Facts Be Bent?" *New York Times*, March 3, 2002.

Marius, Richard. "A Man for All Seasons." In *Past Imperfect: History According to the Movies*, ed. Ted Mico, John Miller-Monzon, and David Rubel. New York: Holt, 1995.

Maslin, Janet. "A Movie's Power Over Attitudes and Action." *New York Times*, February 22, 2004.

_____. "Stone's Embrace of a Despised President." *New York Times*, December 20, 1995, p. C11.

McBride, Joseph. *Searching for John Ford.* New York: St. Martin's, 2001.

McGilligan, Patrick, ed. *Yankee Doodle Dandy.* Madison: University of Wisconsin Press, 1981.

Mico, Ted, John Miller-Monzon, and David Rubel, eds. *Past Imperfect: History According to the Movies.* New York: Holt, 1995.

Napley, D. *Rasputin in Hollywood.* London: Trafalgar Square,1990.

Nizer, Louis. *My Life in Court.* Garden City, N.Y.: Doubleday, 1961.

Owens, F. "Sam Spade, Tarzan, and Copyright Law." *Science Fiction and Fantasy Writers of America Bulletin* 26 (Summer 1992): 14.

Owens, Mackubin Thomas. "History and the Movies: The Lessons of *The Patriot* and *Glory*." *USA Today,* August 1, 2000.

Past Imperfect: History According to the Movies, eds. Ted Mico, John Miller-Monzon, and David Rubel, New York: Henry Holt and Company, 1996.

Rosenberg, Norman. "Young Mr. Lincoln: The Lawyer as Super-Hero." *Legal Studies Forum* 15, no. 3 (1991): 225.

Rosenstone, Robert A. *Revisioning History: Film and the Construction of a New Past.* Princeton, N.J.: Princeton University Press, 1995.

_____. *Visions of the Past: The Challenge of Film to Our Idea of History.* Cambridge, Mass.: Harvard University Press, 1995.

Rusher, William A. "How Dependable Is History?" The Daily Ardmoreite (Ardmore, Okla.), Oct. 29, 1997 (online at http://www.ardmoreite.com).

Schwartz, Amy E. "Get the Crawl." *Washington Post,* Oct. 8, 1994, p. A19.

Seiler, Andy. "An Amused Orlean Plays Along with Preposterous 'Adaptation.'" *USA Today,* January 3, 2003, p. D13.

Shales, Tom. "'The Reagans': Not Quite a Hatchet Job." *Washington Post,* November 30, 2003, p. D1.

Silverberg, H. "Televising Old Films— Some New Legal Questions About Performers' and Proprietors' Rights." 38 *Va. L. Rev.* 615 (1952).

Simon, Art. *Dangerous Knowledge: The JFK Assassination in Art and Film.* Philadelphia: Temple University Press, 1996.

Smirlock, D. "Clear and Convincing Libel: Fiction and the Law of Defamation." 92 *Yale L. J.* 520 (1983).

Stone, Oliver. "Who Is Rewriting History?" *N.Y. Times,* December 20, 1991, p. A35.

Valenti, Jack. "'False History' on a Screen Near You." *Washington Post,* March 23, 2004, p. A23.

Warren, S., and L. Brandes. "The Right of Publicity." 4 *Harv. L. Rev.* 196 (1890).

Weinstein, R. The Legal Effect of Disclaimers of Liability on Motion Pictures Based on Fact." 9 *Glendale L. Rev.* 74, 77 (1990).

Windholz, E. "Comment: Whose Voice Is It Anyway?" 8 *Cardozo Arts & Ent. L. J.* 201 (1989).

Index